Treasure of Ambedkar Series 05

WHO WERE THE SHUDRAS?

Treasure of Ambedkar Series 05

WHO WERE THE SHUDRAS?

How they came to be the
Fourth Varna in the
Indo-Aryan Society

Dr B.R. Ambedkar

KALPAZ

Treasure of Ambedkar Series 05

WHO WERE THE SHUDRAS?

ISBN: 978-93-5128-271-6

First Published 1946
Reprint **2017**, in India by
Kalpaz Publications
C-30, Satyawati Nagar,
Delhi – 110052
E-mail: kalpaz@hotmail.com
Ph.: 9212142040

Printed at: G. Print Process, Delhi

CONTENTS

APPENDICES

PREFACE

In the present stage of the literature on the subject, a book on the Shudras cannot be regarded as a superfluity. Nor can it be said to deal with a trivial problem. The general proposition that the social organization of the Indo-Aryans was based on the theory of *Chaturvarnya* and that *Chaturvarnya* means division of society into four classes—***Brahmins*** (priests), ***Kshatriyas*** (soldiers), ***Vaishyas*** (traders) and ***Shudras*** (menials) does not convey any idea of the real nature of the problem of the Shudras nor of its magnitude. *Chaturvarnya* would have been a very innocent principle if it meant no more than mere division of society into four classes. Unfortunately, more than this is involved in the theory of *Chaturvarnya*. Besides dividing society into four orders, the theory goes further and makes the principle of graded inequality the basis for determining the terms of associated life as between the four *Varnas*. Again, the system of graded inequality is not merely notional. It is legal and penal. Under the system of *Chaturvarnya*, the *Shudra* is not only placed at the bottom of the gradation but he is subjected to innumerable ignominies and disabilities so as to prevent him from rising above the condition fixed for him by law. Indeed until the fifth *Varna* of the Untouchables came into being, the *Shudras* were in the eyes of the Hindus the lowest of the low. This shows the nature of what might be called the problem of the *Shudras*. If people have no idea of the magnitude of the problem it is because they have not cared to know what the population of the *Shudras* is. Unfortunately, the census does not show their population separately. But there is no doubt that excluding the Untouchables the Shudras form about 75 to 80 per cent. of the population of Hindus. A treatise which deals with so vast a population cannot be considered to be dealing with a trivial problem.

The book deals with the *Shudras* in the Indo-Aryan Society. There is a view that an inquiry into these questions is of no present-day moment. It is said by no less a person than Mr. Sherring in his *Hindu Tribes and Castes*[1] that:

> "Whether the Shudras were Aryans, or aboriginal inhabitants of India, or tribes produced by the union of the one with the other, is of little practical moment. They were at an early period placed in a class by themselves, and received the fourth or last degree of rank, yet at a considerable distance from the three superior castes. Even though it be admitted that at the outset they were not Aryans, still, from their extensive intermarriages with the three Aryan Castes, they have become so far Aryanized that, in some instances as already shown, they have gained more than they have lost, and certain tribes now designated as Shudras are in reality more Brahmins and Kshatriyas than anything else. In short, they have become as much absorbed in other races as the Celtic tribes of England have become absorbed in the Anglo-Saxon race; and their own separate individuality, if they ever had any, has completely vanished."

This view is based on two errors. Firstly, the present-day Shudras are a collection of castes drawn from heterogeneous stocks and are racially different from the original Shudras of the Indo-Aryan society. Secondly, in the case of Shudras the centre of interest is not the Shudras as a people but the legal system of pains and penalties to which they are subjected. The system of pains and penalties was no doubt originally devised by the Brahmins to deal with the Shudras of the Indo-Aryan society, who have ceased to exist as a distinct, separate, identifiable community. But strange as it may seem the Code intended to deal with them has remained in

[1] Vol. I, Introduction, p. xxi.

operation and is now applied to all low-class Hindus, who have no lock stock with the original *Shudras*. How this happened must be a matter of curiosity to all. My explanation is that the Shudras of the Indo-Aryan Society in course of time became so degraded as a consequence of the severity of the Brahmanical laws that they really came to occupy a very low state in public life. Two consequences followed from this. One consequence was a change in the connotation of the word Shudra. The word Shudra lost its original meaning of being the name of a particular community and became a general name for a low class people without civilization, without culture, without respect and without position. The second consequence was that the widening of the meaning of the word Shudra brought in its train the widening of the application of the Code. It is in this way that the so-called *Shudras* of the present-day have become subject to the Code, though they are not *Shudras* in the original sense of the word. Be that as it may, the fact remains that the Code intended for the original culprits has come to be applied to the innocents. If the Hindu law-givers had enough historical sense to realize that the original *Shudras* were different from the present-day low-class people, this tragedy—this massacre of the innocents—would have been avoided. The fact, however unfortunate it may be, is that the Code is applied to the present-day *Shudras* in the same rigorous manner in which it was applied to the original *Shudras*. How such a Code came into being cannot therefore be regarded as of mere antiquarian interest to the *Shudras* of to-day.

While it may be admitted that a study of the origin of the *Shudras* is welcome, some may question my competence to handle the theme. I have already been warned that while I may have a right to speak on Indian politics, religion and religious history of India are not my field and that I must not enter it. I do not know why my critics have thought it necessary to give me this warning. If it is an antidote to any extravagant claim made by me as a thinker or a writer, then it is unnecessary. For, I am ready to admit that I am not competent to speak even on Indian politics. If the warning is for the reason that I cannot claim mastery over the Sanskrit language, I admit this deficiency. But I do not see why it should disqualify me altogether from operating in this field. There is very little of literature in the Sanskrit language which is not available in English. The want of knowledge of Sanskrit need not therefore be a bar to my handling a theme such as the present. For I venture to say that a study of the relevant literature, albeit in English translations, for 15 years ought to be enough to invest even a person endowed with such moderate intelligence like myself, with sufficient degree of competence for the task. As to the exact measure of my competence to speak on the subject, this book will furnish the best testimony. It may well turn out that this attempt of mine is only an illustration of the proverbial fool rushing in where the angels fear to tread. But I take refuge in the belief that even the fool has a duty to perform, namely, to do his bit if the angel has gone to sleep or is unwilling to proclaim the truth. This is my justification for entering the prohibited field.

What is it that is noteworthy about this book? Undoubtedly the conclusions which I have reached as a result of my investigations. Two questions are raised in this book : (1) Who were the *Shudras* ? and (2) How they came to be the fourth *Varna* of the Indo-Aryan society ? My answers to them are summarised below :

(1) The *Shudras* were one of the Aryan communities of the Solar race.

(2) There was a time when the Aryan society recognised only three *Varnas*, namely, *Brahmins*, *Kshatriyas* and *Vaishyas*.

(3) The *Shudras* did not form a separate *Varna.* They ranked as part of the Kshatriya *Varna* in the Indo-Aryan society.

(4) There was a continuous feud between the *Shudra* kings and the *Brahmins* in which the *Brahmins* were subjected to many tyrannies and indignities.

(5) As a result of the hatred towards the *Shudras* generated by their tyrannies and oppressions, the *Brahmins* refused to perform the *Upanayana* of the *Shudras.*

(6) Owing to the denial of *Upanayana,* the *Shudras* who were Kshatriyas became socially degraded, fell below the rank of the *Vaishyas* and thus came to form the fourth *Varna.*

I must of course await the verdict of scholars on these conclusions. That these conclusions are not merely original but they are violently opposed to those that are current is of course evident. Whether these conclusions will be accepted or not will depend upon the mentality of a person claiming to have a right to sit in judgment over the issue. Of course, if he is attached to a particular thesis he will reject mine. I would not however bother about his judgment for he would be an adversary from whom nothing can be expected except opposition. But if a person is an honest critic, howsoever cautious, howsoever conservative he may be, provided that he has an open mind and a readiness to accept facts, I do not despair of converting him to my view. This expectation may fail to materialize, but about one thing I am quite certain. My critics will have to admit that the book is rich in fresh insights and new visions.

Apart from scholars, how the Hindu public will react may be an interesting speculation. The Hindus of to-day fall into five definite classes. There is a class of Hindus, who are known as orthodox and who will not admit that there is anything wrong with the Hindu social system. To talk of reforming it is to them rank blasphemy. There is a class of Hindus who are known as Arya Samajists. They believe in the *Vedas* and only in the *Vedas*. They differ from the orthodox in as much as they discard everything which is not in the *Vedas*. Their gospel is that of return to the *Vedas*. There is a class of Hindus who will admit that the Hindu social system is all wrong, but who hold that there is no necessity to attack it. Their argument is that since law does not recognise it, it is a dying, if not a dead system. There is a class of Hindus, who are politically minded. They are indifferent to such questions. To them *Swaraj* is more important than social reform. The fifth class of Hindus are those who are rationalists and who regard social reform as of primary importance, even more important than *Swaraj*.

With the Hindus, who fall into the second category, those who are likely to regard the book as unnecessary I cannot agree. In a way, they are right when they say that the existing law in British India does not recognise the caste system prevalent in the Hindu society. It is true that having regard to section 11 of the Civil Procedure Code, it would not be possible for a Hindu to obtain a declaration from a civil court that he belongs to a particular *Varna*. If courts in British India have to consider the question whether a person belongs to a particular *Varna*, it is only in cases of marriage, inheritance and adoption, the rules of which vary according to the *Varna* to which the party belongs. While it is true that the Law in British India does not recognize the four *Varnas* of the Hindus, one must be careful not to misunderstand what this means. To put it precisely: (1) it does not mean that the observance of the *Varna* system is a crime; (2) it does not mean that the *Varna* system has disappeared; (3) it does not mean that the *Varna* system is not given effect to in cases where the observance of its rules are necessary to acquiring civil rights; (4) it only means that the general legal sanction behind the *Varna* system has been withdrawn. Now law is not the only sanction which goes to sustain social institutions. Institutions are sustained by other sanctions also. Of these, religious sanction and social sanction are the most important. The Varna system has a religious sanction. Because it has a religious sanction, the *Varna* system has the fullest social sanction from the Hindu society. With no legal prohibition, this religious sanction has been more than enough to keep the *Varna* system in full bloom. The best evidence to show that the *Varna* system is alive notwithstanding there is no law to enforce it, is to be found in the fact that the status of the *Shudras* and the Untouchables in the Hindu society has remained just what it has been. It cannot therefore be said that a study such as this is unnecessary.

As to the politically-minded Hindu, he need not be taken seriously. His line of approach is generally governed by a short term view more than by long range considerations. He is willing to follow the line of least resistance and postpone a matter, however urgent, if it is likely to make him unpopular. It is therefore quite natural if the politically-minded Hindu regards this book as a nuisance.

The book treads heavily on the toes of the Arya Samajists. My conclusions have come in sharp conflict with their ideology at two most important points. The Arya Samajists believe that the four *Varnas* of the Indo-Aryan society have been in existence from the very beginning. The book shows that there was a time when there were only three *Varnas* in the Indo-Aryan society. The Arya Samajists believe that the *Vedas* are eternal and sacrosanct. The book shows that portions of the *Vedas* at any rate, particularly the *Purusha Sukta*, which is the mainstay of the Arya Samajists, are fabrications by *Brahmins* intended to serve their own purposes. Both these conclusions are bound to act like atomic bombs on the dogmas of the Arya Samajists.

I am not sorry for this clash with Arya Samajists. The Arya Samajists have done great mischief in making the Hindu society a stationary society by preaching that the Vedas are eternal, without beginning, without end, and infallible, and that the social institutions of the Hindus being based on the Vedas are also eternal, without beginning, without end, infallible and therefore requiring no change. To be permeated with such a belief is the worst thing that can happen to a community. I am convinced that the Hindu society will not accept the necessity of reforming itself unless and until this Arya Samajists' ideology is completely destroyed. The book does render this service, if no other.

What the Orthodox Hindu will say about this book I can well imagine for I have been battling with him all these years. The only thing I did not know was how the meek and non-violent looking Hindu can be violent when anybody attacks his Sacred Books. I became aware of it as never before when last year I received a shower of letters from angry Hindus, who became quite unbalanced by my speech on the subject delivered in Madras. The letters were full of filthy abuse unmentionable and unprintable and full of dire threats to my life. Last time they treated me as a first offender and let me off with mere threats. I don't know what they will do this time. For on reading the book they are sure to find more cause for anger at what in their eyes is a repetition of the offence in an aggravated form for having brought forth chapter and verse to show that what goes by the name of Sacred Books contains fabrications which are political in their motive, partisan in their composition and fraudulent in their purpose. I do not propose to take any notice of their vilifications or their threats. For I know very well that they are a base crew who professing to defend their religion have made religion a matter of trade. They are more selfish than any other set of beings in the world, and are prostituting their intelligence to support the vested interests of their class. It is a matter of no small surprise that when the mad dogs of orthodoxy are let loose against a person who has the courage to raise his voice against the so-called Sacred Books of the Hindus, eminent Hindus occupying lofty places, claiming themselves to be highly educated and who could be expected to have no interest and to have a free and open mind become partisans and join the outcry. Even Hindu Judges of High Courts and Hindu Prime Ministers of Indian States do not hesitate to join their kind. They go further. They not only lead the howl against him but even join in the hunt. What is outrageous is that they do so because they believe that their high stations in life would invest their words with an amount of terror which would be sufficient enough to cow down any and every opponent of orthodoxy. What I would like to tell these amiable gentlemen is that they will not be able to stop me by their imprecations. They do not seem to be aware of the profound and telling words of Dr. Johnson who when confronted with analogous situation said 'I am not going to be deterred from catching a cheat by the menaces of a ruffian.' I do not wish to be rude to these high-placed critics, much less do I want to say that they are playing the part of a ruffian interested in the escape of a cheat. But I do want to tell them two things: Firstly that I propose, no matter what happens, to follow the determination of Dr. Johnson in the pursuit of historical truth by the exposure of the Sacred Books so that the Hindus may know that it is the doctrines contained in their Sacred Books which are responsible for the decline and fall of their country and their society. Secondlv, if the Hindus of this generation do not take notice of what I have to say I am sure the future generation will. I do not despair of success. For I take consolation in the words of the poet Bhavabhuti who said " time is infinite and earth is vast, some day there will be borne a man who will appreciate what I have said." Whatever that be the book is a challenge to orthodoxy.

The only class of Hindus, who are likely to welcome the book are those who believe in the necessity and urgency of social reform. The fact that it is a problem which will certainly take a long time to solve and will call the efforts of many generations to come, is in their opinion, no justification for postponing the study of that problem. Even an ardent Hindu politician, if he is honest, will admit that the problems arising out of the malignant form of communalism, which is inherent in the Hindu social organization and which the politically-minded Hindus desire to ignore or postpone, invariably return to plague those very politicians at every turn. These problems are not the difficulties of the moment. They are our permanent difficulties, that is to say, difficulties of every moment. I am glad to know that such a class of Hindus exists. Small though they be, they are my mainstay and it is to them that I have addressed my argument.

It will be said that I have shown no respect for the sacred literature of the Hindus which every sacred literature deserves. If the charge be true, I can plead two circumstances in justification of myself. Firstly, I claim that in my research I have been guided by the best tradition of the historian who treats all literature as vulgar—I am using the word in its original sense of belonging to the people—to be examined and tested by accepted rules of evidence without recognizing any distinction between the sacred and the profane and with the sole object of finding the truth. If in following this tradition I am found wanting in respect and reverence for the sacred literature of the Hindus my duty as a scholar must serve as my excuse. Secondly, respect and reverence for the sacred literature cannot be made to order. They are the results of social factors which make such sentiments natural in one case and quite unnatural in another. Respect and reverence for the sacred literature of the Hindus is natural to a Brahmin scholar. But it is quite unnatural in a non-Brahmin scholar. The explanation of this difference is quite simple. That a Brahmin scholar should treat this sacred literature with uncritical reverence and forbear laying on it the heavy hands which the detachment of an intellectual as distinguished from the merely educated is what is to be expected. For what is this sacred literature? It is a literature which is almost entirely the creation of the Brahmins. Secondly, its whole object is to sustain the superiority and privileges of the Brahmins as against the non-Brahmins. Why should not the Brahmins uphold the sanctity of such a literature? The very reason that leads the Brahmin to uphold it makes the non-Brahmin hate it. Knowing that what is called the sacred literature contains an abominable social philosophy which is responsible for their social degradation, the non-Brahmin reacts to it in a manner quite opposite to that of the Brahmin. That I should be wanting in respect and reverence for the sacred literature of the Hindus should not surprise any one if it is borne in mind that I am a non-Brahmin, not even a non-Brahmin but an Untouchable. My antipathy to the sacred literature could not naturally be less than that of the non-Brahmin. As Prof. Thorndyke says: that a man thinks is a biological fact what he thinks is a sociological fact.

I am aware that this difference in the attitude of a Brahmin scholar and a non-Brahmin scholar towards this sacred literature—literature which is the main source of the material for the study of the problems of the social history of the Hindus—the former with his attitude of uncritical commendation and the latter with his attitude of unsparing condemnation is most harmful to historical research.

The mischief done by the Brahmin scholars to historical research is obvious. The *Brahmin* scholar has a two-fold interest in the maintenance of the sanctity of this literature. In the first place being the production of his forefathers his filial duty leads him to defend it even at the cost of truth. In the second place as it supports the privileges of the *Brahmins*, he is careful not to do anything which would undermine its authority. The necessity of upholding the system by which he knows he stands to profit, as well as of upholding the prestige of his forefathers as the founders of the system, acts as a silent immaculate premise which is ever present in the mind of the *Brahmin* scholar and prevents him from reaching or preaching the truth. That is why one finds so little that is original in the field of historical research by *Brahmin* scholars unless it be a matter of fixing dates or tracing genealogies. The non-Brahmin scholar has none of these limitations and is therefore free to engage himself in a relentless pursuit of truth. That such a difference exists between the two classes of students is not a mere matter of speculation. This very book is an illustration in point. It contains an exposure of the real character of the conspiracy against the *Shudras*, which no *Brahmin* scholar could have had the courage to present.

While it is true that a non-Brahmin scholar is free from the inhibitions of the Brahmin scholar he is likely to go to the other extreme and treat the whole literature as a collection of fables and fictions fit to be thrown on the dung heap not worthy of serious study. This is not the spirit of an historian. As has been well said an historian ought to be exact, sincere, and impartial; free from passion, unbiased by interest, fear, resentment or affection; and faithful to the truth, which is the mother of history, the preserver of great actions, the enemy of oblivion, the witness of the past, the director of the future. In short he must have an open mind though it may not be an empty mind and readiness to examine all evidence even though it be spurious. The non-Brahmin scholar may find it difficult to remain true to this spirit of the historian. He is likely to import the spirit of non-Brahmin politics in the examination of the truth or falsity of the ancient literature which is not justifiable. I feel certain that in my research I have kept myself free from such prejudice. In writing about the *Shudra* I have had present in my mind no other consideration except that of pure history. It is well known that there is a non-Brahmin movement in this country which is a political movement of the Shudras. It is also well known that I have been connected with it. But I am sure that the reader will find that I have not made this book a preface to non-Brahmin politics.

I am sensible of the many faults in the presentation of the matter. The book is loaded with quotations, too long and too many. The book is not a work of art and it is possible that readers will find it tedious to go through it. But this fault is not altogether mine. Left to myself, I would have very willingly applied the pruning knife. But the book is written for the ignorant and the uninformed *Shudras*, who do not know how they came to be what they are. They do not care how artistically the theme is handled. All they desire is a full harvest of material—the bigger the better. Those of them to whom I have shown the manuscript have insisted upon retaining the quotations. Indeed, their avidity for such material was so great that some of them went to the length of insisting that besides giving translations in English in the body of the book I should also add the original Sanskrit texts in an Appendix. While I had to deny their request for the reproduction of the original Sanskrit texts, I could not deny their request for retaining the translations on the ground that the material is not readily available to them. When one remembers that it is the *Shudras*, who have largely been instrumental in sustaining the infamous system of *Chaturvarnya*, though it has been the primary cause of their degradation and that only the *Shudras* can destroy the *Chaturvarnya*, it would be easy to realise why I allowed the necessity of educating and thereby preparing the *Shudra* fully for such a sacred task to outweigh all other consideration which favoured the deletion or if not deletion the abridgement of the quotations.

There are three persons to whom I owe my thanks. Firstly, to the writer of Adhya LX of the Shanti Parva of the Mahabarata. Whether it is *Vyasa, Vaiashampayana Suta, Lomaharshna* or *Bhrigu* it is difficult to say. But whoever he was, he has rendered great service by giving a full description of *Paijavana.* If he had not described *Paijavana* as a *Shudra,* the clue to the origin of the *Shudra* would have been completely lost. I express my gratitude to the writer for having preserved so important a piece of information for posterity. Without it, this book could not have been written. Secondly, I must thank Prof. Kangle of Ismail Yusuf College, Andheri, Bombay. He has come to my rescue and has checked the translation of Sanskrit shlokas which occur in the book. As I am not a Sanskrit scholar, his help has been to me a sort of an assurance that I have not bungled badly in dealing with the material which is in Sanskrit. The fact that he has helped me does not mean that he is responsible for such faults and errors as may be discovered by my critics. Thanks are also due to Prof. Manohar Chitnis of the Sidharth College, Bombay, who has been good enough to prepare the Index.

I am grateful to Messrs. Charles Scribner's Sons Publishers, New York for their kind permission to reproduce the three maps from Mr. Madison Grant's Passing of the Great Race and which form Appendices II, III and IV of this book.

B. R. AMBEDKAR.

10th October 1946.

"RAJGRAHA,"

DADAR,

BOMBAY 14.

Chapter I

THE RIDDLE OF THE SHUDRAS

Everybody knows that the Shudras formed the fourth Varna of the Indo-Aryan society. But very few have cared to inquire who were these Shudras and how they came to be the fourth Varna. That such an enquiry is of first-rate importance is beyond question. For, it is worth knowing how the Shudras came to occupy the fourth place, whether it was the result of evolut on or it was brought about by revolution.

Any attempt to discover who the Shudras were and how they came to be the fourth Varna must begin with the origin of the *Chaturvarnya* in the Indo-Aryan society. A study of the *Chaturvarnya* must in its turn start with a study of the ninetieth Hymn of the Tenth Mandala of the Rig Veda—a Hymn, which is known by the famous name of *Purusha Sukta.*

What does the Hymn say ? It says[1] :

"1. Purusha has a thousand heads, a thousand eyes, a thousand feet. On every side enveloping the earth he overpassed (it) by a space of ten fingers.

2. Purusha himself is this whole (universe), whatever has been and whatever shall be. He is the Lord of immortality, since (or when) by food he expands.

3. Such is his greatness, and Purusha is superior to this. All existences are a quarter to him ; and three-fourths of him are that which is immortal in the sky.

4. With three-quarters, Purusha mounted upwards. A quarter of him was again produced here. He was then diffused everywhere over things which eat and things which do not eat.

5. From him was born Viraj, and from Viraj, Purusha. When born, he extended beyond the earth, both behind and before.

---

[1] Muir's Original Sanskrit Texts, Vol. I, p. 9.

6. When the gods performed a sacrifice with Purusha as the oblation, the spring was its butter, the summer its fuel, and the autumn its (accompanying) offering.

7. This victim, Purusha, born in the beginning, they immolated on the sacrificial grass. With him the gods, the *Sadhyas*, and the *rishis* sacrificed.

8. From that universal sacrifice were provided curds and butter. It formed those aerial (creatures) and animals both wild and tame.

9. From that universal sacrifice sprang the *rik* and *saman* verses, the metres and the *yajus*.

10. From it sprang horses, and all animals with two rows of teeth ; kine sprang from it ; from it goats and sheep.

11. When (the gods) divided Purusha, into how many parts did they cut him up ? What was his mouth ? What arms (had he) ? What (two objects) are said (to have been) his thighs and feet. ?

12. The Brahmana was his mouth, the Rajanya was made his arms ; the being called the Vaishya, he was his thighs ; the Shudra sprang from his feet.

13. The moon sprang from his soul (manas), the sun from the eye, Indra and Agni from his mouth and Vayu from his breath.

14. From his navel arose the air, from his head the sky, from his feet the earth, from his ear the (four) quarters ; in this manner (the gods) formed the worlds.

15. When the gods, performing sacrifices, bound Purusha as a victim, there were seven sticks (stuck up) for it (around the fire), and thrice seven pieces of fuel were made.

16. With sacrifices the gods performed the sacrifice. These were the earliest rites. These great powers have sought the sky, where are the former *Sadhyas*, gods."

The *Purusha Sukta* is a theory of the origin of the Universe. In other words, it is a cosmogony. No nation which has reached an advanced degree of thought has failed to develop some sort of cosmogony. The Egyptians had a cosmogony somewhat analogous with that set out in the *Purusha Sukta*. According to it[1], it was god *Khnumu* 'the shaper,' who shaped living things on the potter's wheel, 'created all that is, he formed all that

[1] Encyclopædia of Religion and Ethics, Vol. IV, p. 145.

exists, he is the father of fathers, the mother of mothers . . . he fashioned men, he made the gods, he was the father from the beginning . . . he is the creator of the heaven, the earth, the underworld, the water, the mountains . . . he formed a male and a female of all birds, fishes, wild beasts, cattle and of all worms." A very similar cosmogony is found in Chapter I of the Genesis in the Old Testament.

Cosmogonies have never been more than matters of academic interest and have served no other purpose than to satisfy the curiosity of the student and to help to amuse children. This may be true of some parts of the *Purusha Sukta*. But it certainly cannot be true of the whole of it. That is because all verses of the *Purusha Sukta* are not of the same importance and do not have the same significance. Verses 11 and 12 fall in one category and the rest of the verses fall in another category. Verses other than 11 and 12 may be regarded as of academic interest. Nobody relies upon them. No Hindu even remembers them. But it is quite different with regard to verses 11 and 12. *Prima facie* these verses do no more than explain how the four classes, namely, (1) Brahmins or priests, (2) Kshatriyas or soldiers, (3) Vaishyas or traders, and (4) Shudras or menials, arose from the body of the Creator. But the fact is that these verses are not understood as being merely explanatory of a cosmic phenomenon. It would be a grave mistake to suppose that they were regarded by the Indo-Aryans as an innocent piece of a poet's idle imagination. They are treated as containing a mandatory injunction from the Creator to the effect that Society must be constituted on the basis of four classes mentioned in the *Sukta*. Such a construction of the verses in question may not be warranted by their language. But there is no doubt that according to tradition this is how the verses are construed, and it would indeed be difficult to say that this traditional construction is not in consonance with the intention of the author of the *Sukta*. Verses 11 and 12 of the *Purusha Sukta* are, therefore, not a mere cosmogony. They contain a divine injunction prescribing a particular form of the Constitution of society.

The Constitution of society prescribed by the *Purusha Sukta* is known as *Chaturvarnya*. As a divine injunction, it naturally became the ideal of the Indo-Aryan society. This ideal of *Chaturvarnya* was the mould in which the life of the Indo-Aryan community in its early or liquid state was cast. It is this mould, which gave the Indo-Aryan community its peculiar shape and structure.

This reverence, which the Indo-Aryan society had for this ideal mould of *Chaturvarnya*, is not only beyond question, but it is also beyond description. Its influence on the Indo-Aryan Society has been profound and indelible. The social order prescribed by the *Purusha Sukta* has never been questioned by anyone except Buddha. Even Buddha was not able to shake it, for the simple reason that both after the fall of Buddhism and even during the period of Buddhism there were enough law-givers, who made it their business not only to defend the ideal of the *Purusha Sukta* but to propagate it and to elaborate it.

To take a few illustrations of this propaganda in support of the *Purusha Sukta*, reference may be made to the *Apastamba Dharma Sutra* and the *Vasishtha Dharma Sutra*. The *Apastamba Dharma Sutra* states :—

> " There are four castes—Brahmins, Kshatriyas, Vaishyas and Shudras.
>
> Among these, each preceding (caste) is superior by birth to the one following[1].
>
> For all these excepting Shudras and those who have committed bad actions are ordained (1) the initiation (*Upanayan* or the wearing of the sacred thread), (2) the study of the Veda and (3) the kindling of the sacred fire (i.e., the right to perform sacrifice [2])."

---

[1] Prasna 1, Patala 1, Khanda 1, Sutras 4-5.

[2] Prasna 1, Patala 1, Khanda 1, Sutra 6.

This is repeated by *Vasishtha Dharma Sutra* which says :

"There are four castes (Varnas), Brahmins, Kshatriyas, Vaishyas and Shudras.

Three castes, Brahmins, Kshatriyas and Vaishyas (are called) twice-born.

Their first birth is from their mother; the second from the investiture with the sacred girdle. In that (second birth) the Savitri is the mother, but the teacher is said to be the father.

They call the teacher father, because he gives instruction in the Veda[1].

The four castes are distinguished by their origin and by particular sacraments.

There is also the following passage of the Veda. 'The Brahmana was his mouth, the Kshatriya formed his arms, the Vaishya his thighs; the Shudra was born from his feet.'

It has been declared in the following passage that a Shudra shall not receive the sacraments."

Many other law-givers have in parrot-like manner repeated the theme of the *Purusha Sukta* and have reiterated its sanctity. It is unnecessary to repeat their version of it. All those, who had raised any opposition to the sanctity of the ideal set out in the *Purusha Sukta*, were finally laid low by Manu, the architect of the Hindu Society. For Manu did two things. In the first place, he enunciated afresh the ideal of the *Purusha Sukta* as a part of divine injunction. He said :

"For the prosperity of the worlds, he (the creator) from his mouth, arms, thighs and feet created the Brahmin, Kshatriya and Vaishya and the Shudra[2].

The Brahmin, Kshatriya (and) Vaishya (constitute) the three twice-born castes; but the fourth the Shudra has only one birth[3]."

In this he was no doubt merely following his predecessors.

---

[1] Chapter II, Verses 1-4.

[2] Manu, Chapter I, Verse 31.

[3] Manu, Chapter X, Verse 4.

But he went a step further and enunciated another proposition in which he said :—

"Veda is the only and ultimate sanction for Dharma."[1]

Bearing in mind that the *Purusha Sukta* is a part of the Veda, it cannot be difficult to realize that Manu invested the social ideal of *Chaturvarnya* contained in the *Purusha Sukta*, with a degree of divinity and infallibility which it did not have before.

II

A critical examination of the *Purusha Sukta* therefore becomes very essential.

It is claimed by the Hindus that the *Purusha Sukta* is unique. This is no doubt a tall claim for an idea which came to birth when the mind of man was primitive and was without the rich endowment of varied thought available in modern times. But there need not be much difficulty in admitting this claim provided it is understood in what respect the *Purusha Sukta* is unique.

The principal ground for regarding the *Purusha Sukta* as unique is that the ideal of social organization, namely, the ideal of *Chaturvarnya* which it upholds, is unique. Is this a sufficient ground for holding the *Purusha Sukta* as unique ? The *Purusha Sukta* would really have been unique if it had preached a classless Society as an ideal form of society. But what does the *Purusha Sukta* do ? It preaches a class-composed Society as its ideal. Can this be regarded as unique ? Only a nationalist and a patriot can give an affirmative answer to this question. The existence of classes has been the *de facto* condition of every society, which is not altogether primitive. It is a normal state of society all over the world where society is in a comparatively advanced state. Looking at it from

[1] Manu, Chapter II, Verse 6.

this point of view, what uniqueness can there be in the *Purusha Sukta*, when it does no more than recognise the sort of class composition that existed in the Indo-Aryan Society ?

Notwithstanding this, the *Purusha Sukta* must be admitted to be unique, though for quite different reasons. The unfortunate part of the matter is that many people do not know the true reasons why the *Purusha Sukta* should be regarded as unique. But once the true reasons are known, people will not only have no hesitation in accepting that the *Purusha Sukta* is a unique production of the human intellect but will perhaps be shocked to know what an extraordinary production of human ingenuity it is.

What are the features of the social ideal of the *Purusha Sukta*, which give it the hall-mark of being unique? Though the existence of classes is the *de facto* condition of every society, nevertheless no society has converted this *de facto* state of affairs into a *de jure* connotation of an ideal society. The scheme of the *Purusha Sukta* is the only instance in which the real is elevated to the dignity of an ideal. This is the first unique feature of the scheme set forth in the *Purusha Sukta*. Secondly, no community has given the *de facto* state of class composition a legal effect by accepting it as a *de jure* connotation of an ideal society. The case of the Greeks is a case in point. Class composition was put forth as an ideal social structure by no less an advocate than Plato. But the Greeks never thought of making it real by giving it the sanction of law. The *Purusha Sukta* is the only instance in which an attempt was made to give reality to the ideal by invoking the sanction of law. Thirdly, no society has accepted that the class composition is an ideal. At the most they have accepted it as being natural. The *Purusha Sukta* goes further. It not only regards class composition as natural and ideal, but also regards it as sacred and divine. Fourthly, the number of the classes has never been a matter of dogma in any society known to history. The

Romans had two classes. The Egyptians thought three were enough. The Indo-Iranians also had no more than three classes[1] : (1) The *Athravans* (priests) (2) *Rathaeshtar* (warriors) and (3) the *Vastrya-fshuyat* (peasantry). The scheme of the *Purusha Sukta* makes the division of society into four classes a matter of dogma. According to it, there can be neither more nor less. Fifthly, every society leaves a class to find its place *vis-a-vis* other classes according to its importance in society as may be determined by the forces operating from time to time. No society has an official gradation laid down, fixed and permanent, with an ascending scale of reverence and a descending scale of contempt. The scheme of the *Purusha Sukta* is unique, in as much as it fixes a permanent warrant of precedence among the different classes, which neither time nor circumstances can alter. The warrant of precedence is based on the principle of graded inequality among the four classes, whereby it recognises the Brahmin to be above all, the Kshatriya below the Brahmin but above the Vaishya and the Shudra, the Vaishya below the Kshatriya but above the Shudra and the Shudra below all.

III

These are the real reasons why the *Purusha Sukta* is unique. But the *Purusha Sukta* is not merely unique, it is also extraordinary. It is extraordinary because it is so full of riddles. Few seem to be aware of these riddles. But anyone who cares to inquire will learn how real in their nature and how strange in their complexion these riddles are.

The cosmogony set out in the *Purusha Sukta* is not the only cosmogony one comes across in the Rig Veda. There

[1] Geiger—Civilization of the Eastern Iranians in Ancient Times, Vol. II, p. 64.

is another cosmogony which is expounded in the 72nd Hymn of the Tenth Mandala of the Rig Veda. It reads as follows[1] :

1. Let us proclaim with a clear voice of the generation of the gods (the divine company), who, when their praises are recited, look (favourably on the worshipper) in this latter age.

2. Brahmanaspati filled these (generations of the gods) with breath as a blacksmith (his bellows); in the first age of the gods the existent was born of the non-existent.

3. In the first age of the gods the existent was born of the non-existent; after that the quarters (of the horizon) were born, and after them the upward-growing (trees).

4. The earth was born from the upward-growing (tree), the quarters were born from the earth; Daksha was born from Aditi and afterwards Aditi from Daksha.

5. Aditi, who was thy daughter, Daksha, was born; after her, the gods were born, adorable, freed from the bonds of death.

6. When, gods, you abode in this pool well-arranged, then a pungent dust went forth from you as if you were dancing.

7. When, gods, you filled the worlds (with your radiance) as clouds (fill the earth with rain) then you brought forth the sun hidden in the ocean.

8. Eight sons (there were) of Aditi who were born from her body; she approached the gods with seven, she sent forth Martanda on high.

9. With seven sons Aditi went to a former generation, but she bore Martanda for the birth and death (of human beings.) "

The two cosmologies are fundamentally different in principle as well as in detail. The former explains creation *ex nihilo* " being was born of non-being." The latter ascribes creation to a being which it calls *Purusha*. Why in one and the same book two such opposite cosmologies should have come to be propounded ? Why did the author of the *Purusha Sukta* think it necessary to posit a *Purusha* and make all creation emanate from him ?

---

[1] Wilson's Rig Veda, Vol. VI, p. 129.

Any one who reads the *Purusha Sukta* will find that it starts with the creation of donkeys, horses, goats, etc., but does not say anything about the creation of man. At a point when it would have been natural to speak of the creation of man, it breaks off the chain and proceeds to explain the origin of the classes in the Aryan society. Indeed, the *Purusha Sukta* appears to make the explaining of the four classes of the Aryan Society to be its primary concern. In doing this, the *Purusha Sukta* stands in complete contrast not only with other theologies but with the other parts of the Rig Veda also.

No theology has made it its purpose to explain the origin of classes in society. Chapter I of the Genesis in the Old Testament, which can be said to be analogous in intention and purpose to the *Purusha Sukta*, does nothing more than explain how man was created. It is not that social classes did not exist in the old Jewish society. Social classes existed in all Societies. The Indo-Aryans were no exception. Nevertheless, no theology has ever thought it necessary to explain how classes arise. Why then did the *Purusha Sukta* make the explanation of the origin of the social classes its primary concern ?

The *Purusha Sukta* is not the only place in the Rig Veda where a discussion of the origin of creation occurs. There are other places in the Rig Veda where the same subject is referred to. In this connection, one may refer to the following passage in the Rig Veda which reads as follows[1] :—

> *Rig Veda*, i . 96 . 2 . " By the first *nivid*, by the wisdom of Ayu, he (Agni) created these children of men ; by his gleaming light the earth and the waters ; the gods sustained Agni the giver of the riches."

In this, there is no reference at all to the separate creation of classes, though there is no doubt that even at the time of the *Rig Veda*, the Indo-Aryan Society had become differentiated into classes ; yet the above passage

[1] Muir, Vol. I, p. 180.

in the *Rig Veda* ignores the classes and refers to the creation of men only. Why did the *Purusha Sukta* think it necessary to go further and speak of the origin of the classes ?

The *Purusha Sukta* contradicts the *Rig Veda* in another respect. The *Rig Veda* propounds a secular theory regarding the origin of the Indo-Aryans as will be seen from the following texts :

(1) *Rig Veda,* i . 80 . 16 : " Prayers and hymns were formerly congregated in that Indra, in the ceremony which Atharvan, father Manu, and Dadhyanch celebrated."[1]

(2) *Rig Veda,* i . 114 . 2 : " Whatever prosperity or succour father Manu obtained by sacrifice, may we gain all that under thy guidance, O Rudra."[2]

(3) *Rig Veda,* ii . 33 . 13 : " Those pure remedies of yours, O Maruts, those which are most auspicious, ye vigorous gods, those which are beneficent, those which our father Manu chose, those and the blessing and succour of Rudra, I desire."[3]

(4) *Rig Veda,* viii . 52 . 1 : " The ancient friend hath been equipped with the powers of the mighty (gods). Father Manu has prepared hymns to him, as portals of access to the gods."[4]

(5) *Rig Veda,* iii . 3 . 6 : " Agni, together with the gods, and the children (*jantubhih*) of Manush, celebrating a multiform sacrifice with hymns."[5]

(6) *Rig Veda,* iv . 37 . 1 : " Ye gods, Vajas, and Ribhukshana, come to our sacrifice by the path travelled by the gods, that ye, pleasing deities, may institute a sacrifice among these people of Manush (*Manusho vikshu*) on auspicious days."[6]

(7) *Rig Veda,* vi . 14 . 2 : " The people of Manush praise in the sacrifice Agni the invoker."[7]

---

[1] Muir, Vol. I, p. 162.
[2] *Ibid,* p. 163.
[3] *Ibid,* p. 163.
[4] *Ibid,* p. 163.
[5] *Ibid,* p. 165.
[6] *Ibid,* p. 165.
[7] *Ibid,* p. 165.

From these texts it is beyond question that the *rishis* who were the authors of the hymns of the *Rig Veda* regarded *Manu* as the progenitor of the Indo-Aryans. This theory about *Manu* being the progenitor of the Indo-Aryans had such deep foundation that it was carried forward by the *Brahmanas* as well as the *Puranas*. It is propounded in the *Aitareya Brahmana*[1], in the *Vishnu Purana*[2] and the *Matsya Purana*[3]. It is true that they have made Brahma the progenitor of *Manu*; but the *Rig Veda* theory of *Manu* being the progenitor has been accepted and maintained by them.[4] Why does the *Purusha Sukta* make no mention of *Manu*? This is strange because the author of the *Purusha Sukta* seems to be aware of the fact that Manu Svayambhuva is called *Viraj* and *Viraj* is called *Adi Purusha*[5], since he too speaks of *Virajo adhi Purushah* in verse five of the *Sukta*.

There is a third point in which the *Purusha Sukta* has gone beyond the *Rig Veda*. The Vedic Aryans were sufficiently advanced in their civilization to give rise to division of labour. Different persons among the Vedic Aryans followed different occupations. That they were conscious of it is evidenced by the following verse:

> *Rig Veda*, i . 113 . 6 : "That some may go in pursuit of power, some in pursuit of fame, some in pursuit of wealth, some in pursuit of work, Ushas has awakened people so that

---

[1] Quoted by Muir, Vol. I, p. 108.

[2] Quoted by Muir, Vol. I, pp. 105-107.

[3] Quoted by Muir, Vol. I, pp. 110-112.

[4] There is however a great deal of confusion when one comes to details. The *Vishnu Purana* says that *Brahma* divided his person into two parts : with the one half he became a male, with the other half a female. The female was called *Satarupa* who by incessantly practising austere fervour of a highly arduous description acquired for herself as a husband a Male called *Manu Svayambhuva*. There is no suggestion in the Vishnu Purana of incest by Brahma with his daughter. The *Aitareya Brahmana* and the Matsya Purana on the other hand speak of Brahma having begotten Manu by committing incest with his daughter Satarupa; the Matsya Purana adds that Manu by his austerity obtained a beautiful wife named *Ananta*. According to the Ramayana (see Muir I, p. 117) *Manu* was not a male but a female and was a daughter of *Daksha Prajapati* and the wife of *Kasyapa*.

[5] *Matsya Purana*—Muir, Vol. I, p. 111, f.n.

each may go in pursuit of his special and different way of earning his livelihood."

This is as far as the *Rig Veda* had gone. The *Purusha Sukta* goes beyond. It follows up the notion of division of labour and converts the scheme of division of work into a scheme of division of workers into fixed and permanent occupational categories. Why does the *Purusha Sukta* commit itself to such a perversity ?

There is another point in which the *Purusha Sukta* departs from the *Rig Veda*. It is not that the *Rig Veda* speaks only of man. It speaks also of the Indo-Aryan nation. This nation was made up of the five tribes, which had become assimilated into one common Indo-Aryan people. The following hymns refer to these five tribes as moulded into a nation :

(1) *Rig Veda*, vi.11.4: "Agni, whom, abounding in oblations, the five tribes, bringing offerings, honour with prostrations, as if he were a man."[1]

(2) *Rig Veda*, vii.15.2: "The wise and youthful master of the house (Agni) who has taken up his abode among the five tribes in every house."[2]

There is some difference of opinion as to who these five tribes are. *Yaska* in his *Nirukta* says that it denotes *Gandharvas*, *Pitris*, *Devas*, *Asuras* and *Rakshasas*. Aupamanyava says that it denotes the four Varnas and the *Nishadas*. Both these explanations seem to be absurd. Firstly, because the five tribes are praised collectively as in the following hymns :—

(1) *Rig Veda*, ii.2.10: "May our glory shine aloft among the five tribes, like the heaven unsurpassable."[3]

(2) *Rig Veda*, vi.46.7: "Indra, whatever force or vigour exists in the tribe of Nahusha or whatever glory belongs to the five races bring (for us)."[4]

---

[1] Muir, Vol. I, p. 177.
[2] Muir, Vol. I, p. 178.
[3] Muir, Vol. I, p. 178.
[4] Muir, Vol. I, p. 180.

Such laudatory statements could not have been made if the five tribes included the *Shudras*. Besides, the word used is not *Varnas*. The word used is *Janah*. That it refers to the five tribes and not to the four *Varnas* and *Nishadas* is quite clear from the following verse of the *Rig Veda* :

> *Rig Veda*, i . 108 . 8 : " If, O Indra and Agni, ye are abiding among the *Yadus, Turvasas, Druhyus, Anus, Purus*, come hither, vigorous heroes from all quarters, and drink the Soma which has been poured out."[1]

That these five tribes had been moulded into one Aryan people is clear from the *Atharva Veda* (iii . 24 . 2) which says :

> " these five regions ; the five tribes springing from Manu."

A sense of unity and a consciousness of kind can alone explain why the *Rishis* of the *Rig Vedic* hymns came to refer to the five tribes in such manner. The questions are : why did the *Purusha Sukta* not recognise this unity of the five tribes and give a mythic explanation of their origin ? Why instead did it recognise the communal divisions within the tribes ? Why did the *Purusha Sukta* regard communalism more important than nationalism ?

These are some of the riddles of the *Purusha Sukta*, which come to light when one compares it with the *Rig Veda*. There are others, which emerge when one proceeds to examine the *Purusha Sukta* from a sociological point of view.

Ideals as norms are good and are necessary. Neither a society nor an individual can do without a norm. But a norm must change with changes in time and circumstances. No norm can be permanently fixed. There must always be room for revaluation of the values of our norm. The possibility of revaluing values remains open only when the institution is not invested with sacredness. Sacredness prevents revaluation of its values. Once sacred, always sacred. The *Purusha Sukta* makes the

[1] *Ibid* I, p. 179.

Chaturvarnya a sacred institution, a divine ordination. Why did the *Purusha Sukta* make a particular form of social order so sacred as to be beyond criticism and beyond change ? Why did it want to make it a permanent ideal beyond change and even beyond criticism ? This is the first riddle of the *Purusha Sukta* which strikes a student of Sociology.

In propounding the doctrine of *Chaturvarnya*, the *Purusha Sukta* plays a double game. It proceeds first to raise the real, namely, the existence of the four classes in the Indo-Aryan Society to the status of an ideal. This is a deception because the ideal is in no way different from facts as they exist. After raising the real to the status of the ideal, it proceeds to make a show of giving effect to what it regards as an ideal. This again is a deception because the ideal already exists in fact. This attempt of the *Purusha Sukta* to idealize the real and to realize the ideal, is a kind of political jugglery, the like of which, I am sure, is not to be found in any other book of religion. What else is it if not a fraud and a deception ? To idealize the real, which more often than not is full of inequities, is a very selfish thing to do. Only when a person finds a personal advantage in things as they are that he tries to idealize the real. To proceed to make such an ideal real is nothing short of criminal. It means perpetuating iniquity on the ground that whatever is once settled is settled for all times. Such a view is opposed to all morality. No society with a social conscience has ever accepted it. On the contrary, whatever progress in improving the terms of associated life between individuals and classes has been made in the course of history, is due entirely to the recognition of the ethical doctrine that what is wrongly settled is never settled and must be resettled. The principle underlying the *Purusha Sukta* is, therefore, criminal in intent and anti-social in its results. For, it aims to perpetuate an illegal gain obtained by one class and an unjust wrong inflicted upon another.

What can be the motive behind this jugglery of the *Purusha Sukta* ? This is the second riddle.

The last and the greatest of all these riddles, which emerge out of a sociological scrutiny of the *Purusha Sukta*, is the one relating to the position of the *Shudra*. The *Purusha Sukta* concerns itself with the origin of the classes, and says they were created by God—a doctrine which no theology has thought it wise to propound. This in itself is a strange thing. But what is astonishing is the plan of equating different classes to different parts of the body of the Creator. The equation of the different classes to different parts of the body is not a matter of accident. It is deliberate. The idea behind this plan seems to be to discover a formula which will solve two problems, one of fixing the functions of the four classes and the other of fixing the gradation of the four classes after a preconceived plan. The formula of equating different classes to the different parts of the body of the Creator has this advantage. The part fixes the gradation of the class and the gradation in its turn fixes the function of the class. The *Brahmin* is equated to the mouth of the Creator. Mouth being the noblest part of the anatomy, the *Brahmin* becomes the noblest of the four classes. As he is the noblest in the scale, he is given the noblest function, that of custodian of knowledge and learning. The *Kshatriya* is equated to the arms of the Creator. Among the limbs of a person, arms are next below the mouth. Consequently, the *Kshatriya* is given an order of precedence next below the *Brahmin* and is given a function which is second only to knowledge, namely, fighting. The *Vaishya* is equated to the thighs of the Creator. In the gradation of limbs the thighs are next below the arms. Consequently, the *Vaishya* is given an order of precedence next below the *Kshatriya* and is assigned a function of industry and trade which in name and fame ranks or rather did rank in ancient times below that of a warrior. The *Shudra* is equated to the feet of the Creator. The feet fo... the lowest and the most ignoble part of the human frame. Accordingly, the *Shudra* is placed last in the social order and is given the filthiest function, namely, to serve as a menial.

Why did the *Purusha Sukta* choose such a method of illustrating the creation of the four classes ? Why did it equate the *Shudra* to the feet ? Why did it not take some other illustration to show how the four classes were created ? It is not that *Purusha* is the only stock simile used to explain creation. Compare the explanation of the origin of the Vedas contained in the *Chhandogya Upanishad.* It says[1] :

> " Prajapati infused warmth into the worlds, and from them so heated he drew forth their essences, viz., Agni (fire) from the earth, Vayu (wind) from the air, and Surya (the sun) from the sky. He infused warmth into these three deities, and from them so heated he drew forth their essences,—from Agni the *ric* verses, from Vayu the *yajus* verses and from Surya the *saman* verses. He then infused heat into this triple science, and from it so heated he drew forth its essences—from *ric* verses the syllable *bhuh,* from *yajus* verses *bhuvah*, and from *Saman* verses *svar.*"

Here is an explanation of the origin of the Vedas from different deities. So far as the Indo-Aryans are concerned, there was no dearth of them. There were thirty crores of them. An explanation of the origin of the four *Varnas* from four gods would have maintained equality of dignity by birth of all the four classes. Why did the *Purusha Sukta* not adopt this line of explanation ?

Again, would it not have been possible for the author of the *Purusha Sukta* to say that the different classes were born from the different mouths of the *Purusha.* Such a conception could not have been difficult because the *Purusha* of the *Purusha Sukta* has one thousand heads, enough to assign one species of creation to one of his heads. Such a method of explaining creation could not have been unknown to the author of the *Purusha Sukta.*

[1] Muir, Vol. III, p. 5.

For we find it used by the *Vishnu Purana* to explain the origin of the different *Vedas* as may be seen from the following extract[1] :

> "From his eastern mouth Brahma formed the Gayatri, the *ric* verses, the trivrit, the sama-rathantara and of sacrifices, the agnistoma. From his southern mouth he created the yajus verses, the trishtubh metre, the panchadasa stoma, the brihatsaman, and the ukthya. From his western mouth he formed the saman verses, the jagati metre, the saptadasa stoma, the Vairupa, and the atiratra. From his northern mouth he formed the ekavimsa, the atharvan, the aptoryaman with the anushtubh and viraj metres."

The *Harivamsa* has another way of explaining the origin of the Vedas. According to it[2] :

> "The god fashioned the *Rig Veda* with the Yajus from his eyes, the *Sama Veda* from the tip of his tongue, and the *Atharvan* from his head."

Assuming that for some reason the author of the *Purusha Sukta* could not avoid using the body of the Creator and its different parts for explaining the origin and the relation of the four classes, the question still remains as to why he chose to equate the different parts of the *Purusha* to the different classes in the manner in which he does.

The importance of this question is considerably heightened when one realizes that the *Purusha Sukta* is not the only instance in which the different parts of the body of the Creator are used as illustrations to explain the origin of the different classes in society. The same explanation is given by the sage *Vaishampayana* to explain the origin of the various classes of priests employed in the performance of sacrifices. But what a difference is there between the two ! The explanation of *Vaishyampayana* which is reported in the *Harivamsa* reads as follows[3] :

---

[1] Muir, Vol. III, p. 11.

[2] Muir, Vol. III, p. 13.

[3] Muir, Vol. I, pp. 154-155.

"Thus the glorious Lord Hari Narayana, covering the entire waters, slept on the world which had become one sea, in the midst of the vast expanse of fluid (*rajas*), resembling a mighty ocean, himself free from passion (*virajaskah*), with mighty arms; Brahmans know him as the undecaying. Invested through austere fervour with the light of his own form and clothed with triple time (past, present and future) the Lord then slept. *Purushottama* (Vishnu) is whatever is declared to be the highest. *Purusha* the sacrifice, and everything else which is known by the name of *Purusha*. Here how the *Brahmins* devoted to sacrifice, and called *ritvijas*, were formerly produced by him from his own body for offering sacrifices. The Lord created from his mouth the *Brahman*, who is the chief, and the *udgatri*, who chants the *Saman*; from his arms the *hotri* and the *adhvaryu*. He then . . . created the *prastotri*, the *maitravaruna*, and the *pratishthatri*; from his belly the *pratihartri* and the *potri*, from his thighs the *achhavaka* and the *neshtri*, from his hands the *agnidhra* and the sacrificial *brahmanya*, from his arms the *gravan* and the sacrificial *unnetri*. Thus did the divine Lord of the world create the sixteen excellent *ritvijas*, the utterers of all sacrifices. Therefore this *Purusha* is formed of sacrifice and is called the Veda; and all the Vedas with the Vedangas, Upanishads and ceremonies are formed of his essence."

There were altogether seventeen different classes of priests required for the performance of a sacrifice. It could never be possible for anyone attempting to explain the origin of each by reference to a distinct part of the body of the Creator to avoid using the feet of the *Purusha* as the origin of a class, the limbs of the *Purusha* being so few and the number of priests being so many. Yet what does *Vaishampayana* do? He does not mind using the same part of the Creator's body to explain the origin of more than one class of priests. He most studiously avoids using the feet as the origin of anyone of them.

The situation becomes completely intriguing when one compares the levity with which the *Shudras* are treated in the *Purusha Sukta* with the respect with which the *Brahmins* are treated in the *Harivamsa* in the matter of their respective origins. Is it because of malice that the

Purusha Sukta did not hesitate to say that the *Shudra* was born from the feet of the *Purusha* and that his duty was to serve ? If so what is the cause of this malice ?

IV

The riddles about the *Shudras* mentioned above are those which arise out of a sociological scrutiny of the *Purusha Sukta.* There are other riddles regarding the position of the *Shudra* which arise out of later developments of the ideal of *Chaturvarnya.* To appreciate these results it is necessary first to take note of these later developments. The later developments of *Chaturvarnya* are mainly two. First is the creation of the fifth class next below the *Shudras.* The second is the separation of the *Shudra* from the first three *Varnas.* These changes have become so integrated with the original scheme of the *Purusha Sukta* that they have given rise to peculiar terms and expressions so well-known that everybody understands what they stand for. These terms are : *Savarnas, Avarnas, Dvijas, non-Dvijas* and *Traivarnikas.* They stand to indicate the sub-divisions of the original four classes and the degree of separation between them. It is necessary to take note of the relative position of these classes because they disclose a new riddle. If this riddle has not caught the eye of the people, it is because of two reasons. Firstly, because students have not cared to note that these names are not mere names but that they stand for definite rights and privileges and secondly because they have not cared to find out whether the groupings made under these names are logical having regard to the rights and privileges they connote.

Let us therefore see what is the *de jure* connotation of these terms. *Savarna* is generally contrasted with *Avarna. Savarna* means one who belongs to one of the four *Varnas. Avarna* means one who does not belong to any one of the four *Varnas*. The *Brahmins, Kshatriyas, Vaishyas* and *Shudras* are *Savarnas*. The Untouchables or *Ati-Shudras* are called *Avarnas*, those who have no *Varna*. Logically, the *Brahmins, Kshatriyas, Vaishyas* and *Shudras* are within the *Chaturvarnya*. Logically, the Untouchables or the *Ati-Shudras* are outside the *Chaturvarnya*. *Dvija* is generally contrasted with *non-Dvija*. *Dvija* literally means twice-born and *non-Dvija* means one who is born only once. The distinction is based on the right to have *Upanayana*. The *Upanayana* is treated as a second birth. Those who have the right to wear the sacred thread are called *Dvijas*. Those who have no right to wear it are called *non-Dvijas*. The *Brahmins, Kshatriyas* and *Vaishyas* have the right to wear the sacred thread. Logically, they are *Dvijas*. The *Shudras* and the *Ati-Shudras* have no right to wear the sacred thread. Logically, they are both *non-Dvijas*. The *Traivarnika* is contrasted with the *Shudra*. But there is nothing special in this contrast. It conveys the same distinction which is conveyed by the distinction between the *Dvijas* and the *non-Dvijas* except the fact that the contrast is limited to the *Shudra* and does not extend to the *Ati-Shudra*. This is probably because this terminology came into being before the rise of the *Ati-Shudras* as a separate class.

Bearing in mind that both the *Shudra* and the *Ati-Shudra* are *non-Dvijas*, why then is the *Shudra* regarded as *Savarna* and the *Ati-Shudra* as *Avarna* ? Why is the former within and why is the latter outside the *Chaturvarnya* ? The *Brahmins, Kshatriyas, Vaishyas* and *Shudras* are all within the four corners of the *Chaturvarnya*. They are all *Savarnas*. Why then is the *Shudra* denied the right of the *Traivarnikas* ?

Can there be a greater riddle than the riddle of the *Shudras* ? Surely, it calls for investigation and explanation as to who they were and how they came to be the fourth *Varna* in the Aryan Society.

Chapter II

THE BRAHMANIC THEORY OF THE ORIGIN OF THE SHUDRAS

Has the Brahmanic literature any explanation to offer which can account for the origin of the Shudras? There is no doubt that the Brahmanic literature is full of legends regarding creation which touch upon the creation of the universe, of man and of the different Varnas. Whether or not they furnish any clue to discover the origin of the Shudras, there can be no doubt that all such theories should find a place in a book which is concerned with the problem of the Shudras if for no other reason than that of assembling all material relating to the Shudras in one place and making their story complete. It would be better to take each piece of the Brahmanic literature separately, and note what contribution it has to make to the subject.

I

To begin with the *Vedas*. As to the *Rig Veda*, the legend about creation to be found in its *Sukta* known as the *Purusha Sukta* has already been set out in the previous Chapter. It now remains to take note of the legends contained in the other *Vedas*.

There are two recensions of the *Yajur Veda*: (1) the White *Yajur Veda* and (2) the Black *Yajur Veda*. To take the White *Yajur Veda* first. The *Vajasaneyi Samhita* of the White *Yajur Veda* sponsors two theories. One is a mere reproduction of the *Purusha Sukta* of the *Rig Veda* with this difference that it has 22 verses, while the original as it occurs in the *Rig Veda* has only 16 verses. The six additional verses in the White *Yajur Veda* read as follows:

17. Brought forth from the waters and from the essence of the earth, he was produced by Vishvakarman in the beginning. Tvashta gives him form; that is the Universe of Purusha on all sides in the beginning.

18. I know this great Purusha, of the colour of the sun, beyond darkness. Only by knowing him does one go beyond death; there is no other path for going.

19. Prajapati moves in the interior of the womb; though unborn, he is born in many forms. Wise men see his source; wise men desire the place of the Marichis.

20. He who shines for the gods, he who is the priest of the gods, he who was born before the gods,—salutation to that shining offspring of Brahma.

21. The gods, generating the shining offspring of Brahma, said in the beginning: "That Brahmin who knows thus,—the gods will be under his control."

22. Sri and Laxmi are his wives; the day and night his sides; the stars his ornament; the Ashwins his bright face. Grant me my desires; grant me that; grant me everything.

The second explanation contained in the *Vajasaneyi Samhita* is quite different from the *Purusha Sukta.* It reads as follows:

V.S., xiv. 28.[1]—"He lauded with one. Living beings were formed. He lauded with three: the *Brahman* was created; *Brahmanaspati* was the ruler. He lauded with five: existing things were created; *Bhutanampati* was the ruler. He lauded with seven: the seven *rishis* were created: *Dhatri* was the ruler. He lauded with nine; the *Fathers* were created: *Aditi* was the ruler. He lauded with eleven: the seasons were created: the *Artavas* were the rulers. He lauded with thirteen: the months were created: the year was the ruler. He lauded with fifteen: the *Kshattra* (the *Kshatriya*) was created: *Indra* was the ruler. He lauded with seventeen: animals were created: *Brihaspati* was the ruler. He lauded with nineteen: the *Shudra* and the *Arya* (*Vaishya*) were created: day and night were the rulers. He lauded with twenty-one: animals with undivided hoofs were

[1] Muir, Vol. I, p. 18.

created : *Varuna* was the ruler. He lauded with twenty-three : small animals were created : *Pushan* was the ruler. He lauded with twenty-five: wild animals were created: *Vayu* was the ruler (compare *R.V.*, x . 90 . 8). He lauded with twenty-seven : heaven and earth separated : *Vasus, Rudras* and *Adityas* separated after them : they were the rulers. He lauded with thirty-one : living beings were created : the first and second halves of the month were the rulers. He lauded with thirty-one : existing things were tranquillized : *Prajapati Parameshthin* was the ruler."

Now to turn to the Black *Yajur Veda.* The *Taittiriya Samhita* of the Black *Yajur Veda* gives altogether five explanations. The one at iv, 3, 10 is the same as has been put forth by the *Vajasaneyi Samhita* of the White *Yajur Veda* at (xiv. 28) and which has been reproduced earlier. Of the rest those which narrate the origin of the Shudra are set out below :—

T.S., ii . 4 . 13.1.[1]—" The gods were afraid of the *Rajanya* when he was in the womb. They bound him with bonds when he was in the womb. Consequently, this *Rajanya* is born bound. If he were born unbound he would go on slaying his enemies. In regard to whatever *Rajanya* any one desires that he should be born unbound, and should go on slaying his enemies, let him offer for him this *Aindra-Barhaspatya* oblation. A *Rajanya* has the character of *Indra*, and a *Brahman* is *Brihaspati*. It is through the *Brahman* that anyone releases the *Rajanya* from his bond. The golden bond, a gift, manifestly releases from the bond that fetters him."

(2) *T.S.*, vii . 1 . 1 . 4.[2]—" *Prajapati* desired, 'may I propagate.' He formed the Trivrit (stoma) from his mouth. After it were produced the deity Agni, the metre Gayatri, the Saman (called) Rathantara, of men the Brahmin, of beasts the goats. Hence they are the chief (*mukhyah*) because they were created from the mouth (*mukhatah*). From (his) breast, from his arms, he formed the Panchadasa (stoma). After it were created the god, Indra, the Trishtubh metre, the Saman (called) Brihat, of men the *Rajanya*, of

[1] Muir, Vol. I, p. 22.

[2] Muir, Vol. I, p. 16.

beasts the sheep. Hence they are vigorous, because they were created from vigour. From (his) middle he formed the Saptadasa (stoma). After it were created the gods (called) the Visvedevas, the Jagati metre, the Saman called the Vairupa, of men the *Vaishya*, of beasts kine. Hence they are to be eaten, because they were created from the receptacle of food. Wherefore they are more numerous than others, for the most numerous deities were created after (the Saptadasa). From his foot he formed the Ekavimsa (Stoma). After it were created the Anushtubh metre, the Saman called Vairaja, of men the *Shudra*, of beasts the horse. Hence these two, both the horse and the *Shudra*, are transporters of (other) creatures. Hence (too) the *Shudra* is incapacitated for sacrifice, because no deities were created after (the *Ekavimsa*). Hence (too) these two subsist by their feet, for they were created from the foot."

Coming to the *Atharva Veda*, there are altogether four explanations. One of these is the same as the *Purusha Sukta* of the *Rig Veda*. It occurs at xix.6. The others are as stated below :

(1) *A.V.*,[1] iv. 6. 1.—"The *Brahman* was born the first, with ten heads and ten faces. He first drank the soma; he made poison powerless."

(2) *A.V.*,[2] xv. 8. 1.—"He (the *Vratya*) became filled with passion, thence sprang the *Rajanya*."

(3) *A.V.*,[3] xv. 9. 1.—"Let the king to whose house the *Vratya* who knows this, comes as a guest, cause him to be respected as superior to himself. So doing he does no injury to his royal rank, or to his realm. From him arose the *Brahman* (*Brahmin*) and the *Kshattra* (*Kshatriya*). They said 'Into whom shall we enter,' etc."

II

To proceed to the Brahmanas. The *Satapatha Brahmana* contains six explanations. There are two which concern

[1] Muir, Vol. I, p. 21.

[2] Muir, Vol. I, p. 22.

[3] Muir, Vol. I, p. 22.

themselves with the creation of the *Varnas*. Of the two, the one which speaks of the origin of the *Shudras* is given below :

> *S.B.*,[1] xiv . 4 . 2 . 23.—" Brahma (here, according to the commentator, existing in the form of Agni and representing the Brahmana caste) was formerly this (universe), one only. Being one, it did not develope. It energetically created an excellent form, the Kshattra, viz., those among the gods who are powers (Kshattrani), Indra, Varuna, Soma, Rudra, Parjanya, Yama, Mrityu, Isana. Hence nothing is superior to the Kshattra. Therefore the Brahmana sits below the Kshatriya at the Rajasuya sacrifice ; he confers that glory on the Kshattra (the royal power). This, the Brahma, is the source of the Kshattra. Hence, although the king attains supremacy, he at the end resorts to the Brahman as his source. Whoever destroys him (the Brahman) destroys his own source. He becomes most miserable, as one who has injured a superior. He did not develope. He created the Vis, viz., those classes of gods who are designated by troops, Vasus, Rudras, Adityas, Visvedevas, Maruts. He did not develope. He created the Shudra class Pushan. This earth is Pushan ; for she nourishes all that exists. He did not develope. He energetically created an excellent form, Justice (Dharma). This is the ruler (Kshattra) of, the ruler (Kshattra), namely, Justice. Hence nothing is superior to Justice. Therefore the weaker seeks (to overcome) the stronger by Justice, as by a king. This justice is truth. In consequence they say of a man who speaks truth, ' he speaks justice.' For this is both of these. This is the Brahma, Kshattra, Vis and Shudra. Through Agni it became Brahma among the gods, the Brahmana among men, through the (divine) Kshatriya a (human) Kshatriya, through the (divine) Vaishya a (human) Vaishya, through the (divine) Shudra a (human) Shudra. Wherefore it is in Agni among the gods and in a Brahman among men that they seek after an abode."

The *Taittiriya Brahmana* is responsible for the following explanations :

---

[1] Muir, Vol. I, p. 20.

(1) *T.B.*,[1] i. 2. 6. 7.—"The Brahmana caste is sprung from the gods; the Shudras from the Asuras."

(2) *T.B.*,[2] iii. 2. 3. 9.—"This Shudra has sprung from non-existence."

III

Here is a complete collection of all the Brahmanic speculations on the origin of the four classes and of the Shudras. The ancient Brahmins were evidently conscious of the fact that the origin of the four classes was an unusual and uncommon social phenomenon and that the place of the Shudra in it was very unnatural and that this called for some explanation. Otherwise, it would be impossible to account for these innumerable attempts to explain the origin of the *Chaturvarnya* and of the Shudra.

But what is one to say of these explanations? The variety of them is simply bewildering. Some allege that *Purusha* was the origin of the four *Varnas*, and some attribute their origin to Brahma, some to Prajapati and some to Vratya. The same source gives differing explanations. The White *Yajur Veda* has two explanations, one in terms of *Purusha*, the other in terms of *Prajapati*. The Black *Yajur Veda* has three explanations to offer. Two are in terms of *Prajapati*, the third in terms of Brahman. The *Atharva Veda* has four explanations, one in terms of *Purusha*, second in terms of *Brahman* third in terms of *Vratya* and fourth quite different from the first three. Even when the theory is the same, the details are not the same. Some explanations such as those in terms of Prajapati, or Brahma are theological. Others in terms of Manu or Kasyapa are in humanistic terms. It is imagination running riot. There is in them neither history nor sense. Prof. Max Muller commenting on the *Brahmanas* has said:

---

[1] Muir, Vol. I, p. 21.

[2] Muir, Vol. I, p. 21.

"The Brahmanas represent no doubt a most interesting phase in the history of the Indian mind, but judged by themselves, as literary productions, they are most disappointing. No one would have supposed that at so early a period, and in so primitive a state of society, there could have risen up a literature which for pedantry and downright absurdity can hardly be matched anywhere. There is no lack of striking thoughts, of bold expressions, of sound reasoning, and curious traditions in these collections. But these are only like the fragments of a torso, like precious gems set in brass and lead. The general character of these works is marked by shallow and insipid grandiloquence, by priestly conceit, and antiquarian pedantry. It is most important to the historian that he should know how soon the fresh and healthy growth of a nation can be blighted by priestcraft and superstition. It is most important that we should know that nations are liable to these epidemics in their youth as well as in their dotage. These works deserve to be studied as the physician studies the twaddle of idiots, and the raving of madmen." [1]

On reading these Brahmanic speculations on the origin of the four *Varnas* and particularly of the *Shudras* one is very much reminded of these words of Prof. Max Muller. All these speculations are really the twaddles of idiots and ravings of madmen and as such they are no use to the student of history who is in search of a natural explanation of a human problem.

[1] Max Muller : Ancient Sanskrit Literature (Panini office edition) P. 200.

CHAPTER III

THE BRAHMANIC THEORY OF THE STATUS OF THE SHUDRAS

So much for the Brahmanic view of the origin of the Shudra. Turning to the Brahmanic view of the civil status of the Shudra, what strikes one is the long list of disabilities, accompanied by a most dire system of pains and penalties to which the Shudra is subjected by the Brahmanic law-givers.

The disabilities and penalties of the Shudra found in the *Samhitas* and the *Brahmanas* were few, as may be seen from the following extracts :—

I. According to the *Kathaka Samhita* (xxxi.2) and the *Maitrayani Samhita* (iv.1.3; i.8.3)

> " A Shudra should not be allowed to milk the cow whose milk is used for Agnihotra."

II. The *Satapatha Brahmana* (iii.1.1.10), the *Maitrayani Samhita* (vii.1.1.6) and also the *Panchavimsa Brahmana* (vi.1.11) say :—

> " The Shudra must not be spoken to when performing a sacrifice and a Shudra must not be present when a sacrifice is being performed."

III. The *Satapatha Brahmana* (xiv.1.31) and the *Kathaka Samhita* (xi.10) further provide that

> " The Shudra must not be admitted to Soma drink."

IV. The *Aitareya Brahmana* (vii.29.4) and the *Panchavimsa Brahmana* (vi.1.11) reached the culminating point when they say :—

> " Shudra is a servant of another (and cannot be anything else)."

But what in the beginning was a cloud no bigger than a man's hand, seems to have developed into a storm, which has literally overwhelmed the Shudras. For, as will be seen from the extracts given from later penal legislation by the *Sutrakaras* like *Apastamba, Baudhayana,* etc. and the *Smritikaras* like Manu and others, the growth of the disabilities of the Shudras has been at a maddening speed and to an extent which is quite unthinkable.

The disabilities are so deadening that it would be impossible to believe them unless one sees them in cold print. They are, however, so numerous that it is impossible to present them in their fullness. To enable those, who do not know them, to have some idea of these disabilities, I have assembled below in one place illustrative statements by the different *Sutrakaras* and *Smritikaras* relating to the disabilities of the Shudras scattered in their Law Books.

II

(*i*)

(A) The *Apastamba Dharma Sutra* says :

"There are four castes—Brahmanas, Kshatriyas, Vaishyas and Shudras.

Amongst these, each preceding (caste) is superior by birth to the one following[1] :

For all these, excepting Shudras and those who have committed bad actions are ordained (1) the initiation (Upanayana or the wearing of the sacred thread), (2) the study of the Veda and (3) the kindling of the sacred fire (i.e., the right to perform sacrifices)[2]."

(B) This is what the *Vasishtha Dharma Sutra* says :

"There are four castes (Varna) Brahmanas, Kshatriyas, Vaishyas and Shudras.

Three castes, Brahmanas, Kshatriyas and Vaishyas (are called) twice-born.

---

[1] Prasna 1, Patala 1, Khanda 1, Sutras 4-5.

[2] *Ibid*, Sutra 6.

Their first-birth is from the mother; the second from the investiture with the sacred girdle. In that (second birth) the Savitri is the mother, but the teacher is said to be the father.

They call the teacher father, because he gives instruction in the Veda [1].

The four castes are distinguished by their origin and by particular sacraments.

There is also the following passage of the Veda: 'The Brahmana was his mouth, the Kshatriya formed his arms; the Vaishya his thighs; the Shudra was born from his feet.'

It has been declared in the following passage of the Veda that a Shudra shall not receive the sacraments. 'He created the Brahmana with the Gayatri (metre), the Kshatriya with the Trishtubh, the Vaishya with the Jagati, the Shudra without any metre [2].' "

(C) The *Manu Smriti* propounds the following view on the subject:

"For the prosperity of the worlds, he (the creator) from his mouth, arms, thighs and feet created the Brahmana, Kshatriya, Vaishya and Shudra [3].

The Brahmana, Kshatriya (and) Vaishya constitute the three twice-born castes; but the fourth, the Shudra has only one birth [4]."

(*ii*)

(A) The *Apastamba Dharma Sutra* says:

"(A Traivarnika) shall never study (the Veda) in a burial ground nor anywhere near it within the throw of a Samya.

If a village has been built over a burial ground or its surface has been cultivated as a field, the recitation of the Veda in such a place is not prohibited.

But if that place is known to have been a burial ground, he shall not study (there).

A Shudra and an outcaste are (included by the term) burial-ground, (and the rule given, Sutra 6 applies to them).

---

[1] Chapter II, Verses 1-4.

[2] Chapter IV, Verse 3.

[3] Chapter I, Verse 31.

[4] Chapter X, Verse 4.

Some declare, that (one ought to avoid only to study) in the same house (where they dwell).

But if (a student and) a Shudra woman merely look at each other, the recitation of the Veda must be interrupted[1].

Food touched by a (Brahmana or other high-caste person) who is impure, becomes impure but not unfit for eating.

But what has been brought (be it touched or not) by an impure Sudra, must not be eaten.

A Sudra touches him, (then he shall leave off eating)[2]."

(B) The *Vishnu Smriti* says :

" He must not cause a member of a twice born caste to be carried out by a Shudra (even though he be a kinsman of the deceased).

Nor a Shudra by a member of a twice-born caste.

A father and a mother shall be carried out by their sons ; (who are equal in caste to their parents).

But Shudras must never carry out a member of a twice-born caste, even though he be their father." [3]

(C) The *Vasishtha Dharma Sutra* prescribes :—

" Now therefore, we will declare what may be eaten and what may not be eaten.

Food given by a physician, a hunter, a woman of bad character, a mace-bearer, a thief, an Abhisasta, an eunuch, (or) an outcaste must not be eaten.

Nor that given by a miser, one who has performed the initiatory ceremony of a Srauta-sacrifice, a prisoner, a sick person, a seller of the Soma plant, a carpenter, a washerman, a dealer in spirituous liquour, a spy, an usurer, (or) a cobbler.

Nor that given by a Shudra [4].

Some call that Shudra race a burial-ground.

Therefore the Veda must not be recited in the presence of a Shudra.

Now they quote also the (following) verses which Yama proclaimed :

The wicked Shudra-race is manifestly a burial-ground. Therefore (the Veda) must never be recited in the presence of a Shudra [5].

---

[1] Prasna 1, Patala 3, Khanda 9, Sutras 6-11.
[2] Prasna 1, Patala 5, Khanda 16, Sutras 21-22.
[3] Chapter XIX, Sutras 1-4.
[4] Chapter XIV, Verses 1-4.
[5] Chapter XVIII, Verses 11-15.

Some become worthy receptacles of gifts through sacred learning, and some through the practice of austerities. But that Brahmana whose stomach does not contain the food of a Shudra, is even the worthiest receptacle of all [1].

If a Brahmana dies with the food of a Shudra in his stomach, he will become a village pig (in his next life) or be born in the family of that Shudra.

For though a (Brahmana) whose body is nourished by the essence of a Shudra's food may daily recite the Veda, though he may offer (an Agnihotra) or mutter (prayers, nevertheless) he will not find the path that leads upwards.

" But if, after eating the food of a Shudra, he has conjugal intercourse, (even) his sons (begotten on a wife of his own caste) will belong to the giver of the food (i.e., to the Shudra), and he shall not ascend to heaven." [2]

(D) The *Manu Smriti* says :—

" He (Brahmin) may not dwell in the kingdom of a Shudra, nor in one full of unrighteous people, nor in one invaded by hosts of heretics nor in one possessed by low-born men. [3]

A Brahmin who performs a sacrifice for a Shudra should not be invited to dine with other Brahmins at a Shraddha ceremony. His company will destroy all merit that which may otherwise be obtained from such a dinner. [4]

One should carry out by the southern town-gate a dead Shudra, but the twice-born by the western, northern and eastern (gates) respectively." [5]

(iii)

(A) The *Apastamba Dharma Sutra* says :—

" A Brahmana shall salute stretching forward his right arm on a level with his ear, a Kshatriya holding it on a level with the breast, a Vaishya holding it on a level with the waist, a Shudra holding it low (and) stretching forward the joined hands. [6]

---

[1] Chapter VI, Verses 26.

[2] Chapter VI, Verses 27-29.

[3] Chapter IV, Verse 61.

[4] Chapter III, Verse 178.

[5] Chapter V, Verse 92.

[6] Prasna 1, Patala 2, Khanda 5, Sutra 16.

And when returning the salute of (a man belonging) to the first (three) castes, the last syllable of the name of the person addressed is produced to the length of three moras.[1]

If a Shudra comes as a guest (to a Brahmana) he shall give him some work to do. He may feed him, after (that has been performed. To feed him without asking him first to do some work is to do him honour.)

Or the slaves (of the Brahmana householder) shall fetch (rice) from the royal stores, and honour the Shudra as a guest."[2]

(B) The *Vishnu Smriti* prescribes :—

" The same punishment (payment of hundred Panas) is also ordained for hospitably entertaining a Shudra or religious ascetic at an oblation to the gods or to the manes."[3]

(C) The *Manu Smriti* enjoins that :—

" One should consider a Brahmana ten years old and a Kshatriya a hundred years old as father and son ; but of them the Brahman (is) the father.

Wealth, kindred, age, sects (and) knowledge as the fifth ; those are the causes of respect ; the most important (is) the last (mentioned).

In whom among the three (higher) castes the most and the best of (those) five may be he is here worthy of respect ; a Shudra (is not worthy of respect on the ground of his wealth or knowledge no matter how high they are. It is only on the ground of his age and that too only if) he has attained the tenth (decade of his life that he becomes worthy of respect and not before.)[4]

For not by years, nor by grey hair, not by wealth, nor kindred (is superiority); the seers made the rule—Who knows the Veda completely, he is great among us.

Of Brahmins, superiority (is) by knowledge, but of Kshatriyas by valour ; of Vaishyas by reason of property (and) wealth, and of Shudras by age.

One is not, therefore, aged because his head is grey ; whoever, although a youth, has perused (the Vedas), him the gods consider an elder.[5]

---

[1] *Ibid*, Sutra 17.

[2] Prasna II, Patala 2, Khanda 4, Sutras 19-20.

[3] Chapter V, Sutra 115.

[4] Chapter II, Verses 135-37.

[5] Chapter II, Verses 154-156.

Now a Kshatriya is not called a guest in a Brahmin's house, nor a Vaishya nor a Shudra; neither is a friend, the kinsman, nor a Guru (of the householder). (That is, a Brahmin has alone the right to have the honour of being treated as a guest in a Brahmin's house).

But if a Kshatriya come as a guest to the house after the said Brahmins have eaten, one should give him food (if) he wishes.

If a Vaishya (or) Shudra come to the house as guests, the Brahmin should give them food but with the servants, using kindness." [1]

(*iv*)

(A) According to the *Apastamba Dharma Sutra* :—

" He who has killed a Kshatriya shall give a thousand cows (to Brahmins for the expiation of the act).

He shall give, a hundred cows for the killing of a Vaishya, (only) ten for a Shudra." [2]

(B) According to the *Gautama Dharma Sutra* :—

" A Kshatriya (shall be fined) one hundred (Karshapanas) if he abuses a Brahmana.

In case of an assault (on a Brahmana) twice as much.

A Vaishya (who abuses a Brahmana, shall pay) one and a half (times as much as a Kshatriya).

But a Brahmana (who abuses) a Kshatriya (shall pay) fifty (Karshapanas).

One half of that amount (if he abuses) a Vaishya.

And if he abuses a Shudra nothing." [3]

(C) According to *Brihaspati's Dharma Shastra* :—

" For a Brahmin abusing a Kshatriya, the fine shall be half of a hundred (fifty) Panas; for abusing a Vaisya, half of fifty (twenty-five) Panas; for abusing a Shudra twelve and a half."

" This punishment has been declared for abusing a virtuous Shudra (i.e., a Shudra who accepts his low status and does willingly the duties attached to that status) who has committed no wrong; no offence is imputable to a Brahmin for abusing a Shudra devoid of virtue.

[1] Chapter III, Verses 110-112.

[2] Prasna I, Patala 9, Khanda 24, Sutras 1-3.

[3] Chapter XII, Sutras 8-13.

A Vaishya shall be fined a hundred (Panas) for reviling a Kshatriya ; a Kshatriya reviling a Vaishya shall have to pay half of that amount as a fine.

In the case of a Kshatriya reviling a Shudra the fine shall be twenty Panas ; in the case of a Vaishya, the double amount is declared to be the proper fine by persons learned in law.

A Shudra shall be compelled to pay the first fine for abusing a Vaishya ; the middling fine for abusing a Kshatriya ; and the highest fine for abusing a Brahmin."[1]

(D) According to the *Manu Smriti* :—

A Kshatriya who reviles a Brahmin ought to be fined one hundred (Panas) ; a Vaishya one hundred and fifty or two hundred, but a Shudra ought to receive corporal punishment.

A Brahmin should be fined fifty if he has thrown insult on a Kshatriya, but the fine shall be a half of fifty if on a Vaishya and twelve if on a Shudra.[2]

In the murder of a Kshatriya, one fourth (part) of the penance for slaying a Brahman is declared to be the proper penance ; an eighth part in the case of a Vaishya ; and in (the case of) a Shudra (who) lives virtuously, one sixteenth part must be admitted (as the proper penance).

But if one of the highest of the twice-born (a Brahmin) slay a Kshatriya involuntarily he may, in order to cleanse himself give a thousand cows and a bull.

Or let him for three years (with senses) subdued and locks braided, follow the observances of one who has slain a Brahmin, living in a place rather far from the town, his dwelling place the foot of a tree.

The highest of a twice-born (the Brahmin) should practise just this expiation for a year on having slain a Vaishya who lives virtuously and give one hundred and one (heads) of cattle.

The slayer of a Shudra should practise exactly all these observances for six months ; or he may give to a priest ten white cows and a bull."[3]

(E) According to the *Vishnu Smriti* :—

"With whatever limb an inferior insults or hurts his superior in caste, of that limb the king shall cause him to be deprived.

---

[1] Chapter XX, Verses 7-11.

[2] Chapter VIII, Verses 267-268.

[3] Chapter XI, Verses 127-131.

If he places himself on the same seat with his superior, he shall be banished with a mark on his buttocks.

If he spits on him he shall lose both lips.

If he breaks wind against him, he shall lose his hind parts.

If he uses abusive language, his tongue.

If a low-born man through pride give instruction (to a member of the highest caste) concerning his duty, let the king order hot oil to be dropped into his mouth.

If a Shudra man mentions the name or caste of a superior revilingly, an iron pin ten inches long shall be thrust into his mouth (red hot)[1]."

(v)

(A) According to the *Brihaspati Smriti* :—

" A Shudra teaching the precepts of religion or uttering the words of the Veda, or insulting a Brahmin shall be punished by cutting out his tongue[2]."

(B) According to the *Gautama Dharma Sutra* :—

" Now if he listens intentionally to (a recitation of) the Veda, his ears shall be filled with (molten) tin or lac.

If he recites (Vedic texts), his tongue shall be cut out.

If he remembers them, his body shall be split in twain[3]."

(C) According to the *Manu Smriti* :—

" One who teaches for hire, also one who learns by paying hire ; (a Shudra) teacher and one who learns from him are unfit for being invited at the performance in honour of the Devas and Pitris[4].

One may not give advice to a Shudra, nor (give him) the remains (of food) or of butter that has been offered.

And one may not teach him the law or enjoin upon him religious observances.

For he who tells him the law and he who enjoins upon him (religious) observances, he indeed together with that (Shudra) sinks into the darkness of the hell called Asamvrita[5].

One should never recite (the Vedas) indistinctly or in the presence of a Shudra ; nor having recited the Veda at the end of the night, (though) fatigued may one sleep again[6]."

---

[1] Chapter V, Sutras 19-25.
[2] Chapter XII, Verse 12.
[3] Chapter XX, Sutras 4-6.
[4] Chapter III, Verse 156.
[5] Chapter IV, Verses 78-81.
[6] Chapter IV, Verse 99.

(*vi*)

This is what the *Manu Smriti* says :—

" A Brahmin may take possession of the goods of a Shudra with perfect peace of mind, for, since nothing at all belongs to this Shudra as his own, he is one whose property may be taken away by his master [1].

Indeed, an accumulation of wealth should not be made by a Shudra even if he is able to do so, for the sight of mere possession of wealth by a Shudra injures the Brahmin [2]."

(*vii*)

Here is the advice of the *Manu Smriti* to the king :—

" He who can claim to be a Brahmin merely on account of his birth, or he who only calls himself a Brahmin, may be, if desired, the declarer of law for the king, but a Shudra never.

If a king looks on while a Shudra gives a judicial decision, his realm sinks into misfortune, like a cow in a quagmire.

A realm which consists chiefly of Shudras and is overrun by unbelievers and destitute of twice-born men is soon totally destroyed, oppressed by famine and disease.[1]"

(*viii*)

(A) The *Apastamba Dharma Sutra* says :—

And those who perform austerities, being intent on fulfilling the sacred laws.

And a Shudra who lives by washing the feet (of the Brahmin).

Also blind, dumb, deaf and diseased persons (as long as their infirmities last) are exempt from taxes[2].

To serve the other three castes is ordained for the Shudra.

The higher the caste which he serves the greater is the merit[3]."

(B) The *Manu Smriti* has the following :—

" Now, for the sake of preserving all this creation, the most glorious (being) ordained separate duties for those who sprang from (his) mouth, arm, thigh and feet.

---

[1] Chapter VIII, Verse 417.

[2] Chapter X, Verse 129.

[3] Chapter VIII, Verses 20-22.

[4] Prasna II, Patala 10, Khanda 26, Sutras 14-16.

[5] Prasna I, Patala 1 Khanda 1, Sutras 7-8.

For Brahmins he ordered teaching, study, sacrifices and sacrificing (as priests) for others, also giving and receiving gifts.

Defence of the people, giving (alms), sacrifice, also study, and absence of attachment to objects of sense, in short for a Kshatriya.

Tending of cattle, giving (alms), sacrifice, study, trade, usury, and also agriculture for a Vaishya.

One duty the Lord assigned to a Shudra—service to those (before-mentioned) classes without grudging[1]."

(*ix*)

(A) The *Apastamba Dharma Sutra* says :—

"A man of one of the first three castes (who commits adultery) with a woman of the Shudra caste shall be banished.

A Shudra (who commits adultery) with a woman of one of the first three castes shall suffer capital punishment[2]."

(B) The *Gautama Dharma Sutra* says :—

"If (the Shudra) has criminal intercourse with an Aryan woman, his organ shall be cut off, and all his property be confiscated.

If (the woman had) a protector (i.e., she was under the guardianship of some person) he (the Shudra) shall be executed after having undergone the punishments prescribed above[3]."

(C) The *Manu Smriti* says :—

"If a man (of the Shudra caste) makes love to a girl of the highest caste he deserves corporal punishment[4].

A Shudra cohabiting with a woman of twice-born castes, whether she be guarded or not guarded, is (to be) deprived of his member and of all his property if she be not guarded and of everything if she is guarded[5].

For twice-born men, at first, a woman of the same caste is approved for marrying ; but of those who act from lust, those of lower caste may in order (be wives).

A Shudra woman alone (is) a wife for a Shudra ; both she and a woman of his own caste (are) legally (wives) of a

[1] Chapter 1, Verses 87-91.

[2] Prasna II, Patala 10, Khanda 27, Sutras 8-9.

[3] Chapter XII, Sutras 2-3.

[4] Chapter VIII, Verse 366.

[5] *Ibid*, Verse 374.

Vaishya; they two and also a woman of his own caste (are wives) of a Kshatriya; both they and a woman of his own caste (are wives) of a Brahmin.

A Shudra wife is not indicated in any history for a Brahmin and Kshatriya, even though they be in distress.

Twice-born men marrying a (Shudra) woman out of infatuation will surely bring quickly (their) families and descendants to the condition of Shudras[1].

A Brahmin having taken a Shudra woman to his bed goes the lower course; having begotten on her a son, he is surely deprived of his Brahminhood.

Now of (a man) whose offerings towards gods, manes, and guests depend on her, the manes and gods eat not that offering, nor does he go to heaven.

An expiation is not prescribed for him who has drunk the moisture on a Shudra woman's lips, who has been reached by her breath, and who has also begotten a son on her[2]."

(*x*)

(A) The *Vasishtha Dharma Sutra* says :—

"One may know that bearing grudges, envy, speaking untruths, speaking evil of Brahmins, backbiting and cruelty are the characteristics of a Shudra[3]."

(B) The *Vishnu Smriti* prescribes that :—

" (The name to be chosen should be) auspicious in the case of a Brahmin.

Indicating power in the case of a Kshatriya.

Indicating wealth in the case of a Vaishya.

And indicating contempt in the case of a Shudra[4].

(C) The *Gautama Dharma Sutra* says:—

The Shudra belongs to the fourth caste, which has one birth (only).

And serves the higher (castes).

From them he shall seek to obtain his livelihood.

He shall use their cast-off shoes.

And eat the remnants of their food.

---

[1] Chapter III, Verses 12-15.

[2] *Ibid*, Verses 17-19.

[3] Chapter VI, Verse 24.

[4] Chapter XXVII, Sutras 6-9.

A Shudra who intentionally reviles twice-born men by criminal abuse, or criminally assaults them with blows, shall be deprived of the limb with which he offends.

If he assumes a position equal to that of twice-born men in sitting, in lying down, in conversation or on the road, he shall undergo (corporal punishment) [1]."

(D) The *Manu Smriti* follows suit and says :—

"But if a Brahmin through avarice, and because he possesses the power, compel twice-born men, who have received the initiation (into the caste order), to do the work of a slave when they do not wish it, he shall be fined six hundred panas by the king.

But a Shudra, whether bought or not bought (by the Brahmin) may be compelled to practise servitude; for that Shudra was created by the self-existent merely for the service of the Brahmin.

Even if freed by his master, the Shudra is not released from servitude; for this (servitude) is innate in him; who then can take it from him. [2]

Just in proportion as one pursues without complaining the mode of life (practised) by the good, so free from blame, he gains both this and the other world [3].

Now the supreme duty of a Shudra and that which ensures his bliss is merely obedience toward celebrated priests who understand the Veda and live as householders.

"If he be pure, obedient to the higher (castes), mild in speech, without conceit, and always submissive to the Brahmin, he attains (in the next transmigration) a high birth [4].

Now a Shudra desiring some means of subsistence may serve a Kshatriya, so (is the rule); or the Shudra (if) anxious to support life, (may do so by) serving a wealthy Vaishya.

But he should serve the Brahmins for the sake of heaven, or for the sake of both (heaven and livelihood); for by him (for whom) the word Brahmin (is always) uttered is thus attained the state of completing all he ought to do.

Merely to serve the Brahmins is declared to be the most excellent occupation of a Shudra; for if he does anything other than this it profits him nothing.

---

[1] Chapter X, Sutras 50, 56-59 and Chapter XII, Sutras 1, 7.

[2] Chapter VIII, Verses 412-414.

[3] Chapter X, Verse 128.

[4] Chapter IX, Verses 334-335.

His means of life should be arranged by those Brahmins out of their own household (goods) in accordance with what is fitting after examining his ability, cleverness, and (the amount) the dependents embrace.

The leaving of food should be given (to him) and the old clothes ; so too the blighted part of the grain ; so too the old furniture [1].

"Let a Brahmin's name be auspicious, a Kshatriya's full of power ; let a Vaishya's mean wealth, a Shudra's however be contemptible.

Let a Brahmin's (distinctive title) imply prosperity, a Kshatriya's safeguard, a Vaishya's wealth, a Shudra's service[2].

If (a man) of one birth assault one of the twice-born castes with virulent words, he ought to have his tongue cut, for he is of the lowest origin.

If he makes mention in an insulting manner of their name and caste, a red-hot iron rod, ten fingers long, should be thrust into his mouth.

If this man through insolence gives instruction to the priests in regard to their duty, the king should cause boiling hot oil to be poured into his mouth and ear [3].

If a man of the lowest birth should with any member injure one of the highest station, even that member of this man shall be cut (off) ; this is an ordinance of Manu.

If he lift up his hand or his staff (against him), he ought to have his hand cut off ; and if he smites him with his feet in anger, he ought to have his feet cut off."

"If a low-born man endeavours to sit down by the side of a high-born man, he should be banished after being branded on the hip, or (the king) may cause his backside to be cut off.

If through insolence he spit upon him, the king should cause his two lips to be cut off ; and if he makes water upon him, his penis, and if he breaks wind upon him, his anus.

If he seize him by the locks, let the king without hesitation cause both his hands to be cut off, (also if he seize him) by the feet, the beard, the neck or the testicles.

A man who tears (another's) skin and one who causes blood to be seen ought to be fined five hundred (Panas), if he tears

---

[1] Chapter X, Verses 121-125.

[2] Chapter II, Verses 31-32.

[3] Chapter VIII, Verses 270-72.

the flesh (he should be fined) six niskas, but if he breaks a bone he should be banished [1]."

(D) The *Narada Smriti* says :—

"Men of the Shudra caste, who prefer a false accusation against a member of a twice-born Aryan caste, shall have their tongue split by the officers of the king, and he shall cause them to be put on stakes.

A once-born man (or Shudra) who insults members of a twice-born caste with gross invectives, shall have his tongue cut off ; for he is of low origin.

If he refers to their name or caste in terms indicating contempt, an iron-rod, ten angulas long, shall be thrust red-hot into his mouth.

If he is insolent enough to give lessons regarding their duty to Brahmins, the king shall order hot oil to be poured into his mouth and ears.

With whatever limb a man of low caste offends against a Brahmin, that very limb of him shall be cut off ; such shall be the atonement for his crime.

A low-born man, who tries to place himself on the same seat with his superior in caste, shall be branded on his hip and banished, or (the king) shall cause his backside to be gashed.

If through arrogance he spits on a superior, the king shall cause both his lips to be cut off ; if he makes water on him, the penis, if he breaks wind against him, the buttocks. [2]"

III

Such were the laws made against the Shudras by the Brahmanic law-givers. The gist of them may be summarized under the following heads :—

(1) That the Shudra was to take the last place in the social order.

(2) That the Shudra was impure and therefore no sacred act should be done within his sight and within his hearing.

---

[1] Chapter VIII, Verses 279-284.

[2] Chapter XV, Verses 22-27.

(3) That the Shudra is not to be respected in the same way as the other classes.

(4) That the life of a Shudra is of no value and anybody may kill him without having to pay compensation and if at all of small value as compared with that of the Brahmana, Kshatriya and Vaishya.

(5) That the Shudra must not acquire knowledge and it is a sin and a crime to give him education.

(6) That a Shudra must not acquire property. A Brahmin can take his property at his pleasure.

(7) That a Shudra cannot hold office under the State.

(8) That the duty and salvation of the Shudra lies in his serving the higher classes.

(9) That the higher Classes must not inter-marry with the Shudra. They can however keep a Shudra woman as a concubine. But if the Shudra touches a woman of the higher classes he will be liable to dire punishment.

(10) That the Shudra is born in servility and must be kept in servility for ever.

Anyone who reads this summary will be struck by two considerations. He will be struck by the consideration that the Shudra alone has been selected by the Brahmanic law-givers as a victim for their law-making authority. The wonder must be all the greater when it is recalled that in the ancient Brahmanic literature the oppressed class in the ancient Indo-Aryan society was the Vaishya and not the Shudra. In this connection a reference may be made to the *Aitareya Brahmana*. The *Aitareya Brahmana* in telling the story of King Vishvantara and the Shyaparna Brahmanas refers to the sacrificial drink to which the different classes are entitled. In the course of the story, it speaks of the Vaishya in the following terms :—

> "Next, if (the priest bring) curds, that is the Vaishya's draught; with it thou shalt satisfy the Vaishyas. One like a Vaishya shall be born in thy line, one who is tributary to

another, who is to be used (lit. eaten) by another, and who may be oppressed at will[1]."

The question is : why was the Vaishya let off and why the fury directed towards the Shudras ?

He will also be struck by the close connection of the disabilities of the Shudra with the privileges of the Brahmin. The Shudra is below the Traivarnikas and is contrasted with the Traivarnikas. That being so, one would expect all the Traivarnikas to have the same rights against the Shudras. But what are the facts ? The facts are that the Kshatriyas and Vaishyas have no rights worth speaking of against the Shudras. The only Traivarnika who has special rights and privileges is the Brahmin. For instance, if the Shudra is guilty of an offence against the Brahmin, the Brahmin has the privilege of demanding a higher punishment than what a Kshatriya or a Vaishya could. A Brahmin could take the property of the Shudra without being guilty of an offence if he needed it for the purpose of performing a sacrifice. A Shudra should not accumulate property because he thereby hurts the Brahmin. A Brahmin should not live in a country where the king is a Shudra. Why is this so ? Had the Brahmin any cause to regard the Shudra as his special enemy ?

There is one other consideration more important than these. It is, what does the average Brahmin think of these disabilities of the Shudras ? That they are extraordinary in their conception and shameful in their nature will be admitted by all. Will the Brahmin admit it ? It would not be unnatural if this catalogue of disabilities may not make any impression upon him. In the first place, by long habit and usage his moral sense has become so dulled that he has ceased to bother about the how and why of these disabilities of the Shudras. In the second place, those of them who are conscious of them feel that

[1] Muir, Vol. 1, p. 436-40.

similar disabilities have been imposed on particular classes in other countries and there is therefore nothing extraordinary nor shameful in the disabilities of the Shudras. It is the second attitude that needs to be exposed.

This attitude is a very facile one and is cherished because it helps to save reputation and salve conscience. It is, however, no use leaving things as they are. It is absolutely essential to show that these disabilities have no parallel anywhere in the world. It is impossible to compare the Brahmanic Law with every other legal system on the point of rights and disabilities. A comparison of the Brahmanic Law with the Roman Law ought to suffice.

IV

It will be well to begin this comparison by noting the classes which under the Roman Law had rights and those which suffered from disabilities. The Roman jurists divided men into five categories: (1) Patricians and Plebians; (2) Freemen and Slaves; (3) Citizens and Foreigners; (4) Persons who were *sui juris* and persons who were *alieni juris* and (5) Christians and Pagans.

Under the Roman Law, persons who were privileged were: (1) Patricians; (2) Freemen; (3) Citizens; (4) *Sui juris* and (5) Christians. As compared to these, persons who suffered disabilities under the Roman Law were: (1) the Plebians; (2) Slaves; (3) Foreigners; (4) Persons who were *alieni juris* and (5) Pagans.

A Freeman, who was a citizen under the Roman Law, possessed civil rights as well as political rights. The civil rights of a citizen comprised rights of *connubium* and *commercium*. In virtue of the *connubium* the citizen could contract a valid marriage according to the *jus civile*, and acquire the rights resulting from it, and particularly the paternal power and the civil relationship called agnation, which was absolutely necessary to enable him in law to succeed to the property of persons who died intestate. In virtue of the *commercium* he could acquire and dispose of property of all kinds, according to the forms and with the peculiar privileges of the Roman Law. The political rights of the Roman citizen included *jus suffragii* and *jus honorum*, the right to vote in public elections and the right to hold office.

The slave differed from the Freeman in as much as he was owned by the master and as such had no capacity to acquire rights.

Foreigners, who were called *Peregrine*, were not citizens and had none of the political or civil rights which went with citizenship. A Foreigner could obtain no protection unless he was under the protection of a citizen.

The *alieni juris* differed from *sui juris* in as much as the former were subject to the authority of another person, while the latter were free from it. This authority was variously called (1) *Potestas*, (2) *Manus* and (3) *Mancipium*, though they had the same effect. *Potestas* under the Roman Law fell into two classes. Persons subject to *Potestas* were (1) slaves, (2) children, (3) wife in *Manus*, (4) debtor assigned to the creditor by the Court and (5) a hired gladiator. *Potestas* gave to one in whom it was vested rights to exclusive possession of those to whom it extended and to vindicate any wrong done to them by anyone else.

The correlative disabilities which persons *alieni juris* suffered as a result of being subject to *Potestas* were: (1) they were not free, (2) they could not acquire property and (3) they could not directly vindicate any wrong or injury done to them.

The disabilities of the Pagans began with the advent of Christianity. Originally, when all the Romans followed the same Pagan worship, religion could occasion no difference in the enjoyment of civil rights. Under the Christian Emperors, heretics and apostates as well as

Pagans and Jews, were subjected to vexatious restrictions, particularly as regards their capacity to succeed to property and to act as witnesses. Only orthodox Christians who recognised the decisions of the four œcumenical councils had the full enjoyment of civil rights.

This survey of rights and disabilities of the Roman Law may well give comfort to Hindus that the Brahmanic Law was not the only law which was guilty of putting certain classes under disabilities, although the disabilities imposed by the Roman Law have nothing of the cruelty which characterizes the disabilities imposed by the Brahmanic Law. But when one compares the principles of the Roman Law with those of the Brahmanic Law underlying these disabilities, the baseness of the Brahmanic Law becomes apparent.

Let us first ask : What was the basis of rights and disabilities under the Roman Law. Even a superficial student of Roman Law knows that they were based upon (1) *Caput* and (2) *Existimatio.*

Caput meant the civil status of a person. Civil status among the Romans had reference chiefly to three things : liberty, citizenship and family. The *status libertatis* consisted of being a freeman and not a slave. If a freeman was also a Roman citizen, he enjoyed the *status civitatis*. Upon this quality depended not only the enjoyment of political rights, but the capacity of participating in the *jus civile*. Finally, the *status familiæ* consisted in a citizen belonging to a particular family, and being capable of enjoying certain rights in which the members of that family, in their quality of agnates, could alone take part.

If an existing status came to be lost or changed, the person suffered what was called a *capitis diminutio*, which extinguished either entirely or to some extent his former legal capacity. There were three changes of state or condition attended with different consequences, called *maxima*, *media*, and *minima*. The greatest involves the loss of liberty, citizenship, and family; and this happened when a Roman citizen was taken prisoner in war, or condemned to slavery for his crimes. But a citizen who was captured by the enemy, on returning from captivity, was restored to all his civil rights *jure postliminii.*

The next change of status consisted of the loss of citizenship and family rights, without any forfeiture of personal liberty; and this occurred when a citizen became a member of another state. He was then forbidden the use of fire and water, so as to be forced to quit the Roman territory, or was sentenced to deportation under the empire.

Finally, when a person ceased to belong to a particular family, without losing his liberty or citizenship, he was said to suffer the least change of state, as for instance, where one *sui juris* came under the power of another by arrogation, or a son who had been under the *patria potestas* was legally emancipated by his father.

Citizenship was acquired first by birth. In a lawful marriage the child followed the condition of the father, and became a citizen, if the father was so at the time of conception. If the child was not the issue of *justæ nuptiæ*, it followed the condition of the mother at the time of its birth. Secondly, by manumission, according to the formalities prescribed by law, the slave of a Roman citizen became a citizen. This rule was modified by the laws Ælia Sentia and Junia Norbana, according to which, in certain cases, the freedman acquired only the status of a foreigner, *peregrinus dedititius* or of a Latin, *Latinus Junianus.* Justinian restored the ancient principle, according to which every slave, regularly enfranchised, became in full right a Roman citizen. Thirdly, the right of citizenship was often granted as a favour, either to a whole community or to an individual, by the people or the senate during the republic, and by the reigning prince during the empire; and this was equivalent to what the moderns call naturalisation.

Citizenship was lost—Firstly, by the loss of liberty—as, for instance, when a Roman became a prisoner of war; Secondly, by renouncing the character of Roman citizen, which took place when anyone was admitted a citizen of another state; Thirdly, by a sentence of deportation or exile, as a punishment for crime.

The civil status of a person under the Roman Law may or may not be *civis optimo jure*. *Civis optimo jure* included not only capacity for civil rights but also capacity for political rights such as *jus suffragii et honorum*, i.e., the right to vote and the capacity to hold a public office. Capacity for political rights depended upon *existimatio*. *Existimatio* means reputation in the eye of the law. A Roman citizen may have *caput* as well as *existimatio*. On the other hand, a Roman may have *caput* but may not have *existimatio*. Whoever had *caput* as well as *existimatio* had civil rights as well as political rights. Whoever had *caput* but had no *existimatio* could claim civil rights only. He could not claim political rights.

A person's *existimatio* was lost in two ways. It was lost by loss of freedom or by conviction for an offence. If a person lost his freedom, his *existimatio* was completely extinguished. Loss of *existimatio* by conviction for offence varied according to the gravity of the offence[1]. If the offence was serious the diminution of his *existimatio* was called *infamia*. If the offence was less grave it was called *turpitudo*. *Infamia* resulted in the extinguishment of *existimatio*. Under the Roman Law a defendant, in addition to ordinary damages, was subjected to *infamia*. Condemnation for theft, robbery, *injuria* or fraud, entailed infamy. So a partner, a *mandatarius*, a *depositarius*, *tutor*, a mortgagee (in *contractus fiduciæ*) if condemned for wilful breach of duty, was held to be infamous.

The consequence of *infamia* was exclusion from political

[1] Such as robbery, theft, perjury, fraud, appearing on the public stage as an actor or gladiator, ignominious expulsion from the army, gaining a living by aiding in prostitution and other disreputable occupations and other variety of acts involving gross moral turpitude.

rights[1], not merely from office (honours), but even from the right to vote in elections (*suffragium*).

From this brief survey of the basis of rights and disabilities in Roman Law, it will be clear that the basis was the same for all. They did not differ from community to community. Rights and disabilities according to Roman Law were regulated by general considerations, such as *caput* and *existimatio*. Whoever had *caput* and *existimatio* had rights. Whoever lost his *caput* and his *existimatio* suffered disabilities. What is the position under the Brahmanic Law? There again, it is quite clear that rights and disabilities were not based on general uniform considerations. They were based on communal considerations. All rights for the first three *Varnas* and all disabilities for the Shudras was the principle on which the Brahmanic Law was based.

The protagonists of Brahmanic Laws may urge that this comparison is too favourable to Roman Law and that the statement that Roman Law did not distribute rights and liabilities on communal basis is not true. This may be conceded. For so far as the relation between the Patricians and Plebians was concerned the distribution of rights and liabilities was communal. But in this connection the following facts must be noted.

In the first place, it must be noted that Plebians were not slaves. They were freemen in as much as they enjoyed *jus commercii* or the right to acquire, hold and

---

[1] There were other consequences of *infamia* such as exclusion from the office of attorney, disability to act on behalf of another in a lawsuit or giving evidence. *Infamia* was inflicted in two ways, either by the censors or by the judgment of a Court of Law. It was in the power of the censors, in superintending public morality, to deprive senators of their dignity, to remove knights from the equestrian order and even to strip a citizen of all his political rights by classing him among the *ærarii*. The censors also put a *nota censoria* opposite to a man's name in the roll of citizens; and this might be done upon their own responsibility, without special inquiry, though they generally acted in accordance with public opinion. The *nota censoria* produced no effect except during the magistracy of the censor who imposed it. In this respect it differed essentially from infamy, which was perpetual, unless the stigma was removed by the prerogative of the people or the Emperor.

transfer property. Their disabilities consisted in the denial of political and social rights. In the second place, it must be noted that their disabilities were not permanent. There were two social disabilities from which they suffered. One arose from the interdict on intermarriage between them and the Patricians imposed by the Twelve Tables[1]. This disability was removed in B.C. 445 by the passing of the Canulenian Law which legalized intermarriage between Patricians and Plebians. The other disability was their ineligibility to hold the office of Pontiffs and Augurs in the Public Temples of Rome. This disability was removed by the Ogulnian Law passed in B.C. 300.

As to the political disabilities of the Plebians they had secured the right to vote in popular assemblies (*Jus suffragii*) under the Constitution of Servius Tullius the Sixth King of Rome. The political disabilities which had remained unredressed were those which related to the holding of office. This too was removed in course of time after the Republic was established in B.C. 509. The first step taken in this direction was the appointment of Plebian Tribunes in B.C. 494; the Questorship was opened to them, formally in B.C. 421, actually in B.C. 409; the Consulship in B.C. 367; the curule-ædileship in B.C. 366; the dictatorship in B.C. 356; the Censorship in B.C. 351; and the Praetorship in B.C. 336. The Hortensian Law enacted in B.C. 287 marked a complete triumph for the Plebians. By that law the resolutions of the Assembly of the tribes were to be directly and without modification, control or delay, binding upon the whole of the Roman people.

This marks a complete political fusion of Patricians and Plebians on terms of equality.

Not only were the Plebians placed on the same footing as to political capacity and social status with the Patricians but the road to nobility was also thrown open to them.

[1] It was older than the Twelve Tables. The Twelve Tables only recognized it.

In Roman society, birth and fortune were the two great sources of rank and personal distinction. But in addition to this, the office of Curule Magistracy was also a source of ennoblement to the holder thereof. Every citizen, whether Patrician or Plebian, who won his way to a Curule Magistracy, from that *Ædile* upwards, acquired personal distinction, which was transmitted to his descendants, who formed a class called *Nobiles*, or men known, to distinguish them from the *ignobiles*, or people who were not known. As the office was thrown open to the Plebians, many Plebians[1] had become nobles and had even surpassed the Patricians in point of nobility.

It may be that the Roman Law did recognise communal distinction in distributing rights and disabilities. The point is that the disabilities of the Plebians were not regarded as permanent. Although they existed they were in course of time removed. That being so, the protagonists of Brahmanic Law cannot merely take solace in having found a parallel in the Roman Law but have to answer why the Brahmanic Law did not abolish the distinction between the Traivarnikas and the Shudras as the Roman Law did by equating the Plebians with the Patricians ? One can therefore contend that the Roman Law of rights and disabilities was not communal while the Brahmanic Law was.

This is not the only difference between the Roman Law and the Brahmanic Law. There are two others. One is equality before law in criminal matters. The Roman Law may not have recognized equality in matters of civil and political rights. But in matters of criminal law it made no distinction between one citizen and another, not even between Patrician and Plebian. The same offence the same punishment, no matter who the complainant and who the accused was. Once an offence was proved, the punishment was the same. What do the

[1] A Plebian who first attained a Curule office and became the founder of a noble family was called by the Romans a *novus homo* or new man.

Dharma Sutras and the *Smritis* do ? They follow an entirely different principle. For the same offence the punishment varies according to the community of the accused and the community of the complainant. If the complainant is a Shudra and the accused belonged to any one of the three classes the punishment is less than what it would be if the relations were reversed. On the other hand, if the complainant was a Traivarnika and the accused a Shudra, the punishment is far heavier than in the first case. This is another barbarity which distinguishes the Brahmanic Law from the Roman Law.

The next feature of the Roman Law which distinguishes it from the Brahmanic Law is most noteworthy. It relates to the extinction of disabilities. Two points need be borne in mind. First is that the disabilities under the Roman Law were only contingent. So long as certain conditions lasted, they gave rise to certain disabilities. The moment the conditions changed, the disabilities vanished and a step in the direction of equality before law was taken. The second point is that the Roman Law never attempted to fix the conditions for ever and thereby perpetuate the disabilities. On the other hand, it was always ready to remove the conditions to which these disabilities were attached as is evident in the case of the Plebians, the Slaves, the Foreigners and the Pagans.

If these two points about the disabilities under the Roman Law are borne in mind, one can at once see what mischief the *Dharma Sutras* and the *Smritis* have done in imposing the disabilities upon the Shudras. The imposition of disabilities would not have been so atrocious if the disabilities were dependent upon conditions and if the disabled had the freedom to outgrow those conditions. But what the Brahmanic Law does is not merely to impose disabilities but it tries to fix the conditions by making an act which amounts to a breach of those conditions to be a crime involving dire punishment. Thus, the Brahmanic Law not only seeks to impose disabilities but it endeavours to make them permanent. One illustration will suffice. A Shudra is not entitled to perform Vedic sacrifices as he is not able to repeat the Vedic *Mantras*. Nobody would quarrel with such a disability. But the *Dharma Sutras* do not stop here. They go further and say that it will be a crime for a Shudra to study the Vedas or hear it being pronounced and if he does commit such a crime his tongue should be cut or molten lead should be poured into his ear. Can anything be more barbarous than preventing a man to grow out of his disability ?

What is the explanation of these disabilities ? Why did the Brahmanic Law-givers take such a cruel attitude towards the Shudras ? The Brahmanic Law books merely state the disabilities. They say that the Shudras have no right to *Upanayana*. They say that the Shudras shall hold no office. They say that the Shudras shall not have property. But they do not say why. The whole thing is arbitrary. The disabilities of the Shudra have no relation to his personal conduct. It is not the result of infamy. The Shudra is punished just because he was a Shudra. This is a mystery which requires to be solved. As the Brahmanic Law books do not help us to solve it, it is necessary to look for explanation elsewhere.

Chapter IV

SHUDRAS *VERSUS* ARYANS

I

From what has been said before, it is clear that the Brahmanic writers do not give us any clue as to who the Shudras were and how they came to be the fourth *Varna*. It is, therefore, necessary to turn to the Western writers and to see what they have to say about the subject. The Western writers have a definite theory about the origin of the Shudras. Though all of them are not agreed upon every aspect of the theory, there are points on which there seems to be a certain amount of unity among them. They comprise the following :—

(1) The people who created the Vedic literature belonged to the Aryan race.

(2) This Aryan race came from outside India and invaded India.

(3) The natives of India were known as Dasas and Dasyus who were racially different from the Aryans.

(4) The Aryans were a white race. The Dasas and Dasyus were a dark race.

(5) The Aryans conquered the Dasas and Dasyus.

(6) The Dasas and Dasyus after they were conquered and enslaved were called Shudras.

(7) The Aryans cherished colour prejudice and therefore formed the *Chaturvarnya* whereby they separated the white race from the black race such as the Dasas and the Dasyus.

These are the principal elements in the Western theory about the origin and position of the Shudras in the Indo-Aryan society. Whether it is valid or not is another matter. But this much must certainly be said about it that after reading the Brahmanic theories with their long and tedious explanations attempting to treat a social fact as a divine dispensation, one cannot but feel a certain amount of relief in having before oneself a theory, which proceeds to give a natural explanation of a social fact. One can do nothing with the Brahmanic theories except to call them senseless ebullitions of a silly mind. They leave the problem as it is. With the modern theory, one is at least on the road to recover one's way.

To test the validity of the theory, the best thing to do is to examine it piece by piece and see how far each is supported by evidence.

The foundation on which the whole fabric of the theory rests is the proposition that there lived a people who were Aryan by race. It is in the fitness of things therefore to grapple with this question first.

What is this Aryan race? Before we consider the question of Aryan race we must be sure as to what we mean by the word "race." It is necessary to raise this question because it is not impossible to mistake a people for a race. The best illustration of such a mistake is the Jews. Most people believe that the Jews are a race. To the naked eye, they appear to be so. But what is the verdict of the experts? This is what Prof. Ripley[1] has to say about the Jews :—

> "Our final conclusion, then, is this: This is paradoxical yet true, we affirm. The Jews are not a race, but only a people after all. In their faces we read its confirmation; while in respect of their other traits, we are convinced that such individuality as they possess—by no means inconsiderable—is of their own making from one generation to the next, rather than a product of an unprecedented purity of physical descent."

What is a race? A race may be defined as a body of people possessing certain typical traits which are heredi-

1 'The Races of Europe,' by W. E. Ripley, p. 400.

tary. There was a time when it was believed that the traits which constitute a race are: (1) the form of the head, (2) the colour of the hair and eyes, (3) the colour of the skin, and (4) the stature. To-day the general view is that pigmentation and stature are traits, which vary according to climate and habitat, and consequently they must be ruled out as tests for determining the race of the people. The only stable trait is the shape of the human head—by which is meant the general proportions of length, breadth and height and that is why anthropologists and ethnologists regard it as the best available test of race.

The use of head-forms for determining the race to which an individual belongs has been developed by anthropologists into an exact science. It is called anthropometry. This science of anthropometry has devised two ways of measuring the head-form : (1) cephalic index, and (2) facial index. The index is the mark of the race.

Cephalic index is the breadth of the head above the ears expressed in percentage of its length from forehead to back. Assuming that this length is 100, the width is expressed as a fraction of it. As the head becomes proportionately broader—that is more fully rounded, viewed from the top down—this cephalic index increases. When it rises above 80, the head is called brachycephalic. When it falls below 75, the term dolichocephalic is applied to it. Indexes between 75 and 80 are characterized as mesocephalic. These are technical terms. They constantly in literature dealing with crop up questions of race and if one does not know what they denote it obviously becomes very difficult to follow the discussion intelligently. It would not therefore be without advantage if I were to stop to give their popular equivalents. The popular equivalent of mesocephalic is medium-headed, having a medium cephalic index, the breadth of the cranium being between three-fourths and four-fifths of the length.

Dolichocephalic means long-headed, having a low cephalic index, the breadth of the cranium being below four-fifths of the length.

Facial index is the correlation between the proportions of the head and the form of the face. In the majority of cases, it has been found that a relatively broad head is accompanied by a rounded face, in which the breadth back of the cheek bones is considerable as compared with the height from forehead to chin. Lack of uniformity in the mode of taking measurements has so far prevented extended observations fit for exact comparison. All the same, it has been found safe to adopt the rule, long head, oval face : short-head and round face.

Applying these measures of anthropometry, Prof. Ripley, an authority on the question of race, has come to the conclusion that the European people belong to three different races in terms of cephalic and facial index. His conclusions are summarized in the following table[1] :

EUROPEAN RACIAL TYPES.

	Head.	Face.	Hair.	Eyes.	Stature.	Nose.
1. Teutonic ...	Long	Long	Very light	Blue	Tall	Narrow acquiline
2. Alpine (Celtic)..	Round	Broad	Light Chestnut	Hazel Grey	Medium stocky	Variable : rather broad heavy
3. Mediterranean	Long	Long	Dark brown or black	Dark	Medium slender	Rather broad

Is there an Aryan race in the physical sense of the term ? There seem to be two views on the subject.

[1] Ripley's Races of Europe, p. 121.

One view is in favour of the existence of the Aryan race. According to it :—

"The Aryan type . . is marked by a relatively long (dolicho-cephalic) head ; a straight finely-cut (leptorrhine) nose ; a long, symmetrically narrow face ; well developed regular features and a high facial angle. The stature is fairly high—and the general build of the figure well-proportioned and slender rather than massive."

The other view is that of Prof. Max Muller. According to him, the word is used in three different senses. This is what he, in his lectures on the Science of Language[2], says :

" In *ar* or *ara*, I recognise one of the oldest names of the earth, as the ploughed land, lost in Sanskrit but preserved in Greek as (era) so that Arya would have conveyed originally the meaning of landholder, cultivator of the land, while Vaishya from Vis meant householder. *Ida* the daughter of Manu is another name of the cultivated earth and probably a modification of *Ara.*"

The second sense in which it was used was to convey the idea of ploughing or tilling the soil. As to this, Prof. Max Muller makes the following observations :—

" I can only state that the etymological signification of Arya seems to be : One who ploughs or tills. The Aryans would seem to have chosen this name for themselves as opposed to the nomadic races, the Turanians, whose original name *Tura* implies the swiftness of the horsemen."

In the third sense, the word was used as a general name for the Vaishyas, i.e., the general body of the people, who formed the whole mass of the people. For this, Prof. Max Muller relies on Panini (iii . 1 . 103) for his authority. Then, there is the fourth sense, which the word got only towards the later period, in which sense it means ' of noble origin.'

What is however of particular importance is the opinion

---

[1] Ripley's Races of Europe, p. 121.

[2] Vol. I, pp. 276-77.

of Prof. Max Muller on the question of the Aryan race. This is what he[1] says on the subject :—

> "There is no Aryan race in blood; Aryan, in scientific language, is utterly inapplicable to race. It means language and nothing but language; and if we speak of Aryan race at all, we should know that it means no more than . . . Aryan speech.
>
> * * *
>
> I have declared again and again that if I say Aryas, I mean neither blood nor bones, nor hair nor skull; I mean simply those who speak an Aryan language. The same applies to Hindus, Greeks, Romans, Germans, Celts and Slavs. When I speak of them I commit myself to no anatomical characteristics. The blue-eyed and fair-haired Scandinavians may have been conquerors or conquered, they may have adopted the language of their darker lords or their subjects, or *vice versa*. I assert nothing beyond their language, when I call them Hindus, Greeks, Romans, Germans, Celts and Slavs; and in that sense, and in that sense only, do I say that even the blackest Hindus represent an earlier stage of Aryan speech and thought than the fairest Scandinavians. This may seem strong language, but in matters of such importance we cannot be too decided in our language. To me, an ethnologist who speaks of Aryan race, Aryan blood, Aryan eyes and hair, is as great a sinner as a linguist who speaks of a dolichocephalic dictionary or a brachycephalic grammar. It is worse than a Babylonian confusion of tongues —it is downright theft. We have made our own terminology for the classification of language; let ethnologists make their own for the classification of skulls, and hair and blood."

The value of this view of Prof. Max Muller will be appreciated by those who know that he was at one time a believer in the theory of Aryan race and was largely responsible for the propagation of it.

The two views are obviously not in harmony. According to one view, the Aryan race existed in a physiological sense with typical hereditary traits with a fixed cephalic and facial index. According to Prof. Max Muller, the

---

[1] Biography of Words, pp. 89 and 120-21.

Aryan race existed in a philological sense, as a people speaking a common language.

In this conflict of views, one may well ask : what is the testimony of the Vedic literature ? An examination of the Vedic literature shows that there occur two words in the Rig Veda—one is Arya (अर्य) with a short 'a' and the other is Arya (आर्य) with a long 'à'. The word Arya (अर्य) with a short 'a' is used in the Rig Veda[1] in 88 places. In what sense is it used ? The word[2] is used in four different senses ; as (1) enemy, (2) respectable person, (3) name for India, and (4) owner, Vaishya or citizen.

The word (आर्य) with a long 'a' is used in the Rig Veda in 31 places[3]. But in none of these is the word used in the sense of race.

From the foregoing discussion, the one indisputable conclusion which follows is that the terms 'Arya' and 'Arya' which occur in the Vedas have not been used in the racial sense at all.

One may also ask : what is the evidence of anthropometry ? The Aryan race is described as long-headed. This description is not enough. For as will be seen from the table given by Prof. Ripley, there are two races which are long-headed. The question which of the two is the Aryan race still remains open.

II

Let us take the next premise—namely, that the Aryans came from outside India, invaded India and conquered the native tribes. It would be better to take these questions separately.

---

[1] For a list of the references in the Rig Veda, see App. I.

[2] For a list of references showing in which place the word is used and in what sense, see Appendix II.

[3] For a list of references, see Appendix III.

From where did the Aryan race come into India? On the question of locating the original home of the Aryan race, there is a bewildering variety of views and opinions. According to Benfey, the original home of the Aryan race must be determined by reference to the common vocabulary. His views on the subject have been well summarized by Prof. Isaac Taylor[1] in the following words :—

> "The investigation of the vocabulary common to the whole of the Aryan languages might yield a clue to the region inhabited by the Aryans before the linguistic separation. He contended that certain animals, such as the bear and the wolf, and certain trees, such as the beech and the birch with which the primitive Aryans must have been acquainted, are all indigenous to the temperate zone, and above all, to Europe, whereas the characteristic animals and trees of Southern Asia, such as the lion, the tiger and the palm were known only to the Indians and the Iranians. He urged that the absence from the primitive Aryan vocabulary of common names for the two great Asiatic beasts of prey, the lion and the tiger, or for the chief Asiatic beast of transport, the camel, is difficult to explain on the theory of the migration of the Aryans from the region eastward of the Caspian. That the Greeks called the lion by its Semitic name, and the Indians by a name which cannot be referred to any Aryan root, argues that the lion was unknown in the common home of Greeks and Indians.
>
> * * *
>
> Benfey's declaration speedily bore fruit, and Geiger forthwith ranged himself in the same camp, but placing the cradle of the Aryans, not as Benfey had done in the region to the North of the Black Sea, but more to the north-west, in Central and Western Germany. Geiger's contribution to the argument was not without its value. He bases his conclusions largely on the tree names which belong to the primitive Aryan vocabulary. In addition to the fir, the willow, the ash, the alder, and the hazel, he thinks the names of the birch, the beech and the oak are specially decisive. Since the Greek (phegos) which denotes the oak is the linguistic

1 The Origin of the Aryans, by Isaac Taylor, pp. 24-26.

equivalent of the Teutonic *beech* and of the Latin *fague* he draws the conclusion that the Greeks migrated from a land of beeches to a land of oaks, transferring the name which denoted the tree with 'edible' fruit from the one tree to the other."

Another school holds that the original home of the Aryan race was in Caucasia, because the Caucasians like the Aryans are blonds, have a straight, sharp nose and a handsome face. On this point, the view of Prof. Ripley is worth quoting. This is what Prof. Ripley[1] has to say on the subject :—

"The utter absurdity of the misnomer Caucasian, as applied to the blue-eyed and fair-headed 'Aryan' (?) race of Western Europe, is revealed by two indisputable facts. In the first place, this ideal blond type does not occur within many hundred miles of Caucasia; and, secondly, nowhere along the great Caucasian chain is there a single native tribe making use of a purely inflectional or Aryan language.

* * *

Even the Ossetes, whose language alone is possibly inflectional, have not had their claims to the honour of Aryan made positively clear as yet. And even if Ossetian be Aryan, there is every reason to regard the people as immigrants from the direction of Iran, not indigenous Caucasians at all. Their head form, together with their occupation of territory along the only highway—the Pass of Dariel—across the chain from the South, give tenability to the hypothesis. At all events, whether the Ossetes be Aryan or not, they little deserve pre-eminence among the other peoples about them. They are lacking both in the physical beauty for which this region is justly famous, and in courage as well, if we may judge by their reputation in yielding abjectly and without shadow of resistance to the Russians.

* * *

It is not true that any of these Caucasians are even 'somewhat typical.' As a matter of fact they could never be typical of anything. The name covers nearly every physical type and family of language of the Eur-Asian continent except, as we have said, that blond, tall, 'Aryan'

[1] Ripley's Races of Europe, pp. 436-437.

speaking one to which the name has been specifically applied. It is all false; not only improbable but absurd. The Caucasus is not a cradle—it is rather a grave—of peoples, of languages, of customs and of physical types. Let us be assured of that point at the outset. Nowhere else in the world probably is so heterogeneous a lot of people, languages and religions gathered together in one place as along the chain of the Caucasus mountains."

Mr. Tilak has suggested that the original home of the Aryan race was in the Arctic region. His theory may be summarized in his own words. He begins by taking note of the astronomical and climatic phenomenon in the region round about the North Pole. He finds[1] that there are :—

"Two sets of characteristics, or *differentiæ;* one for an observer stationed exactly at the terrestrial North Pole, and the other for an observer located in the Circum-Polar regions, or tracts of land between the North Pole and the Arctic circle."

Mr. Tilak call these two sets of *differentiæ* as Polar and Circum-Polar, and sums them up as follows:

I. The Polar Characteristics.

(1) The sun rises in the south.

(2) The stars do not rise and set; but *revolve* or spin round and round, in horizontal planes, completing one round in 24 hours. The northern celestial hemisphere is alone overhead and visible during the whole year; and the southern or lower celestial world is always invisible.

(3) The year consists only of one long day and one long night of six months each.

(4) There is only one morning and one evening, or the sun rises and sets only once a year. But the *twilight,* whether of the morning or of the evening, lasts continuously for about *two months,* or 60 periods of 24 hours each. The ruddy light of the morn, or the evening twilight, is not again confined to a particular part of the horizon (eastern or western) as with us; but moves, like the stars at the place, round and round along the horizon, like a potter's wheel, completing

[1] 'The Arctic Home in the Vedas,' by Mr. B. G. Tilak, pp. 58-60.

one round in every 24 hours. These rounds of the morning light continue to take place, until the orb of the sun comes above the horizon ; and then the sun follows the same course for six months, that is, moves, without setting, round and round the observer, completing one round every 24 hours.

II. The Circum-Polar Characteristics

(1) The sun will always be to the south of the zenith of the observer ; but as this happens even in the case of an observer stationed in the temperate zone, it cannot be regarded as a special characteristic.

(2) A large number of stars are *circum-polar*, that is, they are above the horizon during the entire period of their revolution and hence always visible. The remaining stars rise and set as in the temperate zone, but revolve in more oblique circles.

(3) The *year* is made up of three parts : (i) one long continuous night, occurring at the time of the winter solstice, and lasting for a period, greater than 24 hours and less than six months, according to the latitude of the place ; (ii) one long continuous day to match, occurring at the time of the summer solstice ; and (iii) a succession of ordinary days and nights during the rest of the year, a nycthemeron, or a day and a night together, never exceeding a period of 24 hours. The day, after the long continuous night, is at first shorter than the night, but it goes on increasing until it developes into the long continuous day. At the end of the long day, the night is, at first, shorter than the day, but, in its turn, it begins to gain over the day, until the commencement of the long continuous night, with which the year ends.

(4) The dawn, at the close of the long continuous night, lasts for several days, but its duration and magnificence is proportionally less than at the North Pole, according to the latitude of the place. For places, within a few degrees of the North Pole, the phenomenon of revolving morning light will still be observable during the greater part of the duration of the dawn. The other dawns, viz., those between ordinary days and nights, will, like the dawns in the temperate zone, only last for a few hours. The sun, when he is above the horizon during the continuous day, will be seen revolving, without setting, round the observer, as at the Pole, but in oblique and not horizontal circles, and during the long night he will be entirely below the horizon ; while during the rest of

the year he will rise and set, remaining above the horizon for a part of 24 hours, varying according to the position of the sun in the ecliptic."

Summing up the position as analysed by him, Mr. Tilak concludes by saying :—

> " Here we have two distinct sets of *differentiæ*, or special characteristics of the Polar and *Circum-Polar* regions—characteristics which are not found anywhere else on the surface of the globe. Again as the Poles of the earth are the same to-day as they were millions of years ago, the above astronomical characteristics will hold good for all times, though the Polar climate may have undergone violent changes in the Pleistocene period."

Having noted the phenomenon in the Arctic region, Mr. Tilak proceeds to argue that :—

> " If a Vedic description or tradition discloses any of the characteristics mentioned above, we may safely infer that the tradition is Polar or Circum-Polar in origin, and the phenomenon, if not actually witnessed by the poet, was at least known to him by tradition faithfully handed down from generation to generation. Fortunately there are many such passages or references in the Vedic literature, and, for convenience, these may be divided into two parts ; the first comprising those passages which directly describe or refer to the long night, or the long dawn ; and the second consisting of myths and legends which corroborate and indirectly support the first."

Mr. Tilak is satisfied that the description of natural phenomenon and the myths and legends contained in the Vedas tally with the natural phenomenon as it exists near the North Pole and concludes that the Vedic poets i.e., the Vedic Aryans must have had the Arctic region as their home.

This is of course a very original theory. There is only one point which seems to have been overlooked. The horse is a favourite animal of the Vedic Aryans. It was most intimately connected with their life and their religion. That the queens vied with one another to copulate with the horse in the Ashvamedha Yajna[1] shows what place the horse had acquired in the life of the Vedic Aryans. Question is : was the horse to be found in the Arctic region ? If the answer is in the negative, the Arctic home theory becomes very precarious.

III

What evidence is there of the invasion of India by the Aryan race and the subjugation by it of the native tribes ? So far as the *Rig Veda* is concerned, there is not a particle of evidence suggesting the invasion of India by the Aryans from outside India. As Mr. P. T. Srinivasa Iyengar[2] points out :—

> " A careful examination of the *Mantras* where the words Arya, Dasa and Dasyu occur, indicates that they refer not to race but to cult. These words occur mostly in *Rig Veda Samhita* where *Arya* occurs about 33 times in *mantras* which contain 153,972 words on the whole. This rare occurrence is itself a proof that the tribes that called themselves *Aryas* were not invaders that conquered the country and exterminated the people. For an invading tribe would naturally boast of its achievements constantly."

So far as the testimony of the Vedic literature is concerned, it is against the theory that the original home of the Aryans was outside India. The language in which reference to the seven rivers is made in the *Rig Veda* (x. 75.5) is very significant. As Prof. D. S. Triveda says[3]—the rivers are addressed as 'my Ganges, my Yamuna, my Sarasvati ' and so on. No foreigner would ever address a river in such familiar and endearing terms unless by long association he had developed an emotion about it.

[1] See Yajur Veda with Madhavacharya's Bhashya.

[2] Life in Ancient India in the age of the Mantras, pp. 11-12.

[3] The Original Home of the Aryans—by D. S. Triveda—Annals of the Bhandarkar Oriental Research Institute, Vol. XX, p. 62.

As to the question of conquest and subjugation, references can undoubtedly be found in the *Rig Veda* where Dasas and Dasyus are described as enemies of the Aryas and there are many hymns in which the Vedic *rishis* have invited their gods to kill and annihilate them. But before drawing any conclusion from it in favour of conquest and subjugation by the Aryans, the following points must be taken into consideration.

First is the paucity of references in the *Rig Veda* to wars between the Aryans on the one hand and the Dasas or Dasyus on the other. Out of the 33 places in which the word occurs in the *Rig Veda* only in 8 places is it used in opposition to Dasas and only in 7 places is it used in opposition to the word Dasyus. This may show the occurrence of sporadic riots between the two. It is certainly not evidence of a conquest or subjugation.

The second point about the Dasas is that whatever conflict there was between them and the Aryans, the two seem to have arrived at a mutual settlement, based on peace with honour. This is borne out by references in the *Rig Veda* showing how the Dasas and Aryans have stood as one united people against a common enemy. Note the following verses from the *Rig Veda* :—

Rig Veda — vi. 33. 3
vii. 83. 1
viii. 51. 9
x. 102. 3

The third point to note is that whatever the degree of conflict, it was not a conflict of race. It was a conflict which had arisen on account of difference of religions. That this conflict was religious and not racial is evidenced by the *Rig Veda* itself. Speaking of the Dasyus, it[1] says :—

"They are *avrata*, without (the Arya) rites (R.V., i . 51 . 8, 9 ; i . 132 . 4 ; iv . 41, 2 ; vi . 14, 3) ; *apavrata* (R.V., v . 42, 2),

---

[1] Iyengar, *Ibid*, p. 13.

anyavrata of different rites (R.V., viii. 59, 11; x. 22, 8), *Anagnitra* fireless (R.V., v. 189, 8), *ayajyu, ayajvan*, non-sacrifices (R.V., i. 131, 44; i. 33, 4; viii. 59, 11), *abramha*, without prayers (or also not having Brahmana priest (R.V., iv. 15, 9; x. 105, 8), *anrichah*, without Riks (R.V., x. 105, 8), *Brahmadvisha*, haters of prayer (or Brahmans) R.V., v. 42, 9), and *anindra*, without Indra, despisers of Indra, (R.V., i. 133, 1; v. 2, 3; vii. 18, 6; x. 27, 6; x. 48, 7). 'They pour no milky draughts they heat no cauldron' (R.V., iii. 53, 4). They give no gifts to the Brahmana (R.V., v. 7, 10)."

Attention may also be drawn to the *Rig Veda* x. 22. 8 which says :—

> "We live in the midst of the Dasyu tribes, who do not perform sacrifices, nor believe in anything. They have their own rites and are not entitled to be called men. O! thou, destroyer of enemies, annihilate them and injure the Dasas."

In the face of these statements from the *Rig Veda*, there is obviously no room for a theory of a military conquest by the Aryan race of the non-Aryan races of Dasas and Dasyus.

IV

So much about the Aryans, their invasion of India and their subjugation of the Dasas and Dasyus. The consideration so far bestowed upon the question has been from the Aryan side of the issue. It might be useful to discuss it from the side of the Dasas and the Dasyus. In what sense are the names Dasa and Dasyu used? Are they used in a racial sense?

Those who hold that the terms Dasa and Dasyu are used in the racial sense rely upon the following circumstances: (1) The use in the *Rig Veda* of the terms *Mridhravak* and *Anasa* as epithets of Dasyus. (2) The description in the *Rig Veda* of the Dasas as being of Krishna Varna.

The term *Mridhravak* occurs in the following places in the *Rig Veda*.

(1) *Rig Veda*, i. 174. 2
(2) *Rig Veda*, v. 32. 8
(3) *Rig Veda*, vii. 6. 3
(4) *Rig Veda*, vii. 18. 3

What does the adjective *Mridhravak* mean ? *Mridhravak* means one who speaks crude, unpolished language. Can crude unpolished language be regarded as evidence of difference of race ? It would be childish to rely upon this as a basis of consciousness of race difference.

The term *Anasa* occurs in Rig Veda v. 29. 10. What does the word mean ? There are two interpretations. One is by Prof. Max Muller. The other is by Sayanacharya. According to Prof. Max Muller, it means 'one without nose' or 'one with a flat nose' and has as such been relied upon as a piece of evidence in support of the view that the Aryans were a separate race from the Dasyus. Sayanacharya says that it means 'mouthless,' i.e., devoid of good speech. This difference of meaning is due to difference in the correct reading of the word '*Anasa*.' Sayanacharya reads it as *an-asa* while Prof. Max Muller reads it as *a-nasa*. As read by Prof. Max Muller, it means 'without nose.' Question is: which of the two readings is the correct one ? There is no reason to hold that Sayana's reading is wrong. On the other hand there is every thing to suggest that it is right. In the first place, it does not make non-sense of the word. Secondly, as there is no other place where the Dasyus are described as noseless, there is no reason why the word should be read in such a manner as to give it an altogether new sense. It is only fair to read it as a synonym of *Mridhravak*. There is therefore no evidence in support of the conclusion that the Dasyus belonged to a different race.

Turning to Dasas, it is true that they are described as *Krishna Yoni*, in Rig Veda vi. 47. 21. But there are various points to be considered before one can accept the inference which is sought to be drawn from it. First is that this is the only place in the Rig Veda where the phrase *Krishna Yoni* is applied to the Dasas. Secondly, there is no certainty as to whether the phrase is used in the literal sense or in a figurative sense. Thirdly, we do not know whether it is a statement of fact or a word of abuse. Unless these points are clarified, it is not possible to accept the view that because the Dasas are spoken of as *Krishna Yoni*, they therefore belonged to a dark race.

In this connection, attention may be drawn to the following verses from the Rig Veda :

1. *Rig Veda*, vi . 22. 10.—" Oh, Vajri, thou hast made Aryas of Dasas, good men out of bad by your power. Give us the same power so that with it we may overcome our enemies."

2. *Rig Veda*, x . 49. 3, (says Indra).—" I have deprived the Dasyus of the title of Aryas."

3. *Rig Veda*, i . 151. 8.—" Oh, Indra, find out who is an Arya and who is a Dasyu and separate them."

What do these verses indicate ? They indicate that the distinction between the Aryans on the one hand and the Dasas and Dasyus on the other was not a racial distinction of colour or physiognomy. That is why a Dasa or Dasyu could become an Arya. That is why Indra was given the task to separate them from the Arya.

V

That the theory of the Aryan race set up by Western writers falls to the ground at every point, goes without saying. This is somewhat surprising since Western scholarship is usually associated with thorough research and careful analysis. Why has the theory failed ? It is important to know the reasons why it has failed. Anyone who cares to scrutinize the theory will find that it suffers from a double infection. In the first place, the theory is based on nothing but pleasing assumptions and inferences based on such assumptions. In the second place, the theory is a perversion of scientific investigation. It is not allowed to evolve out of facts. On the contrary, the theory is preconceived and facts are selected to prove it.

The theory of the Aryan race is just an assumption and no more. It is based on a philological proposition put forth by Dr. Bopp in his epoch-making book called 'Comparative Grammar' which appeared in 1835. In this book, Dr. Bopp demonstrated that a greater number of languages of Europe and some languages of Asia must be referred to a common ancestral speech. The European languages and Asiatic languages to which Bopp's proposition applied are called Indo-Germanic. Collectively, they have come to be called the Aryan languages largely because Vedic language refers to the Aryas and is also of the same family as the Indo-Germanic. This assumption is the major premise on which the theory of the Aryan race is based.

From this assumption are drawn two inferences: (1) Unity of race, and (2) that race being the Aryan race. The argument is that if the languages are descended from a common ancestral speech then there must have existed a race whose mother tongue it was and since the mother tongue was known as the Aryan tongue the race who spoke it was the Aryan race. The existence of a separate and a distinct Aryan race is thus an inference only. From this inference, is drawn another inference which is that of a common original habitat. It is argued that there could be no community of language unless people had a common habitat permitting close communion. Common original habitat is thus an inference from an inference.

The theory of invasion is an invention. This invention is necessary because of a gratuitous assumption which underlies the Western theory. The assumption is that the Indo-Germanic people are the purest of the modern representatives of the original Aryan race. Its first home is assumed to have been somewhere in Europe. These assumptions raise a question : How could the Aryan speech have come to India ? This question can be answered only by the supposition that the Aryans must have come into India from outside. Hence the necessity for inventing the theory of invasion.

The third assumption is that the Aryans were a superior race. This theory has its origin in the belief that the Aryans are a European race and as a European race it is presumed to be superior to the Asiatic races. Having assumed its superiority, the next logical step one is driven to take is to establish the fact of superiority. Knowing that nothing can prove the superiority of the Aryan race better than invasion and conquest of the native races, the Western writers have proceeded to invent the story of the invasion of India by the Aryans and the conquest by them of the Dasas and Dasyus.

The fourth assumption is that the European races were white[1] and had a colour prejudice against the dark races. The Aryans being a European race, it is assumed that it must have had colour prejudice. The theory proceeds to find evidence for colour prejudice in the Aryans who came into India. This it finds in the *Chaturvarnya*—an institution established by the Indo-Aryans after they came to India and which according to these scholars is based upon *Varna* which is taken by them to mean colour.

Not one of these assumptions is borne out by facts. Take the premise about the Aryan race. The theory does not take account of the possibility that the Aryan race in the physiological sense is one thing and an Aryan race in the philological sense quite different, and that it is perfectly possible that the Aryan race, if there is one, in the physiological sense may have its habitat in

---

[1] For a discussion as to who the Dasas and Dasyus were, see Chapter VI.

one place and that the Aryan race, in the philological sense, in quite a different place. The theory of the Aryan race is based on the premise of a common language and it is supposed to be common because it has a structural affinity. The assertion that the Aryans came from outside and invaded India is not proved and the premise that the Dasas and Dasyus are aboriginal tribes[1] of India is demonstrably false.

Again to say that the institution of *Chaturvarnya* is a reflexion of the innate colour prejudice of the Aryans is really to assert too much. If colour is the origin of class distinction, there must be four different colours to account for the different classes which comprise *Chaturvarnya.* Nobody has said what those four colours are and who were the four coloured races who were welded together in *Chaturvarnya.* As it is, the theory starts with only two opposing people, Aryas and Dasas—one assumed to be white and the other assumed to be dark.

The originators of the Aryan race theory are so eager to establish their case that they have no patience to see what absurdities they land themselves in. They start on a mission to prove what they want to prove and do not hesitate to pick such evidence from the Vedas as they think is good for them.

Prof. Michael Foster has somewhere said that 'hypothesis is the salt of science.' Without hypothesis there is no possibility of fruitful investigation. But it is equally true that where the desire to prove a particular hypothesis is dominant, hypothesis becomes the poison of science. The Aryan race theory of Western scholars is as good an illustration of how hypothesis can be the poison of science as one can think of.

The Aryan race theory is so absurd that it ought to have been dead long ago. But far from being dead, the theory has a considerable hold upon the people. There

---

[1] For a discussion whether in their origin the European races were white or dark see the observations of Prof. Ripley, *infra*, p. 76.

are two explanations which account for this phenomenon. The first explanation is to be found in the support which the theory receives from Brahmin scholars. This is a very strange phenomenon. As Hindus, they should ordinarily show a dislike for the Aryan theory with its express avowal of the superiority of the European races over the Asiatic races. But the Brahmin scholar has not only no such aversion but he most willingly hails it. The reasons are obvious. The Brahmin believes in the two-nation theory. He claims to be the representative of the Aryan race and he regards the rest of the Hindus as descendents of the non-Aryans. The theory helps him to establish his kinship with the European races and share their arrogance and their superiority. He likes particularly that part of the theory which makes the Aryan an invader and a conqueror of the non-Aryan native races. For it helps him to maintain and justify his overlordship over the non-Brahmins.

The second explanation why the Aryan race theory is not dead is because of the general insistence by European scholars that the word *Varna* means *colour* and the acceptance of that view by a majority of the Brahmin scholars. Indeed, this is the mainstay of the Aryan theory. There is no doubt that as long as this interpretation of the *Varna* continues to be accepted, the Aryan theory will continue to live. This part of the Aryan theory is therefore very important and calls for fuller examination. It needs to be examined from three different points of view: (1) Were the European races fair or dark? (2) Were the Indo-Aryans fair? and (3) What is the original meaning of the word *Varna*?

On the question of the colour of the earliest Europeans Prof. Ripley is quite definite that they were of dark complexion. Prof. Ripley goes on to say[1]:

> "We are strengthened in this assumption that the earliest Europeans were not only long-headed but also dark-com-

[1] Races of Europe, by Prof. Ripley, p. 466.

plexioned, by various points in our enquiry thus far. We have proved the prehistoric antiquity of the living Cro-Magnon type in Southern France; and we saw that among these peasants, the prevalence of black hair and eyes is very striking. And comparing types in the British Isles we saw that everything tended to show that the brunet populations of Wales, Ireland and Scotland constituted the most primitive stratum of population in Britain. Furthermore, in that curious spot in Garfagnana, where a survival of the ancient Ligurian population of Northern Italy is indicated, there also are the people characteristically dark. Judged, therefore, either in the light of general principles or of local details, it would seem as if this earliest race in Europe must have been very dark. . . . It was Mediterranean in its pigmental affinities, and not Scandinavian."

Turning to the Vedas for any indication whether the Aryans had any colour prejudice, reference may be made to the following passages in the Rig Veda :

In Rig Veda, i . 117 . 8, there is a reference to *Ashvins* having brought about the marriage between *Shyavya* and *Rushati*. *Shyavya* is black and *Rushati* is fair.

In Rig Veda, i . 117 . 5, there is a prayer addressed to *Ashvins* for having saved Vandana who is spoken as of golden colour.

In Rig Veda, ii . 3 . 9, there is a prayer by an Aryan invoking the Devas to bless him with a son with certain virtues but of (*pishanga*) tawny (reddish brown) complexion.

These instances show that the Vedic Aryans had no colour prejudice. How could they have? The Vedic Aryans were not of one colour. Their complexion varied; some were of copper complexion, some white, and some black. Rama the son of Dasharatha has been described as *Shyama* i.e., dark in complexion, so is Krishna the descendant of the Yadus, another Aryan clan. The Rishi Dirghatamas, who is the author of many *mantras* of the Rig Veda must have been of dark colour if his name was given to him after his complexion. Kanva is an Aryan rishi of great repute. But according to the description given in Rig Veda—x . 31 . 11, he was of dark colour.

To take up the third and the last point, namely, the meaning of the word *Varna*[1]. Let us first see in what sense it is used in the Rig Veda. The word *Varna* is used[2] in the Rig Veda in 22 places. Of these, in about 17 places the word is used in reference to deities such as Ushas, Agni, Soma, etc., and means lustre, features or colour. Being used in connection with deities, it would be unsafe to use them for ascertaining what meaning the word *Varna* had in the Rig Veda when applied to human beings. There are four and at the most five places in the Rig Veda where the word is used in reference to human beings. They are :

1. Rig Veda, i . 104 . 2.
2. Rig Veda, i . 179 . 6.
3. Rig Veda, ii . 12 . 4.
4. Rig Veda, iii . 34 . 5.
5. Rig Veda, ix . 71 . 2.

Do these references prove that the word *Varna* is used in the Rig Veda in the sense of colour and complexion ?

Rig Veda, iii . 34 . 5 seems to be of doubtful import. The expression 'caused Shukla Varna to increase' is capable of double interpretation. It may mean Indra made Ushas throw her light and thereby increase the white colour, or it may mean that the hymn-maker being of white complexion, people of his i.e., of white colour increased. The second meaning would be quite far-fetched for the simple reason that the expansion of the white colour is the effect and lightening of Ushas is the cause.

Rig Veda, ix . 71 . 2 the expression 'abandons Asura Varna' is not clear, reading it in the light of the other stanzas in the *Sukta*. The *Sukta* belongs to Soma Pava-

---

[1] On what follows see *Maharashtra Dnyanakosha*, Vol. III, pp. 39-42.

[2] See Appendix IV.

mana. Bearing this in mind, the expression 'abandons Asura Varna' must be regarded as a description of Soma. The word Varna as used here is indicative of '*roopa.*' The second half of the stanza says: 'he throws away his black or dark covering and takes on lustrous covering.' From this it is clear that the word Varna is used as indicative of darkness.

Rig Veda, i . 179 . 6 is very helpful. The stanza explains that Rishi Agasya cohabited with Lopamudra in order to obtain *praja*, children and strength and says that as a result two Varnas prospered. It is not clear from the stanza, which are the two Varnas referred to in the stanzas, although the intention is to refer to Aryas and Dasas. Be that as it may, there is no doubt that the Varna in the stanza means class and not colour.

In Rig Veda, i . 104 . 2 and Rig Veda, ii . 12 . 4 are the two stanzas in which the word Varna is applied to Dasa. The question is: What does the word Varna mean when applied to Dasa? Does it refer to the colour and complexion of the Dasa, or does it indicate that Dasas formed a separate class? There is no way of arriving at a positive conclusion as to which of the two meanings is correct.

The evidence of the Rig Veda is quite inconclusive. In this connection, it will be of great help to know if the word occurs in the literature of the Indo-Iranians and if so, in what sense.[1]

Fortunately, the word Varna does occur in the Zend Avesta. It takes the form of *Varana* or *Varena*. It is used specifically in the sense of "Faith, Religious doctrine, Choice of creed or belief." It is derived from the root *Var* which means to put faith in, to believe in. One comes across the word *Varana* or *Varena* in the Gathas about six times used in the sense of faith, doctrine, creed or belief.

[1] The information relating to the meaning of the word "Varna" in the Indo-Iranian literature, I owe to my friend Dastur Bode, who is well-versed in it.

It occurs in Gatha Ahunavaiti—Yasna Ha 30 Stanza 2 which when translated in English reads as follows :—

> " Give heed with your ears and contemplate the highest Truth I proclaim; with your illumined mind introspect. Each man for himself must determine his (Avarenao) faith. Before the Great Event, let each individually be awake to the Truth we teach."

This is one of the most famous strophes of the Gatha where Zarathushtra exhorts each one individually to use reasoning faculty and freedom of choice in the selection of his or her faith. The words occurring here are "*Avarenao vichithahya,*" *Avarenao* meaning faith, belief and *vichi- thahya* meaning 'of discriminating, of selecting, of determining.'

It occurs in Gatha Ahunavaiti—Yasna Ha 31 Stanza 11. The word used is *Vareneng* accusative plural of *Varena* meaning ' belief, faith.' In this stanza, Zarathushtra propounds the theory of the creation of man. After speaking about man's creation being completed, in the last half line Zarathushtra says " voluntary beliefs are given (to man)."

It occurs in Gatha Ushtavaiti—Yasna Ha 45 Stanza 1 in the form of *Varena.* In the last line of this strophe, Zarathushtra says ' owing to sinful belief (or evil faith) the wicked is of evil tongue (or inverted tongue.)'

It occurs in Gatha Ushtavaiti—Yasna Ha 45 Stanza 2 in the same form as above *Varena* in the clear sense of faith, religion, belief, etc. In this stanza, Zarathushtra is propounding his philosophy of good and evil and speaking of dual aspects of human mind. In this stanza, the two mentalities—the good mentality and the evil mentality—are speaking to each other saying " Neither in thought, word, intelligence, faith (or religion or Creed) utterance, deed, conscience nor soul do we agree."

It occurs in Gatha Spenta Mainyu,—Yasna Ha 48 Stanza 4 in the form of *Vareneng* meaning religion, faith (root *Vere* Persian *gervidan*= to have faith in). In this stanza,

Zarathushtra says that "Whosoever will make his mind more pure and holy and thus keep his conscience pure by deed and word, such man's desire is in accordance with his faith (religion, belief)."

It occurs in Gatha Spenta Mainyu,—Yasna Ha 49 Stanza 3 as *Varenai* in dative case meaning 'religion.' In the same stanza occurs the word *Tkaeshai* which also means religion, creed, religious law. These two words *Varenai* and *Tkaeshai* occurring in the same stanza strengthens our argument, as the word *Tkaesha* clearly means religion as is found in the compound *Ahuratkaesha* meaning 'The Ahurian religion.' This word *Tkaesha* is translated in Pahlavi as *Kish* which means religion.

In Vendidad (a book of Zarathushtrian sanitary law written in Avesta language) we come across a word *Anyo Varena.* Here *Anyo* means other and *Varena* means religion; thus a man of different religion, faith, belief is spoken of as *Anyo-Varena.* Similarly, we come across in Vendidad the word *Anyo-Tkaesha* also meaning a man of different religion.

We come across many verbal forms in the Gatha derived from this root, e.g., Ahunavaiti Gatha Yasna Ha, 31, Stanza 3. Zarathushtra declares *Ya jvanto vispeng vauraya*; here the verb *vauraya* means I may cause to induce belief, faith (in God) (in all the living ones). In Yasna Ha, 28: Stanza 5, we come across the verb *vauroimaidi,* 'We may give faith to.' We come across another interesting form of this word in Gatha Vahishtaishtish, Yasna Ha, 53, Stanza 9 *Duz—Varenaish.* It is instrumental plural. The first part *Duz* means wicked, false and *Varenai* means believer. Thus the word means "A man belonging to false or wicked religion or a false or wicked believer."

In the Zarathushtrian Confession of Faith, which forms Yasna Ha, 12, we come across the word *Fravarane* meaning 'I confess my faith, my belief' in *Mazdayasno Zarathushtrish* 'Mazda-worshipping Zarathushtrian Religion.' This phrase occurs in almost all the

Zarathushtrian prayers. There is yet another form in the Zarathushtrian Confession Yasna, 12, *Ya-Varena.* Here *Ya* is relative pronoun meaning which and *Varena* —faith, religion. Thus, the word means 'the religion to which.' This form *Ya Varena* is used nine times in Yasna 12, and it is used in the clear sense of faith or religion. Here again the word *Varena* is placed along with the word *Tkaesha* which means religion.

A very interesting reference is found in Yasna 16 *Zarathushtrahe varenemcha tkaeshemcha yazamaide.* Here the *Varena* and *Tkaesha* of Zarathushtra is worshipped. It is quite clear from the use of these corresponding and co-relative words that the faith and religion of Zarathushtra is meant. The translation of the above line is 'We worship the faith and religion of Zarathushtra.'

This evidence from the Zenda Avesta as to the meaning of the word *Varna* leaves no doubt that it originally meant a class holding to a particular faith and it had nothing to do with colour or complexion.

The conclusions that follow from the examination of the Western theory may now be summarized. They are :

(1) The Vedas do not know any such race as the Aryan race.

(2) There is no evidence in the Vedas of any invasion of India by the Aryan race and its having conquered the Dasas and Dasyus supposed to be natives of India.

(3) There is no evidence to show that the distinction between Aryans, Dasas and Dasyus was a racial distinction.

(4) The Vedas do not support the contention that the Aryas were different in colour from the Dasas and Dasyus.

CHAPTER V

ARYANS AGAINST ARYANS

ENOUGH has been said to show how leaky is the Aryan theory expounded by Western scholars and glibly accepted by their Brahmin fellows. Yet, the theory has such a hold on the generality of people that what has been said against it may mean no more than scotching it. Like the snake it must be killed. It is therefore necessary to pursue the examination of the theory further with a view to expose its hollowness completely.

Those who uphold the theory of an Aryan race invading India and conquering the Dasas and Dasyus fail to take note of certain verses in the Rig Veda. These verses are of crucial importance. To build up a theory of an Aryan race marching into India from outside and conquering the non-Aryan native tribes without reference to these verses is an utter futility. I reproduce below the verses I have in mind :

(1) *Rig Veda*, vi . 33 . 3.—" Oh, Indra, Thou has killed both of our opponents, the Dasas and the Aryas."

(2) *Rig Veda*, vi . 60 . 3.—" Indra and Agni—these protectors of the good and righteous suppress the Dasas and Aryas who hurt us."

(3) *Rig Veda*, vii . 81 . 1.—" Indra and Varuna killed the Dasas and Aryas who were the enemies of Sudas and thus protected Sudas from them."

(4) *Rig Veda*, viii . 24 . 27.—" Oh you, Indra, who saved us from the hands of the cruel Rakshasas and from the Aryas living on the banks of the Indus, do thou deprive the Dasas of their weapons."

(5) *Rig Veda*, x . 38 . 3.—" Oh you much revered Indra, those Dasas and Aryas who are irreligious and who are our

enemies, make it easy for us with your blessings to subdue them. With your help we shall kill them."

(6) *Rig Veda*, x. 86. 19.—" Oh, You Mameyu, you give him all prowess who prays you. With your help we will destroy our Arya and our Dasyu enemies."

Anyone who reads these verses, notes what they say calmly and coolly and considers them against the postulates of the Western theory will be taken aback by them. If the authors of these verses of the Rig Veda were Aryas then the idea which these verses convey is that there were two different communities of Aryas who were not only different but opposed and inimical to each other. The existence of two Aryas is not a mere matter of conjecture or interpretation. It is a fact in support of which there is abundant evidence.

II

The first piece of such evidence to which attention may be invited, is the discrimination which existed for a long time in the matter of the recognition of the sacred character of the different Vedas. All students of the Vedas know that there are really two Vedas : (1) the Rig Veda and (2) the Atharva Veda. The Sama Veda and the Yajur Veda are merely different forms of the Rig Veda. All students of the Vedas know that the Atharva Veda was not recognised by the Brahmins as sacred as the Rig Veda for a long time. Why was such a distinction made ? Why was the Rig Veda regarded as sacred ? Why was the Atharva Veda treated as vulgar ? The answer, I like to suggest, is that the two belonged to two different races of Aryans and it is only when they had become one that the Atharva Veda came to be regarded on a par with the Rig Veda.

Besides this, there is enough evidence, scattered through

the whole of the Brahmanic literature, of the existence of two different ideologies, particularly relating to creation, which again points to the existence of two different Aryan races. Reference to one of these has already been made in Chapter II. It remains to draw attention to the second type of ideology.

To begin with the Vedas. The following ideology is to be found in the Taittiriya Samhita :

T. S.,[1] vi . 5 . 6 . 1.—" Aditi, desirous of sons, cooked a Brahmaudana oblation for the gods, the Sadhyas. They gave her the remnant of it. This she ate. She conceived seed. Four Adityas were born to her. She cooked a second (oblation). She reflceted, ' from the remains of the oblation these sons have been born to me. If I shall eat (the oblation) first, more brilliant (sons) will be born to me. She ate it first ; she conceived seed ; an imperfect egg was produced from her. She cooked a third (oblation) for the Adityas, repeating the formula ' may this religious toil have been undergone for my enjoyment.' The Adityas said, ' Let us choose a boon ; let anyone who is produced from this be ours only ; let anyone of his progeny who is prosperous be for us a source of enjoyment.' In consequence the Aditya Vivasvat was born. This is his progeny, namely, men. Among them he alone who sacrifices is prosperous, and becomes a cause of enjoyment to the gods."

Turning to the Brahmanas. The stories of creation contained in the Satapatha Brahmanas are set out below :—

S. B.,[2] i . 8 . 1 . 1.—" In the morning they brought to Manu water for washing, as men are in the habit of bringing it to wash with the hands. As he was thus washing, a fish came into his hands (which spake to him) ' preserve me ; I shall save thee.' (Manu enquired) ' From what wilt thou save me ? ' (The fish replied) ' A flood shall sweep away all these creatures ; from it will I rescue thee.' (Manu asked) ' How (shall) thy preservation (be effected) ? ' The fish said : ' So long as we are small, we are in great peril, for fish devours fish ; thou shalt preserve me first in a jar. When I grow too large for the jar, then thou shalt dig a trench, and

[1] Muir, Vol. I, p. 26.

[2] Muir, Vol. I, pp 181-184.

preserve me in that. When I grow too large for the trench, then thou shalt carry me away to the ocean. I shall then be beyond the reach of danger.' Straightaway he became a large fish; for he waxes to the utmost. (He said) 'Now in such and such a year, then the flood will come; thou shalt embark in the ship when the flood rises, and I shall deliver thee from it.' Having thus preserved the fish, Manu carried him away to the sea. Then in the same year which the fish had enjoined, he constructed a ship and resorted to him. When the flood rose, Manu embarked in the ship. The fish swam towards him. He fastened the cable of the ship to the fish's horn. By this means he passed over this northern mountain. The fish said, 'I have delivered thee; fasten the ship to a tree. But lest the water should cut thee off whilst thou art on the mountain, as much as the water subsides so much shalt thou descend after it.' He accordingly descended after it as much (as it subsided). Wherefore also this, viz., 'Manu's descent' is (the name) of the northern mountain. Now the flood had swept away all these creatures, so Manu alone was left here. Desirous of offspring, he lived worshipping and toiling in arduous religious rites. Among these he also sacrificed with the *paka* offering. He cast clarified butter, thickened milk, whey and curds as an oblation into the waters. Thence in a year a woman was produced. She rose up as it were unctuous. Clarified butter adheres to her steps. Mitra and Varuna met her. They said to her 'Who art thou?' 'Manu's daughter' (she replied). 'Say (thou art) ours' (they rejoined). 'No,' she said, 'I am his who begot me.' They desired a share in her. She promised that, or she did not promise that; but passed onward. She came to Manu. Manu said to her, 'Who art thou?' 'Thy daughter' she replied. 'How, glorious one,' asked Manu, '(art thou) my daughter?' 'Thou hast generated me,' she said, 'from those oblations, butter, thick milk, whey and curds, which thou didst cast into the waters. I am a benediction. Apply me in the sacrifice. If thou wilt employ me in the sacrifice, thou shalt abound in offspring and cattle. Whatever benediction thou will ask through me, shall accrue to thee.' He (accordingly) introduced her (as) that (which comes in) the middle of the sacrifice; for that is the middle of the sacrifice which (comes) between the introductory and concluding forms. With her he lived worshipping and toiling in arduous religious rites, desirous of offspring. With her he begot this offspring which is this offspring of Manu. Whatever benediction he asked with her, was all vouchsafed to him. This is essentially that which is Ida. Whosoever, knowing this, lives with Ida, begets this offspring which Manu begot. Whatever benediction he asks with her, is all vouchsafed to him."

(2) *S.B.* [1] vi . 1 . 2 . 11. "Wherefore they say, 'Prajapati having created these worlds was supported upon the earth. For him these herbs were cooked as food. That (food) he ate. He became pregnant. He created the gods from his upper vital airs, and mortal offspring from his lower vital airs. In whatever way he created, so he created. But Prajapati created all this, whatever exists."

(3) *S.B.*,[2] vii . 5 . 2 . 6.—"Prajapati was formerly this (universe), one only. He desired, 'Let me create food, and be propagated.' He formed animals from his breath, a man from his soul, a horse from his eye, a bull from his breath, a sheep from his ear, a goat from his voice. Since he formed animals from his breaths, therefore men say, 'the breaths are animals.' The soul is the first of the breaths. Since he formed a man from his soul, therefore they say 'man is the first of the animals, and the strongest.' The soul is all the breaths; for all the breaths depend upon the soul. Since he formed man from his soul, therefore they say, 'man is all the animals;' for all these are man's."

(4) *S.B.*, [3]x . 1 . 3 . 1.—"Prajapati created living beings. From his upper vital airs he created the gods: from his lower vital airs mortal creatures. Afterwards he created death a devourer of creatures."

(5) *S.B.*,[4] xiv . 4 . 2 . 1.—"This universe was formerly soul only, in the form of Purusha. Looking closely, he saw nothing but himself (or soul). He first said, 'This is I.' Then he became one having the name of I. Hence even now a man, when called, first says, 'this is I,' and then declares the other name when he has. In as much as he, before (*purvah*) all this, burnt up (*aushat*) all sins, he (is called), *purusha*. The man who knows this burns up the person who wishes to be before him. He was afraid. Hence a man when

[1] Muir, Vol. I, p. 30.
[2] Muir, Vol. I, p. 24.
[3] Muir, Vol. I, p. 31.
[4] Muir Vol. I, p. 25.

alone is afraid. This (being) considered that 'there is no other thing but myself; of what am I afraid ?' Then his fear departed. For why should he have feared ? It is of a second person that people are afraid. He did not enjoy happiness. Hence a person when alone does not enjoy happiness. He desired a second. He was so much as a man and a woman when locked in embrace. He caused this same self to fall asunder into two parts. Thence arose a husband and wife. Hence Yajnavalkya has said that 'this one's self is like the half of a split pea.' Hence the void is filled up by woman. He cohabited with her. From them Men were born. She reflected 'how does he, after having produced me from himself, cohabit with me ? Ah! let me disappear'; she became a cow, and the other a bull; and he cohabited with her. From them kine were produced. The one became a mare, the other a stallion, the one a she-ass, the other a male-ass. He cohabited with her. From them the class of animals with undivided hoofs were produced. The one became a she-goat, the other a he-goat, the one a ewe, the other a ram. He cohabited with her. From them goats and sheep were produced. In this manner pairs of all creatures whatsoever down to ants, were produced."

The Taittiriya Brahmana has the following :—

T.B.,[1] ii . 2 . 9 . 1.—"At first this (universe) was not anything. There was neither sky, nor earth, nor air. Being non-existent, it resolved 'let me be.' It became fervent. From that fervour smoke was produced. It again became fervent. From that fervour fire was produced. It again became fervent. From that fervour light was produced. It again became fervent. From that fervour flame was produced. It again became fervent. From that fervour rays were produced. It again became fervent. From that fervour blazes were produced. It again became fervent. It became condensed like a cloud. It clove its bladder. That became the sea. Hence men do not drink of the sea. For they regard it as like the place of generation. Hence water issues forth before an animal when it is being born. After that the Dasahotri (a particular formula) was created. Prajapati is the Dasahotri. That man succeeds, who thus knowing the power of austere abstraction (or fervour) practises it. This was then water, fluid. Prajapati wept (exclaiming), 'For

[1] Muir, Vol. I, pp. 28-29.

what purpose have I been born, if (I have been born) from this which forms no support.' That which fell into the waters became the earth. That which he wiped away, became the air. That which he wiped away, upwards, became the sky. From the circumstance that he wept (*arodit*), these two regions have the name of *rodasi*, (worlds). They do not weep in the house of the man who knows this. This was the birth of these worlds. He who thus knows the birth of these worlds, incurs no suffering in these worlds. He obtained this (earth as a) basis. Having obtained (this earth as a) basis, he desired, 'May I be propagated.' He practised austere fervour. He became pregnant. He created Asuras from his abdomen. To them he milked out food in an earthern dish. He cast off that body of his. It became darkness. He desired 'May I be propagated.' He practised austere fervour. He became pregnant. He created living beings (*prajah*) from his organ of generation. Hence they are the most numerous, because he created them from his generative organ. To them he milked out milk in a wooden dish. He cast off that body of his. It became moonlight. He desired 'May I be propagated.' He practised austere fervour. He became pregnant. He created the seasons from his armpits. To them he milked out butter in a silver dish. He cast off that body of his. It became the period which connects day and night. He desired 'May I be propagated.' He practised austere fervour. He became pregnant. He created the gods from his mouth. To them he milked out Soma in a golden dish. He cast off that body of his. It became day. These are Prajapati's milkings. He who thus knows, milks out offspring. 'Day (*diva*) has come to us:' this (exclamation expresses) the godhead of the gods. He who thus knows the godhead of the gods, obtains the gods. This is the birth of days and nights. He who thus knows the birth of days and nights, incurs no suffering in the days and nights. Mind (or soul, *manas*), was created from the non-existent. Mind created Prajapati. Prajapati created offspring. All this, whatever exists, rests absolutely on mind. This is that Brahma called Svovasyasa. For the man who thus knows, (Ushas), dawning, dawns more and more bright; he becomes prolific in offspring, and (rich) in cattle; he obtains the rank of Parameshthin."

(3) *T.B.*,[1] ii . 3 . 8 . 1.—" Prajapati desired, 'May I propagate.' He practised austerity. He became pregnant. He became yellow-brown. Hence a woman when pregnant, being yellow, becomes brown. Being pregnant with a fœtus, he became exhausted. Being exhausted he became blackish-brown. Hence an exhausted person becomes blackish-brown. His breath became alive. With that breath (*asu*) he created Asuras. Therein consists the Asura-nature of Asuras. He who thus knows this Asura-nature of Asuras becomes a man possessing breath. Breath does not forsake him. Having created the Asuras he regarded himself as a father. After that he created the Fathers (Pitris). That constitutes the fatherhood of the Fathers. He who thus knows the fatherhood of the Fathers, becomes as a father of his own ; the Fathers resort to his oblation. Having created the Fathers, he reflected. After that he created men. That constitutes the manhood of men. He who knows the manhood of men, becomes intelligent. Mind does not forsake him. To him, when he was creating men, day appeared in the heaven. After that he created the gods. This constitutes the godhead of the gods. To him who thus knows the godhead of the gods, day appears in the heavens. These are the four streams, viz., gods, men, fathers and Asuras. In all of these water is like the air."

(4) *T.B.*,[2] iii . 2 . 3 . 9.—" This Shudra has sprung from non-existence."

The following explanation of the origin of creation is given by the Taittiriya Aranyaka :

T.A.,[3] i . 12 . 3 . 1.—" This is water, fluid. Prajapati alone was produced on a lotus leaf. Within, in his mind, desire arose, 'Let me create this.' Hence whatever a man aims at in his mind, he declares by speech, and performs by act. Hence this verse has been uttered, 'Desire formerly arose in it, which was the primal germ of mind, (and which), sages, searching with their intellect, have discovered in the heart as the bond between the existent and the non-existent.' (Rig Veda x . 129 . 4). That of which he is desirous comes to

[1] Muir, Vol. I, p. 23.
[2] Muir, Vol. I, p. 21.
[3] Muir, Vol. I, p. 32.

the man who thus knows. He practised austere fervour. Having practised austere fervour, he shook his body. From its flesh the rishis (called) Arunas, Ketus and Vatarasanas arose. His nails became the Vaikhanasas, his hairs the Valakhilyas. The fluid (of his body became) a tortoise moving amid the waters. He said to him 'Thou hast sprung from my skin and flesh.' 'No,' replied the tortoise, 'I was here before.' In that (in his having been 'before' *purvam*) consists the manhood of a man (*purusha*). Becoming a man, *Purusha* with a thousand heads, a thousand eyes, a thousand feet (R.V. x. 90. 1) he arose. Prajapati said to him, 'thou wert produced before me; do thou first make this.' He took water from this in the cavity of his two hands and placed it on the east, repeating the text, 'so be it, O Sun.' From thence the sun arose. That was the eastern quarter. Then Aruna Ketu placed (the water) to the south, saying 'so be it, O Agni.' Thence Agni arose. That was the southern quarter. Then Aruna Ketu placed (the water) to the west, saying 'so be it, O Vayu.' Thence arose Vayu. That was the western quarter. Then Aruna Ketu placed (the water) to the north, saying 'so be it, O Indra.' Then arose Indra. That is the northern quarter. Then Aruna Ketu placed (the water) in the centre, saying 'so be it, O Pushan.' Thence arose Pushan. That is this quarter. Then Aruna Ketu placed (the water) above, saying 'so be it, gods.' Thence arose gods, men, Fathers, Gandharvas and Apsarasas. That is the upper quarter. From the drops which fell apart arose the Asuras, Rakshasas, and Pisachas. Therefore they perished, because they were produced from drops. Hence this text has been uttered; 'when the great waters became pregnant, containing wisdom, and generating Svayambhu, from them were created these creations. All this was produced from the waters. Therefore all this is Brahma Svayambhu.' Hence all this was as it were loose, as it were unsteady. Prajapati was that. Having made himself through himself, he entered into that. Wherefore this verse has been uttered; 'Having formed the world, having formed existing things and all intermediate quarters and quarters, Prajapati the first born of the ceremonial entered into himself with himself."

VI

The Mahabharata has its own contribution to make to the subject. It propounds the theory of creation by Manu.

The Vanaparvan[1] says :

> " There was a great rishi, Manu, son of Vivasvat, majestic, in lustre equal to Prajapati. In energy, fiery vigour, prosperity and austere fervour he surpassed both his father and his grandfather. Standing with uplifted arm, on one foot, on the spacious Badari, he practised intense austere fervour. This direful exercise he performed with his head downwards, and with unwinking eyes, for 10,000 years. Once, when, clad in dripping rags, with matted hair, he was so engaged, a fish came to him on the banks of the Chirini, and spake : ' Lord, I am a small fish ; I dread the stronger ones, and from them you must save me. For the stronger fish devour the weaker ; this has been immemorially ordained as our means of subsistence. Deliver me from this flood of apprehension in which I am sinking, and I will requite the deed.' Hearing this, Manu filled with compassion, took the fish in his hand, and bringing him to the water threw him into a jar bright as a moonbeam. In it the fish, being excellently tended, grew ; for Manu treated him like a son. After a long time he became very large and could not be contained in the jar. Then, seeing Manu he said again : ' In order that I may thrive, remove me elsewhere.' Manu then took him out of the jar, brought him to a large pond, and threw him in. There he continued to grow for very many years. Although the pond was two *yojanas* long and one *yojana* broad, the lotus-eyed fish found in it no room to move ; and again said to Manu, ' Take me to Ganga, the dear queen of the ocean-monarch ; in her I shall dwell ; or do as thou thinkest best, for I must contentedly submit to thy authority, as through thee I have exceedingly increased.' Manu accordingly took the fish and threw him into the river Ganga. There he waxed for some time, when he again said to Manu, ' From my great bulk I cannot move in the Ganga ; be gracious and remove me quickly to the ocean.' Manu took him out of the Ganga ; and cast him into the sea. Although so huge, the fish was

[1] Muir, Vol. I, pp. 199-201.

easily borne, and pleasant to touch and smell, as Manu carried him. When he had been thrown into the ocean he said to Manu : ' Great Lord, thou hast in every way preserved me ; now hear from me what thou must do when the time arrives. Soon shall all these terrestrial objects, both fixed and moving, be dissolved. The time for the purification of the worlds has now arrived. I therefore inform thee what is for thy greatest good. The period dreadful for the universe, moving and fixed, has come. Make for thyself a strong ship, with a cable attached ; embark in it with the seven rishis and stow in it, carefully preserved and assorted, all the seeds which have been described of old by Brahmins. When embarked in the ship, look out for me. I shall come recognizable by my horn. So shalt thou do ; I greet thee and depart. These great waters cannot be crossed over without me. Distrust not my word.' Manu replied, ' I shall do as thou hast said.' After taking mutual leave they departed each on his own way. Manu then, as enjoined, taking with him the seeds, floated on the billowy ocean in the beautiful ship. He then thought on the fish, which knowing his desire, arrived with all speed, distinguished by a horn. When Manu saw the horned leviathan, lofty as a mountain, he fastened the ship's cable to the horn. Being thus attached, the fish dragged the ship with great rapidity, transporting it across the briny ocean which seemed to dance with its waves and thunder with its waters. Tossed by the tempests, the ship whirled like a reeling and intoxicated woman. Neither the earth nor the quarters of the world appeared ; there was nothing but water, air, and sky. In the world thus confounded, the seven rishis, Manu, and the fish were beheld. So, for very many years, the fish, unwearied, drew the ship over the waters ; and brought it at length to the highest peak of Himavat. He then, smiling gently, said to the rishis, ' Bind the ship without delay to this peak.' They did so accordingly. And that highest peak of Himavat is still known by the name of Naubandhana (' the Binding of the Ship'). The friendly fish (or god, *animisha*) then said to the rishis, ' I am the Prajapati Brahma, than whom nothing higher can be reached. In the form of a fish I have delivered you from this great danger. Manu shall create all living beings, gods, asuras, men, with all worlds, and all things moving and fixed. By my favour and through severe austere fervour, he shall attain perfect insight into his creative work, and shall not become bewildered.' Having thus spoken, the fish in an instant disappeared. Manu, desirous to call creatures into existence and bewildered in his work, performed a great act of austere fervour ; and then began visibly to create all living beings."

The Adi Parvan of the Mahabharata gives a some what different version of the story of creation[1] :

"Vaisahmpayan said : I shall, after making obeisance to Svayambhu relate to thee exactly the production and destruction of the gods and other beings. Six great rishis are known as the mind-born sons of Brahma, viz., Marichi, Atri, Angiras, Pulastya, Pulaha and Kratu. Kasyapa was the son of Marichi : and from Kasyapa sprang these creatures. There were born to Daksha thirteen daughters of eminent rank, Aditi, Diti, Danu, Kala, Danayu, Simuka, Krodha, Pradha, Visva, Vinata, Kapila and Muni. Kadru also was of the number. These daughters had valorous sons and grandsons innumerable."

"Daksha, the glorious rishi, tranquil in spirit, and great in austere fervour, sprang from the right thumb of Brahma. From the left thumb sprang that great Muni's wife on whom he begot fifty daughters. Of these he gave ten to Dharma, twenty-seven to Indu (Soma), and according to the celestial system, thirteen to Kasyapa." Pitamaha's descendant Manu, the god and the lord of creatures, was his (it does not clearly appear whose) son. The eight Vasus, whom I shall detail, were his sons. Dividing the right breast of Brahma, the glorious Dharma (Righteousness), issued in a human form, bringing happiness to all people. He had three eminent sons, Sama, Kama, and Harsha (Tranquillity, Love, and Joy), who are the delight of all creatures, and by their might support the world . . . Arushi, the daughter of Manu, was the wife of that sage (Chyavana, son of Bhrigu) . . . There are two other sons of Brahma, whose mark remains in the world, Dhatri, and Vidhatri, who remained with Manu. Their sister was the beautiful goddess Lakshmi, whose home is the lotus. Her mind-born sons are the steeds who move in the sky . . . When the creatures who were desirous of food, had devoured one another, Adharma (Uprighteousness) was

[1] Muir, Vol. I, pp. 122-126.

produced, the destroyer of all beings. His wife was Nirriti, and hence the Rakshasas are called Nairritas, or the offspring of Nirriti. She had three dreadful sons, continually addicted to evil deeds, Bhaya, Mahabhaya (Fear and Terror) and Mrityu (Death) the ender of beings. He has neither wife, nor any son, for he is the ender."

"Born all with splendour, like that of great rishis, the ten sons of Prachetas are reputed to have been virtuous and holy; and by them the glorious beings were formerly burnt up by the fire springing from their mouths. From them was born Daksha Prachetasa; and from Daksha, the Parent of the world (were produced), these creatures. Cohabiting with Virini, the Muni Daksha begot a thousand sons like himself, famous for their religious observances, to whom Narada taught the doctrine of final liberation, the unequalled knowledge of the Sankhya. Desirous of creating offspring, the Prajapati Daksha next formed fifty daughters, of whom he gave ten to Dharma, thirteen to Kasyapa, and twenty-seven devoted to the regulation of time to Indu (Soma) . . . On Dakshayani, the most excellent of his thirteen wives, Kasyapa, the son of Marichi, begot the Adityas, headed by Indra and distinguished by their energy, and also Vivasvat. To Vivasvat was born a son, the mighty Yama Vaivasvata. To Martanda (i.e., Vivasvat, the Sun) was born the wise and mighty Manu, and also the renowned Yama, his (Manu's) younger brother. Righteous was this wise Manu, on whom a race was founded. Hence this (family) of men became known as the race of Manu. Brahmins, Kshatriyas, and other men sprang from this Manu. From him, O king, came the Brahmin conjoined with the Kshatriya. Among them the Brahmins, children of Manu, held the Veda with the Vedangas. The children of Manu are said to have been Vena, Dhrishnu, Narishyanta, Nabhaga, Ikshvaku, Karusha, Saryati, Ila the eighth, Prishadra the ninth, who was addicted to the duties of a Kshatriya, and Nabhagarishta, the tenth. Manu had also fifty other sons; but they all, as we have heard, perished in consequence of mutual dissensions. Subsequently, the wise Pururavas was born of Ila, who, we heard, was both his mother and his father."

VII

The Ramayana also deals with the subject of creation. One account of it will be found in the second Kanda.[1] It says :

> "Perceiving Rama to be incensed, Vasishtha replied : 'Jabali also knows the destruction and renovation of this world. But he spoke as he did from a desire to induce you to return. Learn from me, lord of the earth, this (account of) the origin of the world. The universe was nothing but water. In it the earth was fashioned. Then Brahma Svayambhu came into existence, with the deities. He next, becoming a boar, raised up the earth, and created the entire world, with the saints, his sons. Brahma, the eternal, unchanging, and undecaying, was produced from the ether (akasa). From him sprang Marichi, of whom Kasyapa was the son. From Kasyapa sprang Vivasvat : and from him was descended Manu, who was formerly the lord of creatures (Prajapati). Ikshvaku was the son of Manu, and to him this prosperous earth was formerly given by his father. Know that this Ikshvaku was the former king in Ayodhya."

There is besides this another story of creation. If occurs in the third Kanda and is in the following terms :[2]

> "Having heard the words of Rama, the bird (Jatayu) made known to him his own race, and himself, and the origin of all beings. 'Listen while I declare to you from the commencement all the Prajapatis (lords of creatures) who came into existence in the earliest time. Kardama was the first, then Vikrita, Sesha, Samsraya, the energetic Bahuputra, Sthanu, Marichi, Atri, the strong Kratu, Pulastya, Angiras, Prachetas, Pulaha, Daksha, then Vivasvat, Arishtanemi, and the glorious Kasyapa, who was the last. The Prajapati Daksha is famed to have had sixty daughters. Of these Kasyapa took in marriage eight elegant maidens, Aditi, Diti, Danu, Kalaka, Tamra, Krodhavasa, Manu and Anala. Kasyapa, pleased, then, said to these maids : 'ye shall bring forth sons like me, preservers of the three worlds.' Aditi, Diti, Danu, and Kalaka assented ; but the others did not agree. Thirty-three gods were borne by Aditi, the Adityas, Vasus, Rudras, and the two Asvins."

---

[1] Muir, Vol. I, p. 115.

[2] *Ibid*, p. 116.

"Manu, (wife) of Kasyapa, produced men, Brahmins, Kshatriyas, Vaishyas, and Shudras. 'Brahmins were born from the mouth, Kshatriyas from the breast, Vaishyas from the thighs, and Shudras from the feet' so says the Veda. Anala gave birth to all trees with pure fruits."

VIII

As an illustration of what the Puranas have to say, I extract the following passages from the Vishnu Purana[1] :—

"Before the mundane egg existed the divine Brahma Hiranyagarbha the eternal originator of all worlds, who was the form and essence of Brahma, who consists of the divine Vishnu, who again is identical with the Rik, Yajus, Saman and Atharva-Vedas. From Brahma's right thumb was born the Prajapati Daksha; Daksha had a daughter Aditi; from her was born Vivasvat; and from him sprang Manu. Manu had sons called Ikshvaku, Nriga, Dhrishta, Saryati, Narishyanta, Pramśu, Nabhaganedishta, Karusha, and Prishadhra. Desirous of a son, Manu sacrificed to Mitra and Varuna; but in consequence of a wrong invocation through an irregularity of the hotri-priest a daughter called Ila was born. Then through the favour of Mitra and Varuna she became to Manu a son called Sudyumna. But being again changed into a female through the wrath of Isvara (Mahadeva) she wandered near the hermitage of Budha the son of Soma (the Moon); who becoming enamoured of her had by her a son called Pururavas. After his birth, the god who is formed of sacrifice, of the Rik, Yajus, Samań, and Atharva Vedas, of all things, of mind, of nothing, he who is in the form of the sacrificial Male, was worshipped by the rishis of infinite splendour who desired that Sudyumna should recover his manhood. Through the favour of this god Ila became again Sudyumna."

The Vishnu Purana then proceeds to give the following particulars regarding the sons of Manu :—

(i) "Prishadhra became a Shudra in consequence of his having killed his religious preceptor's cow."

[1] Muir, Vol. I, pp. 220-221.

(ii) "From Karusha the Karushas, Kshatriyas of great power were descended."

(iii) "Nabhaga, the son of Nedishta became a Vaishya."

The above is the story of the Solar race. The Vishnu Purana[1] has also a parallel story relating to the Lunar race which according to it sprang from Atri just as the Solar race from Manu :

"Atri was the son of Brahma, and the father of Soma (the moon), whom Brahma installed as the sovereign of plants, Brahmins and stars." After celebrating the *rajasuya* sacrifice, Soma became intoxicated with pride, and carried off Tara (Star), the wife of Brihaspati, the preceptor of the gods, whom, although admonished and entreated by Bramha, the gods, and *rishis*, Soma refused to restore. Soma's part was taken by Usanas; and Rudra, who had studied under Angiras, aided Brihaspati. A fierce conflict ensued between the two sides supported respectively by the gods and the Daityas, etc., Bramha interposed, and compelled Soma to restore Tara to her husband. She had, however, in the meantime become pregnant, and bore a son Budha (the planet Mercury), of whom when strongly urged, she acknowledged Soma to be the father. Pururavas[2] was the son of this Budha by Ila, the daughter of Manu. Pururavas[3] had six sons, of whom the eldest was Ayus. Ayus had five sons; Nahusha, Kshattravriddha, Rambha, Raji and Anenas."

"Kshattravriddha had a son Sunahotra who had three sons, Kasa, Lesa and Gritsamada. From the last sprang Saunaka, who originated the system of four castes. Kasa had a son, Kasiraja, of whom again Dirghatamas was the son, as Dhanvantari was of Dirghatamas."

Compare these ideologies of creation with those set out in Chapter II and what do we find ? I think the result of comparison may be set down in the following propositions : (1) One is sacerdotal in colour and character, the other is secular ; (2) One refers to a human being

---

[1] Muir, Vol. I, pp. 225-226.

[2] The loves of Pururavas and the Aspara Urvasi are related in the Satapatha Brahmana, xi.5.1.11 ; in the Vishnu Purana, iv.6.19.ff ; in the Bhagavata Purana, ix.14 ; and in the Harivamsa, section 26. The Mahabharata, Adip. section 75, alludes to Pururavas as having been engaged in a contest with the Brahmins. This passage will be quoted hereafter.

[3] Vishnu Puran iv.7.1.

Manu as the progenitor, the other refers to God Brahma or Prajapati as the originator; (3) One is historical in its drift, the other is supernatural; (4) One speaks of the deluge, the other is completely silent about it; (5) One aims at explaining the four *Varnas*, the other aims at explaining the origin of society only.

These differences are many and fundamental. Particularly fundamental seems to be the difference in regard to *Chaturvarnya.* The sacerdotal ideology recognizes it, but the secular ideology does not. It is true that an attempt is made to combine the two by explaining, as is done in the Ramayana and the Puranas, how Manu's progeny developed into four *Varnas*. But obviously this is an attempt to mould the two ideologies into one. This attempt is deliberate and calculated. But the difference between the two ideologies is so fundamental that in spite of this attempt they persist as two separate ideologies. All that has happened is that instead of one we have two explanations of *Chaturvarnya,* supernatural *Chaturvarnya,* produced by Purusha, and natural *Chaturvarnya* as developed among Manu's sons. That the result should be so clumsy shows that the two ideologies are fundamentally different and irreconcilable. It is a pity that the existence of two such ideologies recorded in the Brahmanic literature has not been noticed by scholars who have dealt with the subject. But the fact of their existence and their significance cannot be ignored. What is the significance of the existence of two such ideologies fundamentally different and irreconcilable? To me, it seems that they are the ideologies of two different Aryan races—one believing in *Chaturvarnya* and the other not believing in *Chaturvarnya*—who at a later stage became merged into one. If this reasoning is well-founded then this difference in ideologies disclosed by the Brahmanic literature furnishes further evidence in support of the new theory.

IX

The third and the most unimpeachable evidence in support of my view comes from the anthropometrical survey of the Indian people. Such a survey was first made by Sir Herbert Risley in 1901. On the basis of cephalic index, he came to the conclusion that the people of India were a mixture of four different races : (1) Aryan, (2) Dravidian, (3) Mongolian, and (4) Scythian. He even went to the length of defining the areas where they were massed. The survey was a very rough one. His conclusions have been tested by Dr. Guha in 1936. His Report on the subject forms a very valuable document in the field of Indian anthropology. The map[1] prepared by Dr. Guha on which he has plotted so to say the distribution of the Indian people according to their head measurements throws a flood of light on the racial composition of the people of India. Dr. Guha's conclusion is that the Indian people are composed of two racial stocks : (1) long-headed, and (2) short-headed, and that the long-headed are in the interior of India and the short-headed are on the outskirts.

The evidence of skulls found in different parts of India also goes to confirm this. This is how Dr. Guha sums up the evidence on this point :

> " The accounts of the human remains from prehistoric sites given above, though extremely meagre, with the exception of those of the Indus Valley, enable us nevertheless to visualise the broad outlines of the racial history of India in these times. From the beginning of the 4th Millennium B.C. North-western India seems to have been in the occupation of a long-headed race with a narrow prominent nose. Side by side with them we find the existence of another very powerfully built race also long-headed, but with lower cranial vault, and equally long-faced and narrow nose, though the latter was not so high pitched as that of the former.

[1] See Appendix v.

A third type with broader head and apparently Armenoid affinities also existed, but its advent occurred probably somewhat later judged by the age of the site at Harappa from which most of these latter type of skulls came."

Speaking in terms of the Alpine and the Mediterranean race, one can say that the Indian people are composed of two stocks : (1) The Mediterranean or the long-headed race, and (2) the Alpine or the short-headed race.

About the Mediterranean race, certain facts are admitted. It is admitted that it is a race which spoke the Aryan language. It is admitted that its home was in Europe round about the Mediterranean basin and from thence it migrated to India. From its localization, it is clear that it must have come to India before the entry of the Alpine race.

Similar facts about the Alpine race remain to be ascertained. First is about the home of the Alpine race and second is about its native speech. According to Prof. Ripley, the home of the Alpine race was in Asia somewhere in the Himalayas. His reasons may be given in his own words. Says Prof. Ripley[1] :

"What right have we for the assertion that this infiltration of population from the East—it was not a conquest, everything points to it as a gradual peaceful immigration, often merely the settlement of unoccupied territory—marks the advent of an overflow from the direction of Asia? The proof of this rests largely upon our knowledge of the people of that continent, especially of the Pamir region, the Western Himalayan highlands. Just here on the 'roof of the world,' where Max Muller and the early philologists placed the primitive home of Aryan civilization, a human type prevails which tallies almost exactly with our ideal Alpine or Celtic European race. The researches of De Ujfalvy, Topinard, and others localize its peculiar traits over a vast territory hereabouts. The Galchas, mountain Tadjiks, and their fellows are grey-eyed, dark-haired, stocky in build, with cephalic indexes ranging above 86 for the most part. From this region a long chain of peoples of a similar physical type extends,

[1] Races of Europe, pp. 473-4.

uninterruptedly westward over Asia Minor and into Europe. The only point which the discovery of a broad area in Western Asia occupied by an ideal Alpine type settles, is that it emphasises the affinities of this peculiar race. It is no proof of direct immigration from Asia at all, as Tappeiner observes. It does, however, lead us to turn our eyes eastward when we seek for the origin of the broad-headed type. Things vaguely point to an original ethnic base of supplies somewhere in this direction. It could not lie westward, for everywhere along the Atlantic the race slowly disappears, so to speak. That the Alpine type approaches all the other human millions on the Asiatic continent, in the head form especially, but in hair, colour and stature as well, also prejudices us in the matter; just as the increasing long-headedness and extreme brunetness of our Mediterranean race led us previously to derive it from some type parent to that of the African Negro. These points are then fixed; the roots of the Alpine race run eastward; those of the Mediterranean type towards the south."

On the question of its language there is a certain amount of dispute[1] as to who introduced the Aryan language in Europe, whether the Nordics (the purest of the Indo-Germans) or the Alpines. But there is no dispute that the language of the Alpine race was Aryan and therefore it is entitled to be called Aryan race in philological sense.

X

From the foregoing statement of facts, it will be seen that there is a solid foundation in anthropometry and history, in support of the Rig Veda that there were in India two Aryan races and not one. Having regard to this, one cannot refuse to admit that here there is a direct conflict between the Western theory and the testimony of the Rig Veda. Whereas the Western theory speaks of one Aryan race, the Rig Veda speaks of two

[1] Madison Grant—'The Passing of the Great Race' (1922), pp. 238-239.

Aryan races. The Western theory is thus in conflict with the Rig Veda on a major issue. The Rig Veda being the best evidence on the subject the theory which is in conflict with it must be rejected. There is no escape.

This conflict on the major issue also creates a conflict on the issue of invasion and conquest. We do not know which of the two Aryan races came to India first. But if they belonged to the Alpine race then its home being near the Himalayas, there is no room for the theory of invasion from outside. As to the conquest of the native tribes, assuming it to be a fact, the matter is not quite so simple as Western writers have supposed. On the footing that the Dasas and Dasyus were racially different from the Aryans, the theory of conquest must take account not merely of a possible conquest of Dasas and Dasyus by Aryans but also of a possible conquest of Aryans by Aryans. It must also explain which of the two Aryans conquered the Dasas and Dasyus if they conquered them at all.

The Western theory, it is clear, is only a hurried conclusion drawn from insufficient examination of facts and believed to be correct because it tallied with certain pre-conceived notions about the mentality of the ancient Aryans which they were supposed to have possessed on no other grounds except that their alleged modern descendents, namely, the Indo-Germanic races are known to possess. It is built on certain selected facts which are assumed to be the only facts. It is extraordinary that a theory with such a slender and insecure foundation in fact should have been propounded by Western scholars for serious scholars and should have held the field for such a long time. In the face of the discovery of new facts set out in this Chapter the theory can no longer stand and must be thrown on the scrap heap.

CHAPTER VI

SHUDRAS AND DASAS

IT has been shown how untenable the Western theory is. The only part of the theory that remains to be considered is : who are the Shudras ? Mr. A. C. Das[1] says :—

> " The Dasas and the Dasyus were either savages or non-Vedic Aryan tribes. Those of them that were captured in war were probably made slaves and formed the Shudra caste."

Mr. Kane[2], another Vedic scholar and upholder of the Western theory, holds the view that :

> " The word 'Dasa' in later literature means a 'serf or a slave.' It follows that the Dasa tribes that we see opposed to the Aryas in the Rig Veda were gradually vanquished and were then made to serve the Aryas. In the Manusmriti (VIII, 418) the Shudra is said to have been created by God for service (*dasya*) of the Brahmana. We find in the Tai. Samhita the Tai. Brahmana and other Brahmana works that the Shudra occupied the same position that he does in the Smritis. Therefore it is reasonable to infer that the *Dasas* or *Dasyus* conquered by the Aryans were gradually transformed into the Shudras."

According to this view the Shudras are the same as Dasas and Dasyus and further the Shudras were the non-Aryan original inhabitants of India and were in a primitive and a savage state of civilization. It is these propositions which we must now proceed to examine.

To begin with the first proposition. It is not one proposition but is really two propositions rolled in one. One is that the Dasas and Dasyus are one and the same people. The other is that they and the Shudras are one and the same people.

---

[1] Rig Vedic Culture, p. 133.

[2] Dharma Shastra, II (I), p. 33.

That the Dasas and Dasyus are one and the same people is a proposition of doubtful validity. Such references to them as are to be found in the Rig Veda are not decisive. In some places the terms *Dasa* and *Dasyu* are used in a way as though there was no difference between the two. Shambara, Shushna, Vritra and Pipru are described both as Dasas and Dasyus. Both Dasas and Dasyus are described as the enemies of Indra and Devas and specially the Ashvins. The cities of both Dasas as well as of the Dasyus are described to have been levelled down by Indra and Devas. The defeat of both Dasas as well as Dasyus is described as producing the same effect, namely, release of water and the emergence of light. In describing the release of Dabhiti both are referred to, at one place he is said to have been released from the Dasas and at another place he is said to have been released from the Dasyus.

While these references suggest that the Dasas and Dasyus were the same, there are other references which suggest that they were different. This is clear from the fact that the Dasas are referred to separately in 54 places and Dasyus are referred to separately in 78 places. Why should there be so many separate references if they did not form two distinct entities ? The probability is that they refer to two different communities.

About the second proposition that the Shudras are the same as the Dasas and Dasyus, one can definitely say that it is without any foundation whatsoever.

To make out a case that the Shudras are the same as the Dasas and Dasyus an attempt is made to treat the word Shudra as a derivative word. The word is said to be derived from *Shuc* (sorrow) and *dru* (overcome) and means one overcome by sorrow. In this connection reliance is placed on the story told in the Vedanta Sutra (i . 3 34) of *Janasruti* who is said to have been overcome by sorrow on hearing the contemptuous talk of the flamingoes about himself[1]. The same derivation is given by the Vishnu Purana[2].

How far are these statements well-founded ? To say that Shudra is not a proper name but is a derivative word is too silly for words. The Brahmanic writers excel everybody in the art of inventing false etymologies. There is no word for which they will not design some sort of etymology. Speaking of the different etymologies of the word Upanishad given by Brahmanic writers, Prof. Max Muller[3] said :

> "These explanations seem so wilfully perverse that it is difficult to understand the unanimity of native scholars. We ought to take into account, however, that very general tendency among half-educated people, to acquiesce in any etymology which accounts for the most prevalent meaning of a word. The Aranyakas abound in such etymologics, which probably were never intended as real etymologies, in our sense of the word, but simply as plays on words, helping to account somehow for their meaning."

This warning equally well applies to the attempt of the Vedanta Sutra and of the Vayu Purana to make the word Shudra a derivative word suggesting that it meant a 'sorrowful people' and we must therefore reject it as being absurd and senseless.

We have, however, direct evidence in support of the proposition that Shudra is a proper name of a tribe or a clan and is not a derivative word as is sought to be made out.

Various pieces of evidence can be adduced in favour of this proposition. The historians of Alexander's invasion of India have described a number of republics as free, independent and autonomous whom Alexander encountered. These are, no doubt, formed of different tribes

---

[1] Referred to by Kane's Dharma Shastra, II (I), p. 155.
[2] Muir, Vol. I, p. 97.
[3] Upanishads—Introduction, pp. lxxix-lxxxi.

and were known by the name borne by those tribes. Among these is mentioned a people called *Sodari*. They were a fairly important tribe, being one of those which fought Alexander though it suffered a defeat at his hands. Lassen identified them with the ancient *Shudras*. Patanjali at 1.2.3 of his Mahabhasya mentions Shudras and associates them with the Abhiras. The Mahabharata in Chapter XXXII of the Sabha Parvan speaks of the republic of the Shudras. The Vishnu Purana as well as the Markandeya Purana and the Brahma Purana refer to the Shudras as a separate tribe among many other tribes and fix their location in the Western part of the country above the Vindhyas[1].

II

Let us now turn to the second proposition and examine the various elements of which it is composed. There are two elements in the proposition. First is: Are the words Dasyus and Dasas used in the racial sense indicative of their being non-Aryan tribes? The second element is that assuming they were is there anything to indicate that they were, the native tribes of India? Unless and until these two questions are answered in the affirmative, there is no possibility of identifying the Dasyus and Dasas with the Shudras.

About the Dasyus, there is no evidence to show that the term is used in a racial sense indicative of a non-Aryan people. On the other hand, there is positive evidence in support of the conclusion that it was used to denote persons who did not observe the Aryan form of religion. In this connection, reference may be made to Verse 28

[1] See References in *Tribes in Ancient India*, by B. C. Law, p. 350.

of Adhyaya 65 of the Shantiparvan of the Mahabharata. It reads as follows :—

> दृश्यन्ते मानुषे लोके सर्ववर्णेषु दस्यवः ।
> लिंगान्तरे वर्तमाना आश्रमेषुचतुर्ष्वपि ॥

The verse says :

" In all the Varnas and in all the Ashramas, one finds the existence of Dasyus."

This statement from the Mahabharata must be accepted as conclusive evidence that Dasyu is not used as the name of a non-Aryan tribe.

What is the origin of the word Dasyu it is difficult to say. But a suggestion[1] has been put forth that it was the word of abuse used by the Indo-Aryans to the Indo-Iranians. There is nothing unnatural or far-fetched in this suggestion. That the two had come into conflict is borne out by history. It is therefore quite possible for the Indo-Aryans to have coined such a contemptuous name for their enemies. If this is true, then Dasyus cannot be regarded as the natives of India.

Regarding the Dasas, the question is whether there is any connection between them and the Azhi Dahaka of the Zend Avesta. The name Azhi-Dahaka is a compound name which consists of two parts. *Azhi* means serpent, dragon and *Dahaka* comes from root *Dah* meaning 'to sting, to do harm.' Thus *Azhi-Dahaka* meaning a stinging dragon. It is a proper name of a person commonly known in Indo-Iranian traditions as Zohak. He is mentioned in Yasht literature many a times. He is credited to have lived in Babylon where he had built a palace. He is also credited to have built a great observatory in Babylon. This mighty devil Azhi Dahaka was created by the Arch-demon Angra Mainyu in order to destroy the kingdom of holiness of the corporeal world.

---

[1] I am sorry I have lost the reference.

This Azhi-Dahaka went to war against Yima the renowned king of the Indo-Iranians and not only vanquished him, but killed him in battle.

Yima is always spoken of in Avesta as *Kshaeta* meaning shining or ruling. Root *Kshi* has two meanings, to shine or to rule. There is another ephithet commonly used for Yima and that is *Hvanthwa* meaning 'possessing good flock.' This Avesta Yima Khshaita became in later Persian language *Jamshid*. According to traditions, king Jamshid son of Vivanghvant was the great hero of the Iranian history, the founder of a great Persian civilization. He was a king of the Peshdiadyan dynasty. In Yasna 9 and 5 (Koema Yashi) it is stated that 'Vivanshas' was the first man who unceremoniously pounded Hasma (Sk. Sasma) in this corporeal world and the boon he received was: to him was born a son nobly who was Yima the shining and of good flock, who was most glorious amongst the living ones, who was like a glowing sun amongst mankind, during whose kingship he made noblemen and cattle (animals) immortal, made waters and trees undrying. He possessed undiminishing (ever fresh) divine glory. During the kingship of famous Yima there was neither extreme cold nor extreme heat, there was no old age, death and envy.

Is Dahaka of the Zenda Aveshta the same as Dasa of the Rig Veda ? If similarity in name can be relied upon as evidence, then obviously it points to their being the names of one and the same person. Dasa in Sanskrit can easily be Daha in Aveshta since *sa* in the former is natural conversion to *ha* in the latter. If this were the only evidence the suggestion that Dasa of the Rig Veda and Dahaka of the Zenda Avesta are the same could have been no better than a conjecture. But there is other and more cogent evidence which leaves no doubt about their identity. In Yasna Ha 9 (which is the same as Horn Yashe) Azhi-Dahaka is spoken of as 'Three-mouthed, three-headed and six-eyed'. What is striking is that this physical description of Dahaka in Avesta is exactly similar to the description of Dasa in Rig Veda (x . 99 . 6) where he is also described as having three heads and six eyes.[1] If the suggestion that the Dasa in the Rig Veda is the same as Dahaka in the Avesta, is accepted, then obviously the Dasas were not native tribes aboriginal to India.

III

Were they savages ? The Dasas and Dasyus were not a primitive people. They were as civilized as the Aryans and in fact more powerful than the Aryans. Such is the testimony of the Rig Veda. It is well epitomized by Mr. Iyengar when he says that :—

> "The Dasyus lived in cities (R.V., i . 53 . 8 ; i . 103 . 3) and under kings the names of many of whom are mentioned. They possessed 'accumulated wealth' (R.V., viii . 40 . 6) in the form of cows, horses and chariots (R.V., ii . 15 . 4) which though kept in 'hundred-gated cities' (R.V., x . 99 . 3), Indra seized and gave away to his worshippers, the Aryas (R.V., i . 176 . 4). The Dasyus were welathy (R.V., i . 33 . 4) and owned property 'in the plains and on the hills' (R.V., x . 69 . 6). They were 'adorned with their array of gold and jewels' (R.V., i . 33 . 8). They owned many castles (R.V., i . 33 . 13 ; viii . 17 . 14). The Dasyu demons and the Arya gods alike lived in gold, silver and iron castles (SS.S., vi . 23 ; A.V., v . 28 . 9 ; R.V., ii . 20 . 8). Indra overthrew for his worshipper, Divodasa, frequently mentioned in the hymns, a 'hundred stone castles' (R.V., iv . 30 . 20) of the Dasyus. Agni, worshipped by the Arya, gleaming in behalf of him, tore and burnt the cities of the fireless Dasyus. (R.V., vii . 5 . 3). Brihaspati broke the stone prisons in which they kept the cattle raided from the Aryas (R.V., iv . 67 . 3). The Dasyus owned chariots and used them in war like the Aryas and had the same weapons as the Aryas (R.V., viii . 24 . 27 ; iii . 30 . 5 ; ii . 15 . 4)."

[1] For the identification of Dasa with Dahaka I am indebted to the Maharashtra Dnyana Kosha, Vol. III, p. 53.

That the Dasas and Dasyus were the same as the Shudras is a pure figment of imagination. It is only a wild guess. It is tolerated because persons who make it are respectable scholars. So far as evidence is concerned, there is no particle of it, which can be cited in support of it. As has been said before, the word Dasa occurs in the Rig Veda 54 times and Dasyu 78 times. The Dasas and the Dasyus are sometimes spoken together. The word Shudra occurs only once and that too in a context in which the Dasas and Dasyus have no place. In the light of these considerations, it is difficult to say how anyone in his senses can say that Shudras are the same as the Dasas and Dasyus. Another fact which is to be noted is that the names Dasas and Dasyus completely disappear from the later Vedic literature. It means they were completely absorbed by the Vedic Aryans. But it is quite different with the Shudras. The early Vedic literature is very silent about them. But the later Vedic literature is full of them. This shows that the Shudras were different from the Dasas and Dasyus.

IV

Were the Shudras non-Aryans ? Mr. Kane says :[1]

> " A clear line of demarcation was kept between the Arya and the Shudra in the times of the Brahmana works and even in the Dharmasutras. The Tandya Brahmana speaks of a mock fight : ' the Shudra and Arya fight on a hide; out of the two they so arrange that the Arya colour becomes the victor.' The Ap. Dh. S. (I, i . 3 . 40-41) says that a *brahmachari* if he cannot himself eat all the food he has brought by begging, may keep it near an Arya (for his use) or he may give it to a Shudra who is a Dasa (of his teacher).' Similarly, Gautama x . 69 used the word ' anarya ' for Shudra."

---

[1] Kane's Dharma Shastra, II (I), p. 35.

On the question of the line of demarcation between the Shudras and Aryans, the matter needs to be carefully examined.

The strength of the argument that the Shudras were non-Aryans is to be found in the following statements :

> *A.V.*, iv . 20.4.—" The thousand-eyed god shall put this plant into my right hand ; with that do I see everyone, the Shudra as well as the Arya."
>
> *Kathaka Samhita*, xxxiv . 5.—" The Shudra and the Arya quarrel about the skin. The gods and the demons quarrelled about the sun ; the gods won it (the sun). (By this act of quarrelling with Shudras) the Arya makes the Arya Varna win, makes himself successful. The Arya shall be inside the altar, the Shudra outside the altar. The skin shall be white, circular—the form of the sun."
>
> *Vajasaneyi Samhita*, xxiii . 30-31.—" When a deer eats the barley in the field, the (owner of the field) is not pleased with the nourished animal ; when a Shudra woman has an Arya as a lover, (the husband) does not long for (the consequent) prosperity ;
>
> When a deer eats barley, the (owner of the field) does not approve of the nourished animal. When a Shudra is the lover of an Arya woman, the (husband) does not consent to the prosperity."

These stanzas, which speak of the Shudra and the Arya as separate and opposed form the foundation of the theory that the Shudras are non-Aryans. To say the least, such a conclusion would be a very hasty one. Two considerations must be borne in mind before any conclusion is drawn from the aforementioned statements. In the first place, it must be borne in mind that according to what has been said before and according to the evidence of the Rig Veda, there are two categories of Aryans, the Vedic and the non-Vedic. Given this fact, it would be quite easy for an Arya of one class to speak of an Arya of another class, as though the two were separate and opposed. Interpreted in this way, the above statements, in which Shudras are set against the Aryans, do not mean that they were not Aryas. They were Aryas of a different sect or class.

That this is possible can be seen from the following statements in the sacred literature of the Hindus :

(1) *A.V.*, xix.32.8.—" Make me, Oh, Darbha (grass), dear to the Brahmin, and the Rajanya (i.e., Kshatriya), to the Shudra and to the Arya and to him whom we love and to everyone who is able to see."

(2) *A.V.*, xix.62.1.—" Make me beloved among the gods, make me beloved among the princes ; make me dear to everyone who sees, to the Shudra and to the Arya."

(3) *Vajasaneyi Samhita*, xviii.48.—" (Oh, Agni), give to us lustre among Brahmins, give us lustre among kings ; lustre among Vaishyas and among Shudras ; give to me lustre added to lustre."

(4) *Vajasaneyi Samhita*, xx.17.—" Whatever sin we have committed in the village, in the forest, in the assembly, with our senses, against the Shudra or against the Arya, whatever sin one of us (two, the sacrificer and his wife) has committed in the matter of his duty (towards the other),—of that sin, you are the destroyer."

(5) *Vajasaneyi Samhita*, xviii.48.—" As I speak these auspicious words to the people, to the Brahmin and the Rajanya, to the Shudra and to the Arya and to my own enemy, may I be dear to the gods and to the giver of *dakshinas* here in this world. May this desire of mine be granted. May that (enemy of mine) be subjected to me."

What do these statements show ? The first one makes a distinction between the Brahmins and the Aryas. Can it be said that the Brahmins were non-Aryans ? The other statements pray for the love and goodwill of the Shudras. If the Shudra was a primitive aboriginal non-Aryan, is such a prayer conceivable ? The statements on which reliance is placed do not prove that the Shudras were non-Aryans.

That the Dharma Sutras call the Shudra Anarya and the statements in the Vajasaneyi Samhita pouring scorn on the Shudra woman, do not mean anything. There are two arguments against accepting the testimony of the

Dharma Sutra. In the first place, as will be shown later, the Dharma Sutras and other treatises are books written by the enemies of the Shudra. As such, they have no evidentiary value. It is also doubtful whether such anti-Shudra statements are mere imprecations or statements of facts as they existed. They seem to contradict facts reported in other works.

The Dharma Sutras say that a Shudra is not entitled to the Upanayana ceremony and the wearing of the sacred thread. But in Samskara Ganapati there is an express provision declaring the Shudra to be eligible for Upanayana.[1]

The Dharma Sutras say that a Shudra has no right to study the Vedas. But the Chhandogya Upanishad (iv : 1—2) relates the story of one Janasruti to whom Veda Vidya was taught by the preceptor Raikva. This Janasruti was a Shudra. What is more is that Kavasha Ailusha,[2] was a Shudra. He was a Rishi and the author of several hymns of the Tenth Book of the Rig Veda.

The Dharma Sutras say that a Shudra has no right to perform Vedic ceremonies and sacrifices. But Jaimini, the author of the Purva Mimamsa[3] mentions an ancient teacher by name Badari—whose work is lost—as an exponent of the contrary view that even *Shudras* could perform Vedic sacrifices. The Bharadvaja Srauta Sutra (v.28) admits that there exists another school of thought which holds that a Shudra can consecrate the three sacred fires necessary for the performance of a Vedic sacrifice. Similarly, the commentator of the Katyayana Srauta Sutra (1 . 4 . 16) admits that there are certain Vedic texts which lead to the inference that the Shudra was eligible to perform Vedic rites.

The Dharma Sutras say that a Shudra is not entitled to the sacred drink of Soma. But in the story of the

[1] Referred to by Max Muller in Ancient Sanskrit Literature (1860), p. 207.

[2] Max Muller—Ancient Sanskrit Literature (1860), p. 58.

[3] Adhyaya 6, Pada 1, Sutra 27.

Ashvins, there is definite evidence that the Shudra had a right to the divine drink of Soma. The Ashvins, as the story goes, once happened to behold Sukanya when she had just bathed and when her person was bare. She was a young girl married to a Rishi by name Chyavana who at the time of marriage was so old as to be dying almost any day. The Ashvins were captivated by the beauty of Sukanya and said " Accept one of us for your husband. It behoveth thee not to spend thy youth fruitlessly." She refused, saying " I am devoted to my husband." They again spoke to her and this time proposed a bargain : " We two are the celestial physicians of note. We will make thy husband young and graceful. Do thou then select one of us as thy husband." She went to her husband and communicated to him the terms of the bargain. Chyavana said to Sukanya " Do thou so" ; and the bargain was carried out and Chyavana was made a young man by the Ashvins. Subsequently, a question arose whether the Ashvins were entitled to Soma, which was the drink of the Gods. Indra objected saying that the Ashvins were Shudras and therefore not entitled to Soma. Chyavana, who had received perpetual youth from the Ashvins, set aside the contention and compelled Indra to give them Soma.[1]

There is another reason why the evidence of the Dharma Sutras that the Shudras are non-Aryans should not be accepted. In the first place, it is contrary to the view taken by Manu. In the decision of the issue whether the Shudra was an Aryan or a non-Aryan, the following verses from Manu require to be carefully considered :—

> " If a female of the caste sprung from a Brahmana and a Shudra female, bear (children) to one of the highest castes, the inferior (tribe) attains the highest caste within the seventh generation."
>
> " (Thus) a Shudra attains the rank of a Brahmana and (in a similar manner) a Brahmana sinks to the level of a

[1] V. Fausboll—Indian Mythology, pp. 128-134.

Shudra ; but know that it is the same with the offspring of a Kshatriya or of a Vaishya."

"If (a doubt) should arise, with whom the pre-eminence (is, whether) with him whom an Aryan by chance begot on a non-Aryan female, or (with the son) of a Brahmana woman by a non-Aryan ; "

"The decision is as follows : 'He who was begotten by an Aryan on a non-Aryan female, may become (like to) an Aryan by his virtues ; he whom an Aryan (mother) bore to a non-Aryan father (is and remains) unlike to an Aryan." [1]

Verse 64 from Manu is also to be found in Gautama Dharma Sutra (uv.22). There seems to be some controversy as to the correct interpretation of this verse. In summing up the different interpretations, Buhler says :

"According to Medh., Gov., Kull., and Ragh., the meaning is that, if the daughter of a Brahmana and of a Shudra female and her descendants all marry Brahmanas, the offspring of the sixth female descendant of the original couple will be a Brahmana. While this explanation agrees with Haradatta's comment on the parallel passage of Gautama, Nar. and Nan. take the verse very differently. They say that if a Parasava, the son of a Brahmana and of a Shudra female, marries a most excellent Parasava female, who possesses a good moral character and other virtues, and if his descendants do the same, the child born in the sixth generation will be a Brahmana. Nandana quotes in support of his view, Baudhayana i.16.13-14 (left out in my translation of the Sacred Books of the East, ii, p. 197) . . . '(offspring) begotten by a Nishada on a Nishadi, removes within five generations the Shudrahood ; one may initiate him (the fifth descendant) ; one may sacrifice for the sixth.' This passage of Baudhayana the reading of which is supported by a new MS from Madras clearly shows that Baudhayana allowed the male offspring of Brahmanas and Shudra females to be raised to the level of Aryans. It is also not impossible that the meaning of Manu's verse may be the same, and that the translation should be, 'if the offspring of a Brahmana and of a Shudra female begets children with a most excellent (male of the Brahmana caste or female of the Parasava tribe), the inferior (tribe) attains the highest caste in the seventh generation."

[1] Chapter X, verses 64-67.

Whatever be the interpretation, the fact remains that in the seventh generation[1] a Shudra under certain circumstances could become a Brahmin. Such a conception would have been impossible if the Shudra was not an Aryan.

That the Shudra is a non-Aryan is contrary to the view taken by the school of Arthashtra. As a representative of that school, the opinion of Kautilya on that question is of great value. In laying down the law of slavery, Kautilya says[2] :

> " The selling or mortgaging by kinsmen of the life of a Shudra who is not a born slave, and has not attained majority, but is Arya in birth shall be punished with a fine of 12 panas.
>
> Deceiving a slave of his money or depriving him of the privileges he can exercise as an Arya (*Aryabhava*) shall be punished with half the fine (levied for enslaving the life of an Arya).
>
> Failure to set a slave at liberty on the receipt of a required amount of ransom shall be punished with a fine of 12 panas ; putting a slave under confinement for no reason (*samrodhaschakaranat*) shall likewise be punished.
>
> The offspring of a man who has sold himself off as a slave shall be an Arya. A slave shall be entitled not only to what he has earned himself without prejudice to his master's work but also to the inheritance he has received from his father."

Here is Kautilya, who calls the Shudra an Aryan in the most emphatic and express terms possible.

V

Coming to the question of Shudras having been made slaves, it is nonsense, if not mendacious. It is founded on two assumptions. First is that the Dasas are described

[1] The rule which requires that for establishing his nobility a man must be able to trace his six uninterrupted degrees of unsullied lineage of not merely free-born, but full-born, appears to be universal rule in ancient times—See W. E. Hearn, The Aryan Household, Chapter VIII.

[2] Book III, Chapter 13.

as slaves in the Rig Veda. The second is that the Dasas are the same as Shudras.

It is true that the word Dasa is used in the Rig Veda in the sense of slave or servant. But the word in this sense occurs in only 5 places and no more. But even if it did occur more than five times, would it prove that the Shudras were made slaves ? Unless and until it is proved that the two were the same people, the suggestion is absurd. It is contrary to known facts.

Shudras participated in the coronotion of kings. In the post-vedic or the period of the Brahmanas, the coronotion of a king was in reality an offer of sovereignty by the people to the king. This was done by the representatives of the people called Ratnis who played a very important part in the investiture of the king. The Ratnis were so-called because they held the Ratna (jewel), which was a symbol of sovereignty. The king received his sovereignty only when the Ratnis handed over to him the jewel of sovereignty, and on receiving his sovereignty the king went to the house of each of the Ratnis and made an offering to him. It is a significant fact that one of the Ratnis was always a Shudra.[1]

Nilakantha, the author of *Nitimayukha*, describes the coronation ceremony of a later time. According to him, the four chief ministers, Brahmin, Kshatriya, Vaishya and Shudra, consecrated the new king. Then the leaders of each Varna and of the castes lower still, consecrated him with holy water. Then followed acclamation by the twice-born.[2]

That the Shudras were invited to be present at the coronation of the king along with Brahmins is evidenced by the description of the coronation of Yudhishthira, the eldest brother of the Pandavas, which is given in the Mahabharata.[3]

[1] On this point see Jayaswal—Hindu Polity (1943), pp. 200-201.

[2] See Jayaswal—Hindu Polity (1943), p. 223.

[3] Mahabharata Sabha Parvan, Chapter XXXIII, Verses 41-42.

Shudras were members of the two political assemblies of ancient times, namely, the Janapada and Paura and as a member of these the Shudra was entitled to special respect even from a Brahmin.[1]

This was so even according to the Manusmriti (iv.61) as well as to the Vishnu Smriti (xxi.64). Otherwise there is no meaning in Manu saying that a Brahmin should not live in a country where the king is a Shudra. That means Shudras were kings.

In the Shanti Parvan of the Mahabharata,[2] Bhishma in his lessons on Politics to Yudhishthira says :

> "I shall, however, tell thee what kinds of ministers should be appointed by thee. Four Brahmins learned in the Vedas, possessed of a sense of dignity, belonging to the *Snataka* order, and of pure behaviour, and eight Kshatriyas, all of whom should be possessed of physical strength and capable of wielding weapons, and one and twenty Vaishyas, all of whom should be possessed of wealth, and three Shudras, everyone of whom should be humble and of pure conduct and devoted to his daily duties, and one man of the Suta caste, possessed of a knowledge of the Puraṇas and the eight cardinal virtues should be thy ministers."

This proves that the Shudras were ministers and that they were almost equal to the Brahmins in number.[3]

The Shudras were not poor and lowly. They were rich. This fact is testified by the Maitrayani Samhita (iv.2.7.10) and the Panchavimsa Brahmana (vi.1.11).[4]

There are two other aspects to this question. What significance can there be to the enslavement of the Shudras, assuming it was a fact ? There would be some significance if the Aryans did not know slavery or were not prepared to turn the Aryans into slaves. But the fact is that the Aryans knew slavery and permitted the Aryans to be made slaves. This is clear from Rig Veda,

[1] See Jayaswal—Hindu Polity, p. 248.
[2] Roy's Translation, Vol. II, p. 197.
[3] Bhishma believed in communal representation.
[4] Referred to in the Vedic Index, Vol. II, p. 390.

(vii.86.7; viii.19.36 and viii.56.3). That being so, why should they particularly want to make slaves of the Shudras ? What is more important is, why should they make different laws for the Shudra slaves ?

In short, the Western theory does not help us to answer our questions, who were the Shudras and how did they become the fourth Varna ?

Chapter VII

THE SHUDRAS WERE KSHATRIYAS

Who were the Shudras if they were not a non-Aryan aboriginal race ? This question must now be faced. The theory I venture to advance may be stated in the following three propositions :—

(1) The Shudras were Aryans.
(2) The Shudras belonged to the Kshatriya class.
(3) The Shudras were so important a class of Kshatriyas that some of the most eminent and powerful kings of the ancient Aryan communities were Shudras.

This thesis regarding the origin of the Shudras is a startling if not a revolutionary thesis. So startling it is that not many people will be ready to accept it, even though there may be enough evidence to support it. My obligation is to produce the evidence, leaving the people to judge its worth.

The primary piece of evidence on which this thesis rests is a passage which occurs in Verses 38-40 of Chapter 60 of the Shanti Parvan of the Mahabharata. It reads as follows :

> *"It has been heard by us that in the days of old a Shudra of the name of Paijavana gave a Dakshina (in his own sacrifice) consisting of a hundred thousand Purnapatras according to the ordinance called Aindragni."*

The important statements contained in this passage are three : (1) that Paijavana was a Shudra, (2) that this Shudra Paijavana performed sacrifices, and (3) the Brahmins performed sacrifices for him and accepted Dakshina from him.

The passage quoted above is taken from Mr. Roy's edition of the Mahabharata. The first thing is to ascertain whether the text is accurate or whether there are any variant readings. As regards the authenticity of his text, this is what Mr. Roy[1] says :

> "As far as my edition is concerned it is substantially based on that of Royal Asiatic Society of Bengal published about forty-five years ago under the superintendence of a few learned Pandits of Bengal aided, as I believe, by an English Orientalist of repute. Manuscripts had been procured from all parts of India (the South unexcepted) and these were carefully collated. Although edited with such care, I have not, however, slavishly followed the Society's edition. I have compared it carefully with the Maharajah of Burdwan's text in the Bengalee character which was edited with still greater care. About 18 manuscripts procured from different parts of India (the South not excepted) were carefully collated by the Burdwan Pandits before they admitted a single *sloka* as genuine."

Prof. Sukthankar, the erudite editor of the critical edition of the Mahabharata, after examining many editions of the Mahabharata, concluded by saying that[2] :

> "The *editio princeps* (Calcutta 1856) remains the best edition of the Vulgate, after the lapse of nearly a century."

Although the authenticity of Mr. Roy's edition of the Mahabharata cannot be doubted, it would not be unreasonable if critics were to say that they would like to know what other manuscript support there is behind this text, which is made the basis of this new theory of the origin of the Shudras. In undertaking such an inquiry it is necessary to point to two considerations. One[3] is that there is no such thing as a Mahabharata manuscript in the sense of complete sets of manuscripts covering all the eighteen Parvans. Each Parvan is treated as a separate unit with the result that the number of copies of the different Parvans to be found differ by a vast margin. Consequently, the number of manuscripts

[1] Quoted in Sukthankar Memorial Edition, Vol. I, pp. 43-44.
[2] Quoted in Sukthankar Memorial Edition, Vol. I, p. 131.
[3] Sukthankar, op. cit., p. 14.

to be taken as a basis for deciding which is the correct text must vary with each Parvan.

The second[1] consideration to which attention must be drawn is the fact that the text of the Mahabharata has been handed down in two divergent forms; a Northern and a Southern recension, texts, typical of the Aryavrata and the Dakshinapatha.

It is obvious that an examination of manuscript support must be based upon collation from a fair number of manuscripts and a fair distribution of the manuscripts between the Northern and the Southern recensions. Bearing these considerations in mind, the results of the collation[2] of the text of Shloka 38 of the 60th chapter of the Shanti Parvan of the Mahabharata with which we are primarily concerned from different manuscripts is presented below:—

1.	शूद्र: पैजवनो नाम Shudrah Paijavano nama	(K) S
2.	शूद्र: पैलवनो नाम Shudrah Pailavano nama	(M/1; M/2) S
3.	शूद्र: यैलननो नाम Shudrah Yailanano nama	(M/3; M/4) S
4.	शूद्र: यैजननो नाम Shudrah Yaijanano nama	(F)
5.	शूद्रोपि यजने नाम Shudropi Yajane nama	(L).
6.	शूद्र: पौंजल्क नाम Shudrah Paunjalka nama	(TC) S
7.	शुद्धो वैभवनो नाम Shuddho Vaibhavano nama	(G) N

[1] Sukthankar, op. cit., pp. 9-42.

[2] I am grateful to the Bhandarkar Oriental Research Institute for allowing me to use their collation sheet. Letters in brackets indicate the index number given by the Institute to the manuscript. N or S indicate whether the manuscript comes from the North or South. K is Kumbhakonam.

8. पुरा वैजवनो नाम (A, D/2)
Pura Vaijavano nama

9. पुरा वैजननो नाम (M) N
Pura Vaijanano nama

Here is the result of the collation of nine manuscripts. Are nine manuscripts enough for constituting a text which has a number of variant readings ? It is true that the number of manuscripts taken for the critical edition of the different Parvans of the Mahabharata exceeds nine. For the entire Mahabharata the minimum number of manuscripts taken for constituting the text is only ten.[1] It cannot therefore be contended that nine is an insufficient number. The nine manuscripts fall into two geographical divisions, Northern and Southern. M1, M2, M3, M4 and TC belong to the Southern recension. A, M, G, D2 belong to the Northern recension. The selections of the manuscripts therefore satisfy the two tests which experts have laid down.

A scrutiny of the readings shows that :

(1) there is a variation in the description of Paijavana ;
(2) there is a variation in the name of Paijavana ;
(3) of the nine texts, six agree in describing him as a Shudra. One describes him as Shuddha and two instead of speaking of the class to which he belonged refer to the time when he lived and use the word 'Pura' ;
(4) with regard to the name, there is no agreement between any two of the nine manuscripts. Each gives a different reading.

Given this result, the question is what is the real text ? Taking first the texts relating to the name, it is obvious that this is not a matter in which the question of meaning is involved. It does not raise any questions such as

[1] Sukthankar, Vol. I, p. 14.

interpretation *versus* emendation, or of giving preference to a reading which suggests how other readings might have arisen. The question is which is the correct name and which readings are scriptoral blunders committed by the scribes. There seems to be no doubt that the correct text is Paijavana. It is supported by both the recensions, Southern as well as Northern. For Vaijavano in No. 8 is the same as Paijavano. All the rest are variations which are due to the ignorance of the scribes in not being able to read the original copy correctly and then trying to constitute the text in their own way.

Turning to the description of Paijavana, the change from *Shudrah* to *Pura*, it must be granted, is not accidental. It appears to be deliberate. Why this change has occurred it is difficult to say categorically. Two things appear to be quite clear. In the first place, the change appears to be quite natural. In the second place, the change does not militate against the conclusion that Paijavana was a Shudra. The above conclusion will be obvious if the context, in which verses 38-40 occur, is borne in mind. The context will be clear from the following verses which precede them :

> "The Shudra should never abandon his master whatever the nature or degree of the distress into which the latter may fall. If the master loses his wealth, he should with excessive zeal be supported by the Shudra servant. A Shudra cannot have any wealth that is his own. Whatever he possesses belongs to his master. Sacrifice has been laid down as a duty of the three other orders. It has been ordained for the Shudra also, O! Bharata. A Shudra however is not competent to utter *swaha* and *svadha* or any other *mantra*. For this reason, the Shudra, without observing the vows laid down in the Vedas, should worship the gods in minor sacrifices called *Pakayajnas*. The gift called Purnapatra is declared to be the *Dakshina* of such sacrifices."

Taking the verses 38 to 40 in the context of these verses preceding them, it becomes clear that the whole passage deals with the Shudra. The story of Paijavana is a mere illustration. Against this background, it is unnecessary to repeat the word 'Shudra' before Paijavana. This explains why the word Shudra does not occur before Paijavana in the two manuscripts. As to the reason for the use of the word *Pura* in place of Shudra it must be remembered that the case of Paijavana had occurred in very ancient times. It was therefore quite natural for the scribe to feel that it was desirable to put this fact in express terms. The writer being aware that there was no necessity for describing Paijavana as Shudra since that was made clear from the context, it was not necessary to emphasize it. On the other hand, knowing that Paijavana had lived in very ancient times and that that fact was not made very clear from the context, the writer thought it more appropriate to add the word *Pura* which was necessary and omit the word *Shudrah* which having regard to the context was unnecessary.

If this explanation is well-founded, we may take it as well-established that the person referred to in the passage in the Shanti Parvan of the Mahabharata is Paijavana and that this Paijavana was a Shudra.

II

The next question that falls due for consideration is the identification of Paijavana. Who is this Paijavana ?

Yaska's Nirukta seems to give us a clue. In Nirukta ii.24[1] Yaska says :—

> "The seer Vishvamitra was the purohita of Sudas, the son of Pijavana. Vishvamitra, friend of all. All, moving together. Sudas a bountiful giver. *Paijavana*, son of Pijavana. Again *Pi-javana* one whose speed is enviable or whose gait is inimitable."

From Yaska's Nirukta we get two very important facts : (1) Paijavana means son of Pijavana, and (2) the person

[1] Lakshman Sarup—The Nighantu and Nirukta, pp. 35-36,

who is the son of Pijavana is Sudas. With the help of Yaska, we are able to answer the question: who is Paijavana referred to in the passage in the Shanti Parvan of the Mahabharata? The answer is that Paijavana is simply another name for Sudas.

The next question is who is this Sudas and what do we know about him? A search in the Brahmanic literature discloses three persons with the name Sudas. One Sudas is mentioned in the Rig Veda. His family particulars are given in the following stanzas of the Rig Veda:[1]

1. *Rig Veda*, vii.18.21.—"Parashara, the destroyer of hundreds (of Rakshasas), and Vasishtha, they who, devoted to thee, have glorified thee in every dwelling, neglect not the friendship of thee (their) benefactor; therefore prosperous days dawn upon the pious."

2. *Rig Veda*, vii.18.22.—"Praising the liberality of Sudas, the grandson of Devavata, the son of Pijavana, the donor of two hundred cows, and of two chariots with two wives, I, worthy (of the gift), circumambulate thee, Agni, like the ministrant priest in the chamber (of sacrifice).

3. *Rig Veda*, vii.18.23.—"Four (horses), having golden trappings, going steadily on a difficult road, celebrated on the earth, the excellent and acceptable gifts (made) to me by Sudas, the son of Pijavana; bear me as a son (to obtain) food and progeny."

4. *Rig Veda*, vii.18.24.—"The seven worlds praise (Sudas) as if he were Indra; him whose fame (spreads) through the spacious heaven and earth; who, munificent, has distributed (wealth) on every eminent person, and (for whom) the flowing (rivers) have destroyed Yudhyamadhi in war."

5. *Rig Veda*, vii.18.25.—"*Maruts*, leaders (of rites), attend upon this (prince) as you did upon Divodasa, the father of Sudas; favour the prayers of the devout son of Pijavana, and may his strength be unimpaired, undecaying."

[1] Wilson's Rig Veda, Vol. IV (Poona Reprint), p. 146.

The two others are mentioned by the Vishnu Purana. One Sudas is mentioned in Chapter IV as the descendant of Sagara. The genealogical tree connecting this Sudas with Sagara is as follows[1] :—

"Sumati the daughter of Kasyapa and Kesini the daughter of Raja Vidarbha, were the two wives of Sagara. Being without progeny, the king solicited the aid of the sage Aurva with great earnestness, and the Muni pronounced this boon, that one wife should bear one son, the upholder of his race, and the other should give birth to sixty thousand sons; and he left it to them to make their election. Kesini chose to have the single son; Sumati the multitude; and it came to pass in a short time that the former bore Asamanjas, a prince through whom the dynasty continued; and the daughter of Vinata (Sumati) had sixty thousand sons. The son of Asamanjas was Ansumat.

* * *

The son of Ansumat was Dilipa; his son was Bhagiratha, who brought Ganga down to earth, whence she is called Bhagirathi. The son of Bhagiratha was Sruta; his son was Nabhaga; his son was Ambarisha; his son was Sindhudvipa; his son was Ayutashva; his son was Rituparna, the friend of Nala, skilled profoundly in dice. The son of Rituparna was Sarvakama; his son was Sudasa; his son was Saudasa, named also Mitrasaha."

Another Sudas is mentioned in Chapter XIX as a descendant of Puru. The genealogical tree connecting this Sudas with Puru is as follows[2] :—

"The son of Puru was Janamejaya; his son was Prachinvat; his son was Pravira; his son was Manasyu; his son was Bhayada; his son was Sudyumna; his son was Bahugava; his son was Samyati; his son was Ahamyati; his son was Raudrashva, who had ten sons, Riteyu, Kaksheyu, Sthandileyu, Ghriteyu, Jaleyu, Sthaleyu, Santateyu, Dhaneyu, Vaneyu, and Vrateyu. The son of Riteyu was Rantinara whose sons were Tansu, Apratiratha, and Dhruva. The son of the

[1] Wilson's Vishnu Purana, pp. 377-380.

[2] Wilson's Vishnu Purana, pp. 447-456.

second of these was Kanva, and his son was Medhatithi, from whom the Kanvayana Brahmanas are descended. Anila was the son of Tansu, and he had four sons, of whom Dushyanta was the elder. The son of Dushyanta was the emperor Bharata; . . .

Bharata had by different wives nine sons, but they were put to death by their own mothers, because Bharata remarked that they bore no resemblance to him, and the women were afraid that he would therefore desert them. The birth of his sons being thus unavailing, Bharata sacrificed to the Maruts, and they gave him Bharadvaja, the son of Brihaspati by Mamata the wife of Utathya, . . .

* * *

He was also termed Vitatha, in allusion to the unprofitable (*vitatha*) birth of the sons of Bharata. The son of Vitatha was Bhavanmanyu; his sons were many, and amongst them the chief were Brihatkshatra, Mahavirya, Nara and Garga. The son of Nara was Sankriti; his sons were Ruchiradhi and Rantideva. The son of Garga was Sini; and their descendants called Gargyas and Sainyas, although Kshatriyas by birth, became Brahmins. The son of Mahavirya was Urukshaya, who had three sons, Trayyaruna, Pushkarin and Kapi, the last of whom became a Brahmin. The son of Brihatkshatra was Suhotra, whose son was Hastin, who founded the city of Hastinapur. The sons of Hastin were Ajamidha, Dvimidha and Purumidha. One son of Ajamidha was Kanva, whose son was Medhatithi, his other son was Brihadishu, whose son was Brihadvasu; his son was Brihatkarman; his son was Jayadratha, his son was Vishvajit, his son was Senajit, whose sons were Ruchirashva, Kasya, Dridhadhanush, and Vasahanu. The son of Ruchiraswa was Prithusena; his son was Para; his son was Nipa; he had a hundred sons, of whom Samara, the principal, was the ruler of Kampilya. Samara had three sons, Para, Sampara, Sadashva. The son of Para was Prithu; his son was Sukriti; his son was Vibhratra; his son was Anuha, who married Kritvi, the daughter of Shuka (the son of Vyasa), and had by her Brahmadatta; his son was Vishvaksena; his son was Udaksena; and his son was Bhallata.

The son of Dvimidha was Yavinara; his son was Dhritimat; his son was Satyadhriti; his son was Dridhanemi; his son was Suparshva; his son was Sumati; his son was Sannatimat;

his son was Krita, to whom Hiranyanabha taught the philosophy of the Yoga, and he compiled twenty-four Sanhitas (or compendia) for the use of the eastern Brahmins, who study the Sama-Veda. The son of Krita was Ugrayudha, by whose prowess the Nipa race of Kshatriyas was destroyed; his son was Kshemya; his son was Suvira; his son was Nripanjaya; his son was Bahuratha. These were all called Pauravas.

Ajamidha had a wife called Nilini, and by her he had a son named Nila; his son was Santi; his son was Susanti; his son was Purujanu; his son was Chakshu; his son was Haryashva, who had five sons Mudgala, Srinjaya, Brihadishu, Pravira, and Kampilya. Their father said, 'These my five (pancha) sons are able (alam) to protect the countries'; and hence they were termed the Panchalas. From Mudgala descended the Maudgalya Brahmins; he had also a son named Bahvashva, who had two children, twins, a son and daughter, Divodasa and Ahalya.

* * *

The son of Divodasa was Mitrayu; his son was Chyavana; his son was Sudasa; his son was Saudasa, also called Sahadeva; his son was Somaka; he had a hundred sons, of whom Jantu was the eldest, and Prishata the youngest. The son of Prishata was Drupada; his son was Dhrishtadyumna; his son was Drishtaketu.

Another son of Ajamidha was named Riksha; his son Samvarana; his son was Kuru, who gave his name to the holy district Kurukshetra; his sons were Sudhanush, Parikshit, and many others. The son of Sudhanush was Suhotra; his son was Chyavana; his son was Kritaka; his son was Uparichara the Vasu, who had seven children Brihadratha, Pratyagra, Kushamba, Mavella, Matsya, and others. The son of Brihadratha was Kusagra; his son was Rishabha; his son was Pushpavat; his son was Satyadhrita; his son was Sudhanvan; and his son was Jantu. Brihadratha had another son, who being born in two parts, which were put together (*sandhita*) by a female fiend named Jara, he was denominated Jarasandha; his son was Sahadeva; his son was Somapi; his son was Srutasravas. These were kings of Magadha."

The immediate ancestry of the three Sudasas is put below in parallel columns to facilitate the settlement of the question whether they are one or three different persons :

Sudas in Rig Veda			Sudas in Vishnu Purana	
VII, 18 : 22	VII, 18 : 23	VII, 18 : 25	In the Sagar Family	In the Puru Family
Devavata Pijavana Sudas	Pijavana Sudas	Divodasa= Pijavana Sudas	Rituparna Sarvakama Sudas Saudasa= Mitrasaha	Bahvashva Divodasa Mitrayu Chyavana Sudas Saudasa Somaka

From the table two things are as clear as day-light. First is that neither Sudas mentioned in the Vishnu Purana has anything to do with the Sudas mentioned in the Rig Veda. The second point which is clear is that if the Paijavana mentioned in the Mahabharata can be identified with anybody who lived in ancient times it can only be with Sudas mentioned in Rig Veda who was called Paijavana because he was the son of Pijavana which was another name of Divodasa[1].

[1] Some difficulty is felt about the genealogy of this Sudas in the Rig Veda, which is sought to be got over by identifying Devavata with Divodasa. This difficulty has mainly arisen because of the different texts of Stanzas 22, 23 and 25 which nobody seems to have cared to collect properly. Chitrava Shastri's edition of Rig Veda has Pijavana throughout. Satavalekar's edition has Paijavana throughout. Wilson has Paijavana in 22 and 23 and Pijavana in 25. Wilson's text seems to be accurate. For even Yaska has noticed the existence of the name Paijavana in his Nirukta which he endeavours to explain. If Wilson's text in 25 is taken as correct no difficulty can arise. Pijavana would then appear to be another name of Divodasa and Paijavana would be another name of Sudas.

Fortunately for me my conclusion is the same as that of Prof. Weber. In commenting upon the passage in the Shanti Parvan of the Mahabharata on which my thesis is based Prof. Weber[1] says :

> " Here the remarkable tradition is recorded that Paijavana, i.e., Sudas who was so famous for his sacrifices and who is celebrated in the Rig Veda as the patron of Vishvamitra and enemy of Vasishtha, was a Shudra."

Prof. Weber unfortunately did not realize the full significance of this passage. This is another matter. It is enough for my purpose to find that he too thinks that the Paijavana of the Mahabharata is no other than Sudas of the Rig Veda.

III

What do we know about Sudas, the Paijavana ?

The following particulars are available about him.

I. Sudas was neither Dasa nor Arya. Both the Dasas as well as the Aryas were his enemies[2]. This means that he was a Vedic Aryan.

II. The father of Sudas was Divodasa. He seems to be the adopted son of Vadhryashva[3]. Divodasa was a king. He fought many battles against Turvasas and Yadus[4], Shambara[5], Parava, and Karanja[6] and Gungu.[7] There was a war between Turyavana and Divodasa and his allies Ayu and Kutsa. The victory went to Turyavana[8].

---

1 Muir, Vol. I, p. 366.
2 Rig Veda, VII. 83 . 1.
3 Rig Veda, IX. 61 . 2.
4 Rig Veda, VI. 61 . 1 ; VII. 19 . 8.
5 Rig Veda, I. 130 . 7.
6 Rig Veda, I. 53 . 10.
7 Rig Veda, X. 48.
8 Rig Veda, I. 53 . 8 ; VI. 18 . 13.

It seems that at one time Indra was against him, particularly in the battle of Turyavana. His purohita was Bharadvaja[1], to whom Divodasa gave many gifts[2]. Bharadvaja seems to have played the part of a traitor by joining Turyavana against Divodasa[3].

There is no reference to the mother of Sudas. But there is a reference to the wife of Sudas. His wife's name is given as Sudevi[4]. It is said that the Ashvins procured her for Sudas.

III. Sudas was a king and his coronation ceremony was performed by the Brahma-rishi, Vasishtha.

The Aitareya Brahmana gives the following list of the kings who had the Mahabhisheka ceremony performed and the name of the Purohita who officiated at it.[5]

> "With this ceremony Sharyata, the son of Manu, was inaugurated by Chyavana, the son of Bhrigu. Thence Sharyata went conquering all over the earth, and sacrificed the sacrificial horse, and was even at the sacrificial session held by the gods, the house-father."
>
> "With this ceremony Samasushama, the son of Vajaratna, inaugurated Shatanika, the son of Satrajit. Thence Shatanika went conquering everywhere over the whole of earth up to its ends, and sacrificed the sacrificial horse."
>
> "With this ceremony Parvata and Narada inaugurated Ambashthya. Thence Ambashthya went conquering everywhere over the whole earth up to its ends, and sacrificed the sacrificial horse.
>
> "With this ceremony Parvata and Narada inaugurated Yudhamasraushti, the son of Ugrasena. Thence Yudhamasraushti went conquering everywhere over the whole earth up to its ends, and sacrificed the sacrificial horse."
>
> "With this inauguration ceremony Kashyapa inaugurated Vishvakarma, the son of Bhuvana. Thence Vishvakarma went conquering everywhere over the whole earth up to its ends, and sacrificed the sacrificial horse.

---

1 Rig Veda, I. 116. 18.
2 Rig Veda, VI. 16. 5.
3 Rig Veda, VI. 18. 13.
4 Rig Veda, I. 112. 19.
5 Martin Haug, Vol. II, pp. 523-524.

"They say that the earth sang to Vishvakarma the following stanza :

'No mortal is allowed to give me away (as donation [1]),
O, Vishvakarma, thou hast given me, (therefore) I shall plunge into the midst of the sea. In vain was thy promise made to Kashyapa.'"

"With this ceremony Vasishtha inaugurated Sudas, the son of Pijavana. Thence Sudas went conquering everywhere over the whole earth up to its ends, and sacrificed the sacrificial horse.

"With this inauguration ceremony Samvarta, the son of Angiras, inaugurated Marutta, the son of Avikshit. Thence Marutta went conquering everywhere over the whole earth up to its ends, and sacrificed the sacrificial horse."

In this list there is a specific mention of Sudas and of his coronation having been performed by Vasishtha.

Sudas was the hero in the famous Dasharajna Yuddha or the battle of the ten kings described in the Rig Veda. References to this famous battle occur in the various Suktas of the Seventh Mandala of the Rig Veda.

Sukta 88 says :

4. "Indra and Varuna, you protected Sudas, overwhelming the yet unassailed Bheda with your fatal weapons ; hear the prayers of these Tritsus in time of battle, so that my ministration may have borne them fruit."

6. "Both (Sudas and the Tritsus) call upon you two, (Indra and Varuna), in combats for the acquirement of wealth, when you defend Sudas, together with the Tritsus, when attacked by the ten Rajas."

7. "The ten confederated irreligious Rajas did not prevail, Indra and Varuna, against Sudas ; the praise of the leaders (of rites), the offerers of sacrificial food, was fruitful ; the gods were present at their sacrifices.

9. "One of you destroys enemies in battle, the other ever protects religious observances ; we invoke you, showerers (of benefits), with praises ; bestow upon us, Indra and Varuna, felicity."

[1] The king had promised the whole earth as gift to his officiating priest.

Sukta 33 says :

2. "Disgracing (Pashadyumna), they brought from afar the fierce Indra, when drinking the ladle of Soma at his sacrifice, to (receive) the libation (of Sudas); Indra hastened from the effused Soma of Pashadyumna, the son of Vayata, to the Vasishthas."

3. "In the same manner was he, (Sudas), enabled by them easily to cross the Sindhu river; in the same manner, through them he easily slew his foe; so in like manner, Vasishthas, through your prayers, did Indra defend Sudas in the war with the ten kings.

"Suffering from thirst, soliciting (rain), supported (by the Tritsus) in the war with the ten Rajas, (the Vasishthas) made Indra radiant as the sun; Indra heard (the praises) of Vasishtha glorifying him, and bestowed a spacious region on the Tritsus."

Sukta 19 says :

3. "Undaunted (Indra), thou hast protected with all thy protections Sudas, the offerer of oblations; thou hast protected, in battles with enemies for the possession of the earth, TRASADASYU, the son of PURUKUTSA, and PURU.

6. "Thy favours, Indra, to Sudas, the donor (of offerings), the presenter of oblations, are infinite; showerer (of benefits), I yoke for thee (thy vigorous) steeds; may our prayers, reach thee who art mighty, to whom many rites are addressed."

Sukta 18 of the Seventh Mandala says :

5. "The adorable Indra made the well-known deep waters (of the Parushni) fordable for Sudas, and converted the vehement awakening imprecation of the sacrificer into the calumniation of the rivers."

6. "TURVASHA, who was preceding (at solemn rites), diligent in sacrifice, (went to Sudas) for wealth; but like fishes restricted (to the element of water), the Bhrigus and Druhyus quickly assailed them; of these two everywhere going, the friend (of Sudas, Indra) rescued his friend."

7. "Those who dress the oblation, those who pronounce auspicious words, those who abstain from penance, those who bear horns (in their hands), those who bestow happiness (on the world by sacrifice), glorify that Indra, who recovered the cattle of the Arya from the plunderers, who slew the enemies in battle."

8. "The evil-disposed and stupid (enemies of Sudas), crossing the humble Parushni river, have broken down its banks ; but he by his greatness pervades the earth, and KAVI, the son of CHAYAMANA, like a falling victim, sleeps (in death)."

9. "The waters followed their regular course to the Parushni, nor (wandered) beyond it ; the quick course (of the king) came to the accessible places, and INDRA made the idly-talking enemies, with their numerous progeny, subject among them (to Sudas)."

10. "They who ride on parti-coloured cattle, (the Maruts), despatched by PRISHNI, and recalling the engagement made by them with their friend (Indra), came like cattle from the pasturage, when left without a herdsman ; the exulting Niyut steeds brought them quickly (against the foe)."

11. "The hero INDRA created the Maruts (for the assistance of the Raja), who, ambitious of fame, slew one and twenty of the men on the two banks (of the Parushni), as a well-looking priest lops the sacred grass in the chamber of sacrifice."

12. "Thou, the bearer of the thunderbolt, didst drown SHRUTA, KAVASHA, VRIDDHA, and afterwards DRUHYU in the waters ; for they, Indra, who are devoted to thee, and glorify thee, preferring thy friendship, enjoy it."

13. "Indra, in his might, quickly demolished all their strongholds, and their seven (kinds of) cities ; he has given the dwelling of the son of ANU to TRITSU ; may we, (by propitiating), (Indra) conquer in battle the ill-speaking man."

14. "The warriors of the ANUS and DRUHYUS, intending (to carry off the) cattle, (hostile) to the pious (SUDAS), perished to the number of sixty-six thousand six hundred and sixty ; such are all the glorious acts of INDRA."

15. "These hostile Tritsus, ignorantly contending with INDRA, fled, routed as rapidly as rivers on a downward course, and being discomfited, abandoned all their possessions to SUDAS."

16. "INDRA has scattered over the earth the hostile rival of the hero (SUDAS), the senior of INDRA, the appropriator of the oblation ; INDRA has baffled the wrath of the wrathful enemy, and the (foe) advancing on the way (against SUDAS) has taken the path of flight."

17. "INDRA has effected a valuable (donation) by a pauper ; he has slain an old lion by a goat ; he has cut the

angles of the sacrificial post with a needle; he has given all the spoils (of the enemy) to SUDAS."

18. "Thy numerous enemies, INDRA, have been reduced to subjugation; effect at some time or other the subjugation of the turbulent BHEDA, who holds men praising thee as guilty of wickedness; hurl, INDRA, thy sharp thunderbolt against him."

19. "The dwellers on the Yamuna and Tritsus glorified INDRA when he killed BHEDA in battle; the Ajas, the Shigrus, the Yakshas, offered to him as a sacrifice the heads of the horses (killed in the combat)."

20. "Thy favours, INDRA, and thy bounties, whether old or new, cannot be counted like the (recurring) dawns; thou hast slain DEVAKA, the son of MANYAMANA and of thine own will hast cast down SHAMBARA from the vast (mountain)."

In this battle the kings who fought against Sudas were[1] : (1) Shinyu, (2) Turvasha, (3) Druhyu, (4) Kavasha, (5) Puru, (6) Anu, (7) Bheda, (8) Shambara, (9) Vaikarna, (10) another Vaikarna, (11) Yadu, (12) Matsya, (13) Paktha, (14) Bhalanas, (15) Aleena, (16) Vishanin, (17) Aja, (18) Shiva, (19) Shigru, (20) Yakshu, (21) Yudhyamadhi, (22) Yadva, (23) Devaka Manyamana, (24) Chayamana Kavi, (25) Sutuka, (26) Uchatha, (27) Shruta, (28) Vriddha, (29) Manyu, and (30) Prithu.

Obviously, the war was a much bigger war than its name indicates. The war must have been a very great event in the history of the Indo-Aryans. No wonder the victorious Sudas became a great hero of his time[2]. We do not know what exactly led to this war. Some indication is given by Rig Veda, vii. 83. 7, where the kings arrayed against Sudas are described as irreligious which suggests that it was probably a religious war.

---

[1] The list is taken from Chitrava Shastri's *Prachin Charitra Kosha*, p. 624. There is no unanimity whether all the names are of kings. Sayanacharya says that 13-16 are names of Purohitas. There is also doubt about 27-29.

[2] The name of Sudas occurs in the Rig Veda in 27 places. It shows what a great hero he must have been regarded by the Vedic people.

IV. Sayanacharya, as well as tradition, declare the following hymns of the Rig Veda to have had the undermentioned kings for their rishis :[1]

> " Vitahavya (or Bharadvaja). x : 9, Sindhudvipa, son of Ambarisha (or Trisiras, son of Tvashtri) x . 75, Sindhukshit, son of Priyamedha ; x . 133, Sudas, son of Pijavana ; x . 134, Mandhatri, son of Yuvanasa ; x . 179, Sibi, son of Usinara, Pratardana, son of Divodasa and king of Kasi, and Vasumanas, son of Rohidasva ; and x . 148 is declared to have had Prithi Vainya."

It will be noticed that in this list there occurs the name of Sudas as a composer of Vedic hymns.

V. Sudas performed Ashvamedha Yajna. There is reference to this in Rig Veda, iii . 53.

> 9. " The great *Rishi*, the generator of the gods, attracted by the deities, the overlooker of the leaders (at holy rites), VISHVAMITRA arrested the watery stream when he sacrificed for SUDAS ; INDRA with the *Kushikas*, was pleased."
>
> 11. " Approach, *Kushikas*, the steed of SUDAS ; animate (him), and let him loose to (win) riches (for the raja) ; for the king (of the gods), has slain VRITRA in the East, in the West, in the North, therefore let (SUDAS) worship him in the best (regions) of the earth."

VI. Sudas was known for charity to the Brahmins who called him Atithigva (the doyen) of Philanthrophists. How the Brahmins have praised him for his philanthrophy appears from the following references in the Rig Veda :

> i . 47 . 6. " O, impetuous Ashvins, possessing wealth in your car, bring sustenance to Sudas. Send to us from the (aerial) ocean, or the sky, the riches which are much coveted."
>
> i . 63 . 7. " Thou didst then, O, thundering Indra, war against, and shatter, the seven cities for Purukutsa, when thou, o king, didst without effort hurl away distress from Sudas like a bunch of grass, and bestow wealth on Puru."
>
> i . 112 . 19. "Come, of Ashvins, with those succours whereby ye brought glorious power to Sudas."
>
> vii . 19 . 3. " Thou, o fierce Indra, hast impetuously protected Sudas, who offered oblations, with every kind of

succour. Thou hast preserved Trasadasyu the son of Purukutsa, and Puru in his conquest of land and in his slaughter of enemies."

vii . 20 . 2. "Indra growing in force slays Vritra; the hero protects him who praises him; he makes room for Sudas (or the liberal sacrificer—Sayana); he gives riches repeatedly to his worshippers."

vii . 25 . 3. "Let a hundred succours come to Sudas, a thousand desirable (gifts) and prosperity. Destroy the weapon of the murderous. Confer renown and wealth on us."

vii . 32 . 10. "No one can oppose or stop the chariot of Sudas. He whom Indra, whom the Marutas, protect, walks in a pasture filled with cattle."

vii . 53 . 3. "And ye, O, Heaven and Earth, have many gifts of wealth for Sudas."

vii . 60 . 8. "Since Aditi, Mitra, and Varuna, afford secure protection to Sudas (or the liberal man), bestowing on him offspring;—may we not, o, mighty deities, commit any offence against the gods . . . May Aryaman rid us of our enemies. (Grant) ye vigorous gods, a wide space to Sudas."

These are the biographical bits regarding Paijavana referred to in the Shanti Parvan of the Mahabharata gleaned from the most authentic source, namely, the Rig Veda. From the Rig Veda, we know that his real name was Sudas, that he was a Kshatriya. He was more than a Kshatriya. He was a king and a mighty king. To this, the Mahabharata adds a fresh and a new detail, namely, that he was a Shudra. A Shudra to be an Aryan, a Shudra to be a Kshatriya and a Shudra to be a king!! Can there be a greater revelation? Can there be anything more revolutionary?

This search for biographical details may be closed with a discussion of three important questions: Was Sudas an Aryan? If Sudas is an Aryan what is the tribe to which he belonged? If Sudas is a Shudra, what does Shudra signify?

It might be well to begin with the second. For the determination of this question it is possible to derive some assistance from certain reference in the Rig Veda. The

Rig Veda mentions many tribes, most important of which are Tritsus, Bharatas, Turvasas, Durhyus, Yadus, Purus and Anus. But according to the references in the Rig Veda there are only three with whom Sudas was connected. They are Purus, Tritsus and the Bharatas. It is enough to confine ourselves to these three and to find out if possible to which of these tribes he belonged. The most important stanzas bearing on the relation between Tritsus and Sudas are the Rig Veda, i . 63 . 7 ; i . 130 . 7 ; vii . 18 . 15 ; vii : 33 : 5 ; vii . 83 . 6 ; vii . 83 : 4 , 6.

In i : 63 : 7, Divodasa is spoken of as the king of the Purus and in i . 130 . 7, Divodasa is spoken of as Paurvé, i.e., belonging to the Purus.

Rig Veda, vii . 18 . 15 and vii . 83 . 6, suggest that Sudas was not a Tritsu. The first suggests that Sudas raided the camp of Tritsus who ran away and Sudas took possession of their wealth. The second suggests that Tritsus and Sudas were on one side in the war against the ten kings, but they are shown as separate. But in vii . 35 . 5 and in vii . 83 . 4, Sudas becomes fully identified with Tritsus ; indeed, in the former Sudas becomes a king of the Tritsus.

On this question of the relation between the Tritsus and the Bharatas and between them and Sudas, we have as our evidence Rig Veda, vii . 33 : 6 and vi : 16 . 4 , 6 , 19 ; According to the first, Tritsus are the same as the Bharatas. According to the second, Divodasa the father of Sudas is spoken of as belonging to the Bharatas.

From these references one thing is certain that the Purus, Tritsus and Bharatas were either different branches of one and the same folk or that they were different tribes, who in the course of time became one people, folk. This is not impossible. The only question is : assuming they were different, to whom did Sudas originally belong ? To the Purus, the Tritsus or to the Bharatas ? Having regard to the connection of the Purus and the Bharatas with Divodasa, his father, it seems natural to suppose that Sudas originally belonged either to the Purus or to the Bharatas—which, it is difficult to say.

Whether he belonged to the Purus or not, there is no doubt that Sudas belonged to the Bharatas if regard is had to the fact that his father Divodasa is spoken of as belonging to the Bharatas. The next question is : who were these Bharatas and whether they are the people after whom India got the name Bharata Bhumi or the land of the Bharatas. This question is important because most people are not aware of the true facts. When Hindus talk of the Bharatas they have in mind the Daushyanti Bharatas, Bharatas descended from Dushyanta and Shakuntala and who fought the war which is described in the Mahabharata. Not only are they not aware of any other Bharatas but they believe that the name Bharata Bhumi which was given to India was given after the Daushyanti Bharatas.

There are two Bharatas quite distinct from each other. One tribe of the Bharatas are the Bharatas of the Rig Veda, who were descended from Manu and to whom Sudas belonged. The other tribe of Bharatas are the Daushyanti Bharatas. What is more important is that if India has been named Bharata Bhumi it is after the Bharatas of the Rig Veda and not after the Daushyanti Bharatas. This is made clear by the following stanzas from the Bhagavata Purana :[1]

प्रियंवदो नाम सुतो मनो : स्वायंभुवस्य ह ।
तस्याग्नीध्रस्ततो नाभिर्ऋषभश्च सुतस्ततः ॥
अवतीर्णं पुत्रशतं तस्यासीद्ब्रह्मपारगम् ।
तेषां वै भरतो ज्येष्ठो नारायणपरायण : ।
विख्यातं वर्षमेतद्यन्नाम्ना भारतमुत्तमम् ॥

"Manu, the son of Svayambhu, had a son named Priyamvada ; his son was Agnidhra ; his son was Nabhi ; he had a son Rishabha. He had a hundred sons born to him, all learned in the Veda ; of them, Bharata was the eldest,

[1] Quoted by Vaidya in Mahabharatacha Upasamhara, p. 200.

devoted to Narayana, by whose name this excellent land is known as Bharata."

This shows to what illustrious line of kings this Shudra Sudas belonged.

The next thing to find out is whether Sudas was an Aryan. The Bharatas were of course Aryans and therefore Sudas must have been an Aryan. If reference is had to Rig Veda, vii . 18 . 7, this connection with the Tritsus to the Aryans seems to throw some doubt on his Aryan origin. This stanza says that Indra rescued the cows of the Aryas from the Tritsus and killed the Tritsus, thereby suggesting that the Tritsus were the enemies of the Aryas. Griffiths is very much perturbed by the Tritsus being shown as non-Aryans which is the result of a literal translation of the stanza, and to avoid it he understands cows to mean comrade.[1] This of course is unnecessary if one bears in mind that the Rig Veda contains the story of two sorts of Aryas, whether differing in race or religion, it is difficult to say. Interpreted in the light of this fact, all that the stanza means is that at the time when it was written the Tritsus had not become Aryans by religion. It does not mean that they were not Aryans by race. It is therefore indisputable that Sudas, whether taken as a Bharata or as a Tritsu was an Aryan.

And now to the last question, though it is by no means the least. What does Shudra signify ? In the light of this new discovery that Sudas was a Shudra, the word now stands in a totally different light. To old scholars to whom the word was just the name of a servile and aboriginal class, this new discovery must come as a surprise for which their past researches cannot possibly furnish an answer. As for myself, I am in no better position. The reason is that the social organization of the Vedic Aryans has yet to be studied. We know from the study of primitive societies that they are organized in groups

---

[1] His rendering is " yet to the Tritsus came the Arya's comrade, through love of spoil and heroes' war, to lead them."

and they act as groups. The groups are of various sorts. There are clans, phratries, moieties and tribes. In some cases, the tribe is the primary unit, in others it is the clan, in others the phratry. In some cases tribes are sub-divided into clans. In other cases there are no clans. It is a single clanless tribe.

The clan embraces the descendants of a single ancestor held together by a sense of common descent. Clans often become associated through common social and ceremonial interests into major units, called phratries or brotherhoods of clans. The bond within the phratry may be relatively loose, that is, the association may not imply more than an informal feeling of preferential friendship. The phratry may become a moiety in which each clan is recognized as part of one of two major units. But moieties may occur without any sub-division, that is, the entire clan may consist of two clans. All these organizations whether it is a clan, a phratry, a moiety or a tribe, are all based on the tie of kinship.

The Vedic Aryans had no doubt some such forms of social organization. That is clear from the nomenclature. As pointed out by Prof. Senart :[1]

> " The Vedic hymns are all too indefinite concerning the details of external and social life. We at least see from them that the Aryan population was divided into a number of tribes or small peoples (*janas*), subdivided into clans united by the ties of kinship (*visas*), which in their turn were split up into families. The terminology of the Rig Veda is in this respect somewhat indecisive, but the general fact is clear. *Sajata*, that is to say, ' kinsman ' or ' fellow in *Jati*,' of race, seems in the Atharva-Veda to denote fellow in clan (*vis*). Jana, which assumes a wider significance, recalls the Avestic equivalent of the clan, the *zantu*, and the *jati* or caste. A series of terms, *vra*, *vrijana*, *vraja*, *vrata*, appear to be synonyms or subdivisions either of the clan or of the tribes. The Aryan population then lived, at the epoch to which the hymns refer, under the rule of an organization dominated by

[1] ' Castes in India,' by Emile Senart, p. 192.

the traditions of the tribe and the lower or similar groupings. The very variety of names indicates that this organization was somewhat unsettled."

We have, however, no information to determine which of these corresponds to the clan, which to the phratry and which to the tribe[1]. That being so, it is difficult to say whether Shudra was the name of a clan, a phratry or a tribe. It is, however, interesting to refer to the view of Prof. Weber when he comments on the passage from the Satapatha Brahmana (i . 1 . 4 . 12) where it says that different modes of address should be adopted inviting the sacrificer to proceed with the sacrifice, addressing him as 'come' if he is a Brahmin, 'hasten hither' if he is a Kshatriya, 'hasten hither' if he is a Vaishya and 'run hither' if he is a Shudra.

Prof. Weber says[2] :—

> "The entire passage is of great importance, as it shows (in opposition to what Roth says in the first Volume of this Journal, p. 83) that the Shudras were then admitted to the holy sacrifices of the Aryans, and understood their speech, even if they did not speak it. The latter point cannot certainly be assumed as a necessary consequence, but it is highly probable and I consequently incline to the view of those who regard the Shudras as an Aryan tribe which immigrated into India before the others."

His conclusion that the Shudras were Aryans hits the nail squarely on the head. The only point of doubt is whether the Shudras were a tribe. That they were Aryans and Kshatriyas is beyond doubt.

---

[1] What are called Aryan tribes appear to be a phratry in view of their changing alliances.

[2] Muir, Vol. I, p. 366.

CHAPTER VIII

THE NUMBER OF VARNAS, THREE OR FOUR?

I

THAT there were from the very beginning four *Varnas* in the Indo-Aryan society is a view which is universally accepted by all classes of Hindus, and also by European scholars. If the thesis advanced in the last chapter, namely, that the Shudras were Kshatriyas is accepted, then it follows that this theory is wrong and that there was a time when there were only three *Varnas* in the Indo-Aryan society, viz., Brahmins, Kshatriyas and Vaishyas. Thus, the thesis, while it solves one problem, at the same time creates another. Whether anybody else sees the importance of this problem or not, I do. Indeed, I am aware of the fact that unless I succeed in proving that there were originally only three *Varnas*, my thesis that the Shudras were Kshatriyas may not be said to be proved beyond the shadow of a doubt.

While it is unfortunate that I should have landed on a thesis, which, while holding out a promise of solving the problem, creates another, I feel fortunate in having strong and cogent evidence to show that there were originally only three *Varnas* among the Indo-Aryans.

The first piece of evidence I rely upon is that of the Rig Veda itself. There are some scholars who maintain that the *Varna* system did not exist in the age of the Rig Veda. This statement is based on the view that the Purusha Sukta is an interpolation which has taken place long after the Rig Veda was closed. Even accepting that the Purusha Sukta is a later interpolation, it is not possible to accept the statement that the *Varna* system did not exist in the time of the Rig Veda. Such a system is in open conflict with the text of the Rig Veda. For, the Rig Veda, apart from the Purusha Sukta, does mention Brahmins, Kshatriyas and Vaishyas not once but many times. The Brahmins are mentioned as a separate *Varna* fifteen times, Kshatriyas nine times. What is important is that the Rig Veda does not mention Shudra as a separate *Varna*. If Shudras were a separate *Varna* there is no reason why the Rig Veda should not have mentioned them. The true conclusion to be drawn from the Rig Veda is not that the *Varna* system did not exist, but that there were only three *Varnas* and that Shudras were not regarded as a fourth and a separate *Varna*.

The second piece of evidence I rely on is the testimony of the two Brahmanas, the Satapatha and the Taittiriya. Both speak of the creation of three Varnas only. They do not speak of the creation of the Shudra as a separate.

The Satapatha Brahmana says[1] :

> II. 1 . 4 . 11.—" (Uttering), 'bhuh,' Prajapati generated this earth. (Uttering) 'bhuvah' he generated the air, and (Uttering) 'svah' he generated the sky. This universe is co-extensive with these worlds. (The fire) is placed with the whole. Saying 'bhuh,' Prajapati generated the Brahman; saying 'bhuvah,' he generated the Kshattra; (and saying) 'svah,' he generated the Vis. The fire is placed with the whole. (Saying) 'bhuh,' Prajapati generated himself; (saying) 'bhuvah,' he generated offspring; saying 'svah,' he generated animals. This world is so much as self, offspring, and animals. (The fire) is placed with the whole."

The Taittirya Brahmana[2] says :

> III. 12 . 9 . 2.—" This entire (universe) has been created by Brahma. Men say that the Vaishya class was produced from *ric* verses. They say that the Yajur Veda is the womb from which the Kshattriya was born. The Sama Veda is the source from which the Brahmins sprang. This word the ancients declared to the ancients."

---

[1] Muir, Vol. I, page 17.

[2] Quoted by Muir, Vol. I, p. 17.

Here is my evidence. It consists of an inference from the Rig Veda and two statements from two Brahmanas which in point of authority are co-equal with the Vedas. For both are Shruti both say in definite and precise terms that there were only three *Varnas*. Both agree that the Shudras did not form a separate and a distinct *Varna*, much less the fourth *Varna*. There cannot, therefore, be better evidence in support of my contention that there were originally only three *Varnas* and that the Shudras were only a part of the second *Varna*.

II

Such is my evidence. On the other side, there is, of course, the evidence contained in the Purusha Sukta of the Rig Veda, which maintains that there were four *Varnas* from the very beginning. The question now is : Which of the two should be accepted as the correct ? How is this question to be decided ? It cannot be decided by applying the rules of Mimamsa. If we did apply it, we will have to admit that both the statements, one in the Purusha Sukta that there were four *Varnas* and the statement in the two Brahmanas that there were three *Varnas*, are true. This is an absurd position. We must decide this matter in the light of the canons of historical criticism, such as sequence of time and intrinsic criticism, etc. The main question is whether the Purusha Sukta is a later composition added to the original Rig Veda. The question has been dealt with on the basis of the language of the Sukta as compared with the language of the rest of the Rig Veda. That it is a late production is the opinion of all scholars. This is what Colebrooke says[1]:—

[1] Quoted in Muir, Vol. I, p. 13.

" That remarkable hymn (the Purusha Sukta) is in language, metre, and style, very different from the rest of the prayers with which it is associated. It has a decidedly more modern tone; and must have been composed after the Sanskrit language had been refined, and its grammar and rhythm perfected. The internal evidence which it furnishes serves to demonstrate the important fact that the compilation of the Vedas, in their present arrangement, took place after the Sanskrit tongue had advanced from the rustic and irregular dialect in which the multitude of hymns and prayers of the Veda was composed, to the polished and sonorous language in which the mythological poems, sacred and profane (puranas and kavyas), have been written."

In the opinion of Prof. Max Muller[1]:—

" There can be little doubt, for instance, that the 90th hymn of the 10th book . . . is modern both in its character and in its diction. It is full of allusions to the sacrificial ceremonials, it uses technically philosophical terms, it mentions the three seasons in the order of Vasanta, spring, Grishma, summer and Sharad, autumn; it contains the only passage in the Rig Veda where the four castes are enumerated. The evidence of language for the modern date of this composition is equally strong. Grishma, for instance, the name for the hot season, does not occur in any other hymn of the Rig Veda; and Vasanta also, the name of spring does not belong to the earliest vocabulary of the Vedic poets. It occurs but once more in the Rig Veda (x . 161 . 4), in a passage where the three seasons are mentioned in the order of Sharad, autumn; Hemanta, winter; and Vasanta, spring."

Prof. Weber observes[2]:—

" That the Purusha Sukta, considered as a hymn of the Rig Veda, is among the latest portions of that collection, is clearly perceptible from its contents. The fact that the Sama Samhita has not adopted any verse from it, is not without importance (compare what I have remarked in my Academical Prelections). The Naigeya school, indeed, appears (although it is not quite certain) to have extracted the first five verses in the seventh prapathaka of the first Archika, which is peculiar to it."

---

[1] Quoted Muir, Vol. I, p. 13.

[2] Quoted in Muir, Vol. I, p. 14.

III

This is one line of argument. There is also another line of argument which also helps us to determine whether the Purusha Sukta is an earlier or later production. For this it is necessary to find out how many Samhitas of the Vedas have adopted the Purusha Sukta. Examining the different Vedas and the Samhitas, the position is as follows :

The Sama Veda produces only 5 verses from the Purusha Sukta. As to the White Yajur Veda, the Vajasaneyi Samhita includes it but the difference between the two is great. The Purusha Sukta, as it stands, in the Rig Veda, has only 16 verses. But the Purusha Sukta in the Vajasaneyi Samhita has 22 verses. Of the Black Yajur Veda there are three Samhitas available at present. But none of the three Samhitas, the Taittriya, the Katha and the Maitrayani, gives any place to the Purusha Sukta. The Atharva Veda is the only Veda which contains a more or less exact reproduction of the Purusha Sukta of the Rig Veda.

The text of the Purusha Sukta, as it occurs in the different Vedas, is not uniform. The six additional verses of the Vajasaneyi Samhita are special to it and are not to be found in the text as it occurs in the Rig Veda, the Sama Veda or the Atharva Veda. There is another difference which relates to verse 16. The 16th verse of the Rig Veda is to be found neither in the Atharva Veda nor in the Sama Veda nor in the Yajur Veda. Similarly, the 16th verse of the Atharva Veda is to be found neither in the Rig Veda nor in the Yajur Veda. Of the fifteen verses, which are common to the three Vedas, their texts are not identical. Nor is the order in which the verses stand in the three Vedas the same as may be seen from the following table :

Yajur Veda.	*Rig Veda.*	*Sama Veda.*	*Atharva Veda.*
1	1	3	1
2	2	5	4
3	3	6	3
4	4	4	2
5	5	7	9
6	8	*	10
7	9	*	11
8	10	*	14
9	7	*	13
10	11	*	12
11	12	*	5
12	13	*	6
13	14	*	7
14	6	*	8
15	15	*	15
16†	16	*	16†
17	*	*	*
18	*	*	*
19	*	*	*
20	*	*	*
21	*	*	*
22	*	*	*

The point is that if the Purusha Sukta had been an old, hoary text, sanctified by ancient tradition, could the other Vedas have taken such a liberty with it ? Could they have changed it and chopped it as they have done ?

The place of the Purusha Sukta in the hymns of the different Vedas is also very significant. In the Rig Veda it occurs in the miscellaneous part and in the Atharva Veda it occurs in what is known as the supplementary part. If it was the earliest composition of the Rig Veda, why should it have been placed in such inconsequential

* Means that these Verses are not to be found.

† Means that they are not identical.

collection ? What do these points suggest ? They suggest that :

(1) If the Purusha Sukta was not incorporated in the Taittiriya Kathaka and Maitrayani Samhitas of the Black Yajur Veda, it follows, that the Purusha Sukta was added to the Rig Veda after the Taittiriya Samhitra, the Kathak a Samhita, the Maitrayani Samhita of the Black Yajur Veda.

(2) That it had to be put in the miscellaneous and supplementary portions of the Vedas shows that it was composed at a later stage.

(3) That the freedom which the authors of the different Samhitas took in adding, omitting and recording the verses shows that they did not regard it as an ancient hymn, which they were bound to reproduce in its exact original form.

These points go a long way in furnishing corroborative evidence in support of the views held by Prof. Max Muller and others that the Purusha Sukta is a later interpolation.

IV

The difference in the form of the stanzas in the Purusha Sukta is also very noteworthy. Anyone who reads the Purusha Sukta will find that except for these two verses, viz., 11 and 12, the whole of it is in the narrative form. But the two verses, which explain the origin of the four *Varnas*, are in the form of question and answer. The point is: Why should these verses be introduced in a question form breaking the narrative form ? The only explanation is that the writer wanted to introduce a new matter and in a pointed manner. This means that not only the Purusha Sukta is a later addition to the Rig Veda, but these particular verses are much later than even the Purusha Sukta.

Some critics have gone to the length of saying that the Purusha Sukta is a forgery by the Brahmins to bolster up their claim to superiority. Priests are known to have committed many forgeries. The Donations of Constantine and Pseudo-Isidore Decretals are well-known forgeries in the history of the Papacy. The Brahmins of India were not free from such machinations. How they changed the original word 'Agre' into 'Agne' to make Rig Veda give support to the burning of widows has been pointed out by no less an authority than Prof. Max Muller. It is well-known how in the time of the East India Company a whole Smriti was fabricated to support the case of a plaintiff. There is, therefore, nothing surprising if the Brahmins did forge the Purusha Sukta, if not the whole, at least the two verses 11 and 12, at some later stage, long after the fourth *Varna* had come into being, with a view to give the system of *Chaturvarnya* the sanction of the Veda.

V

Is the Purusha Sukta earlier than the Brahmanas? This question is distinct and separate from the first. It may be that the Purusha Sukta belongs to the later part of the Rig Veda. Yet, if the Rig Veda as a whole is earlier than the Brahmanas, the Purusha Sukta would still be earlier than the Brahmanas. The question, therefore, needs to be separately considered.

It is Prof. Max Muller's view that in the growth of the Vedic literature the order was Vedas, then Brahmanas and thereafter the Sutras. If this proposition was adopted, it would mean that the Purusha Sukta must be earlier than the Brahmanas. Question is: Can Prof. Max Muller's proposition be accepted as absolute ? If it was accepted as absolute, the proposition would lead to two conclusions :

(1) That in the time of the Rig Veda there were four *Varnas* and at the time of the Satapatha Brahmana they became three ; or

(2) that the tradition is not completely recorded in the Satapatha Brahmana.

It is obvious that both these conclusions are absurd and must be rejected. The first is absurd on the face of it. The second is untenable because the theory of the evolution of the *Varnas* by the two Brahmanas is different from that set out in the Purusha Sukta and is complete in itself. The absurdity of the result is inevitable if one were to take Max Muller's proposition as absolute. The proposition cannot be taken as absolute to mean that no Brahmana was composed until all the Samhitas had come into being. On the other hand, it is quite possible as pointed out by Professors Belvalkar and Ranade that most of these compositions are composite and synchronous and, therefore, one part of the Vedas can be earlier than another part and that a part of the Brahmanas can be earlier than parts of the Vedas. If this is a correct view then there is nothing inherently improbable in holding that the parts of the Satapatha Brahmana and of the Taittiriya Brahmana, which record the legend that there were at one time only three *Varnas*, are earlier than the Purusha Sukta of the Rig Veda.

What is the conclusion which follows from this examination of the Purusha Sukta ? There is only one conclusion, that the Sukta is an addition to the Rig Veda made at a later stage and is, therefore, no argument that there were four *Varnas* from the very beginning of the Aryan Society.

For the reasons given above, it will be seen that my thesis about the origin of the Shudras creates no problem such as the one mentioned in the beginning of this Chapter.

If it did appear to create a problem, it was because of the assumption that the Purusha Sukta was an authentic and genuine record of what it purports to say. That assumption has now been shown to be quite baseless. I, therefore, see no difficulty in concluding that there was a time when the Aryan Society had only three *Varnas* and the Shudras belonged to the second or the Kshatriya *Varna*.

CHAPTER IX

BRAHMINS *VERSUS* SHUDRAS

THE thesis that the Shudras were Kshatriyas and that if they became the fourth *Varna* it was because they were degraded to that position does not wholly solve the problem. It only raises another problem. This problem is why were the Shudras degraded ?

The problem is new. It has never been raised before. The existing literature on the subject cannot, therefore, be expected to contain an answer. The question is raised by me for the first time. As it is a question on which my theory of the Shudras rests, the burden of giving a satisfactory answer must rest on me. I believe, I can give a satisfactory answer to this question. My answer is that the degradation of the Shudras is the result of a violent conflict between the Shudras and the Brahmins. Fortunately for me, there is abundant evidence of it.

I

There is direct evidence of a violent conflict between the Shudra king, Sudas and Vasishtha, the Brahmin rishi. The facts relating to this conflict however are stated in a very confused manner. In the narration which follows, I have made an attempt to state them in a neat and an orderly fashion.

To understand the nature of the conflict, it is necessary first to understand the relations between Vasishtha and Vishvamitra.

Vasishtha and Vishvamitra were enemies and were enemies first and enemies last. There was no incident to which one of them was a party in which the other did not know himself as an opponent. As evidence of their enmity, I will refer to some of the episodes. The first one is that of Satyavrata otherwise called Trishanku. The story as told in the Harivamsha[1] is as follows :

> " Meanwhile Vasishtha, from the relation subsisting between the king (Satyavrata's father) and himself, as disciple and spiritual preceptor, governed the city of Ayodhya, the country, and the interior apartments of the royal palace. But Satyavrata, whether through folly or the force of destiny, cherished constantly an increased indignation against Vasishtha, who for a (proper) reason had not interposed to prevent his exclusion from the royal power by his father. 'The formulæ of the marriage ceremonial are only binding' said Satyavrata, 'when the seventh step has been taken, and this had not been done when I seized the damsel ; still Vasishtha, who knows the precepts of the law, does not come to my aid.' Thus Satyavrata was incensed in his mind against Vasishtha, who, however, had acted from a sense of what was right. Nor did Satyavrata understand (the propriety of) that silent penance imposed upon him by his father . . . When he had supported this arduous rite, (he supposed that) he had redeemed his family position. The venerable muni Vasishtha did not, however, (as has been said), prevent his father from setting him aside, but resolved to install his son as king. When the powerful prince Satyavrata had endured the penance for twelve years he beheld, when he was without flesh to eat, the milch cow of Vasishtha which yielded all objects of desire, and under the influence of anger, delusion, and exhaustion, distressed by hunger, and failing in the ten duties he slew . . . and both partook of her flesh himself, and gave it to Vishvamitra's sons to eat. Vasishtha hearing of this, became incensed against him and imposed on him the name of Trishanku as he had committed three sins. On his return home, Vishvamitra

[1] Quoted by Muir, Vol. I, pp. 377-378.

was gratified[1] by the support which his wife had received, and offered Trishanku the choice of a boon. When this proposal was made, Trishanku chose his boon of ascending bodily to heaven. All apprehension from the twelve years' drought being now at an end, the muni (Vishvamitra) installed Trishanku in his father's kingdom and offered sacrifice on his behalf. The mighty Kaushika then, in spite of the resistance of the gods and of Vasishtha exalted[1] the king alive to heaven."

The next episode in which they appear on opposite sides is that of Harishchandra, the son of Trishanku. The story is told in the Vishnu Purana and in the Markandeya Purana. The following account is given[2]. The story runs :

"On one occasion, when hunting, the king heard a sound of female lamentation which proceeded, it appears, from the sciences who were becoming mastered by the austerely fervid sage Vishvamitra, in a way they had never been before by anyone else ; and were consequently crying out in alarm at his superiority. For the fulfilment of his duty as a Kshatriya to defend the weak, and inspired by the god Ganesha, who had entered into him, Harishchandra exclaimed 'What sinner is this who is binding fire in the hem of his garment, while I, his lord, am present, resplendent with force and fiery vigour ? He shall to-day enter on his long sleep, pierced in all his limbs by arrows, which, by their discharge from my bow, illuminate all the quarters of the firmament.' Vishvamitra was provoked by this address. In consequence

---

1 It is stated in the Harivamsha :—

"In consequence of the wickedness which had been committed, Indra did not rain for a period of twelve years. At that time Vishvamitra had left his wife and children and gone to practise austerities on the seashore. His wife, driven to extremity by want, was on the point of selling her second son for a hundred cows, in order to support the others ; but this arrangement was stopped by the intervention of Satyavrata who liberated the son when bound, and maintained the family by providing them with the flesh of wild animals and according to his father's injunction, consecrated himself for the performance of a silent penance for twelve years."

As stated in another place in the Harivamsha Trishanku had been expelled from his home by his father for the offence of carrying off the young wife of one of the citizens under the influence of a criminal passion and Vasishtha did not interfere to prevent his banishment. It is to this that the text refers.

2 Muir, Vol. I, pp. 379-387.

of his wrath the Sciences instantly perished, and Harishchandra, trembling like the leaf of an ashvattha tree, submissively represented that he had merely done his duty as a king, which he defined as consisting in the bestowal of gifts on eminent Brahmins and other persons of slender means, the protection of the timid, and war against enemies. Vishvamitra hereupon demands a gift as a Brahmin intent upon receiving one. The king offers him whatsoever he may ask: Gold, his own son, wife, body, life, kingdom, good fortune. The saint first requires the present for the Rajasuya sacrifice. On this being promised, and still more offered, he asks for the empire of the whole earth, including everything but Harishchandra himself, his wife and son, and his virtue which follows its possessor wherever he goes. Harishchandra joyfully agrees. Vishvamitra then requires him to strip off all his ornaments, to clothe himself in the bark of trees, and to quit the kingdom with his wife Shaivya and his son. When he is departing the sage stops him and demands payment of his yet unpaid sacrificial fee. The king replies that he has only the persons of his wife, his son and himself left. Vishvamitra insists that he must nevertheless pay, and that unfulfilled promises of gifts to Brahmins bring destruction. The unfortunate prince, after being threatened with a curse, engages to make the payment in a month; and commences his journey with a wife unused to such fatigues, amid the universal lamentations of his subjects. While he lingers, listening to their affectionate remonstrances against his desertion of his kingdom, Vishvamitra comes up, and being incensed at the delay and the king's apparent hesitation, strikes the queen with his staff, as she is dragged on by her husband. Harishchandra then proceeded with his wife and little son to Benares, imagining that this divine city, as the special property of Siva, could not be possessed by any mortal. Here he found the relentless Vishvamitra waiting for him, and ready to press his demand for the payment of his sacrificial gift, even before the expiration of the full period of grace. In this extremity, Shaivya the queen suggests with a sobbing voice that her husband should sell her. On hearing this proposal Harishchandra swoons, then recovers, utters lamentations and swoons again, and his wife seeing his sad condition, swoons also. While they are in a state of unconsciousness their famished child exclaims in distress. 'O, father, father, give me bread; O, mother, mother, give me food; hunger overpowers me and my tongue is parched.' At this moment Vishvamitra returns, and after recalling Harishchandra to consciousness by sprinkling water over him, again urges payment of the present. The king again swoons, and is again restored. The sage threatens to curse him if his engagement is not fulfilled by sunset. Being now pressed by his wife, the king agrees to sell her, adding, however, 'If my voice can utter such a wicked word, I do what the most inhuman wretches cannot perpetrate.' He then goes into the city, and in self-accusing language offers his queen for sale as a slave. A rich old Brahmin offers to buy her at a price corresponding to her value, to do his household work. Seeing his mother dragged away the child ran after her, his eyes dimmed with tears, and crying 'mother.' The Brahmin purchaser kicked him when he came up; but he would not let his mother go, and continued crying 'mother, mother.' The queen then said to the Brahmin, 'Be so kind, my master, as to buy also this child, as without him I shall prove to thee but a useless purchase. Be thus merciful to me in my wretchedness, unite me with my son, like a cow to her calf.' The Brahmin agrees: 'Take this money and give me the boy.' After the Brahmin had gone out of sight with his purchases, Vishvamitra again appeared and renewed his demands; and when the afflicted Harishchandra offered him the small sum he had obtained by the sale of his wife and son, he angrily replied, 'If, miserable Kshatriya, thou thinkest this a sacrificial gift befitting my deserts, thou shalt soon behold the transcendent power of my ardent austere-fervour of my terrible majesty, and of my holy study.' Harishchandra promises an additional gift, and Vishvamitra allows him the remaining quarter of the day for its liquidation. On the terrified and afflicted prince offering himself for sale, in order to gain the means of meeting this cruel demand, Dharma (Righteousness) appears in the form of a hideous and offensive Chandala, and agree to buy him at his own price, large or small. Harishchandra declines such a degrading servitude, and declares that he would rather be consumed by the fire of his persecutor's curse than submit to such a fate. Vishvamitra, however, again comes on the scene, asks why he does not accept the large sum offered by the Chandala; and when he pleads in excuse his descent from the solar race, threatens to fulminate a curse against him if he does not accept that method of meeting his liability. Harishchandra implores that he may be spared this extreme of degradation, and offers to become Vishvamitra's slave in payment of the residue of his debt; whereupon the sage rejoins, 'if thou art my slave, then I sell thee as such to the Chandala for a hundred millions of money.' The Chandala, delighted, pays down the money, and carries off Harishchandra bound, beaten, confused, and afflicted, to his own place of abode. Harishchandra is sent by the Chandala to steal grave clothes in a cemetery and is told that he will receive two-sixths of the value for his hire; three-sixths going to his master, and one-sixth to the king. In this horrid spot, and in this degrading occupation he spent, in great misery twelve months, which seemed to him like a hundred years. He then falls asleep and has a series of dreams suggested by the life he had been leading. After he awoke, his wife came to the cemetery to perform the obsequies of their son, who had died from the bite of a serpent. At first, the husband and wife did not recognize each other, from the change in appearance which had been wrought upon them both by their miseries. Harishchandra, however, soon discovered from the tenor of her lamentations that it is his wife, and falls into a swoon; as the queen does also when she recognizes her husband. When consciousness returns they both break out into lamentations, the father bewailing in a touching strain the loss of his son, and the wife the degradation of the king. She then falls on his neck, embraces him and asks 'whether all this is a dream, or a reality, as she is utterly bewildered'; and adds, that 'if it be a reality, then righteousness is unavailing to those who practise it.' After hesitating to devote himself to death on his son's funeral pyre without receiving his master's leave, Harishchandra resolves to do so, braving all the consequences and consoling himself with the hopeful anticipation; 'If I have given gifts and offered sacrifices and gratified my religious teachers, then may I be reunited with my son and with thee (my wife) in another world.' The queen determines to die in the same manner. When Harishchandra, after placing his son's body on the funeral pile, is meditating on the Lord Hari Narayana Krishna, the supreme spirit, all the gods arrive, headed by Dharma (Righteousness), and accompanied by Vishvamitra. Dharma entreats the king to desist from his rash intention; and Indra announces to him that, he, his wife, and son have conquered heaven by their good works, Ambrosia, the antidote of death, and flowers are rained by the gods from the sky;

and the king's son is restored to life and the bloom of youth. The king adorned with celestial clothing and garlands, and the queen, embrace their son. Harishchandra, however, declares that he cannot go to heaven till he has received his master the Chandala's permission, and has paid him a ransom. Dharma then reveals to the king that it was he himself who had miraculously assumed the form of a Chandala. The king next objects that he cannot depart unless his faithful subjects, who are sharers in his merits, are allowed to accompany him to heaven, at least for one day. This request is granted by Indra; and after Vishvamitra has inaugurated Rohitashva the king's son to be his successor, Harishchandra, his friends and followers, all ascend in company to heaven. Even after this great consummation, however, Vasishtha the family priest of Harishchandra, hearing, at the end of a twelve years' abode in the waters of the Ganges, an account of all that has occurred, becomes vehemently incensed at the humiliation inflicted on the excellent monarch, whose virtues and devotion to the gods and Brahmins he celebrates, declares that his indignation had not been so greatly roused even when his own hundred sons had been slain by Vishvamitra, and in the following words dooms the latter to be transformed into a crane: 'Wherefore that wicked man, enemy of the Brahmins, smitten by my curse, shall be expelled from the society of intelligent beings, and losing his understanding shall be transformed into a Baka.' Vishvamitra reciprocates the curse, and changes Vasishtha into a bird of the species called Ari. In their new shapes the two have a furious fight, the Ari being of the portentous height of two thousand yojanas =18,000 miles, and the Baka of 3090 yojanas. They first assail each other with their wings; then the baka smites his antagonist in the same manner, while the Ari strikes with his talons. Falling mountains, overturned by the blasts of wind raised by the flapping of their wings, shake the whole earth, the waters of the ocean overflow, the earth itself, thrown off its perpendicular slopes downwards to Patala, the lower regions. Many creatures perished by these various convulsions. Attracted by the dire disorder, Brahma arrives, attended by all the gods, on the spot, and commands the combatants to desist from their fray. They were too fiercely infuriated to regard this injunction; but Brahma put an end to the conflict by restoring them to their natural forms and counselling them to be reconciled."

The next episode in which they came in as opponents is connected with Ambarisha, king of Ayodhya :

"The story[1] relates that Ambarisha was engaged in performing a sacrifice, when Indra carried away the victim. The priest said that this ill-omened event had occurred owing to the king's bad administration ; and would call for a great expiation, unless a human victim could be produced. After a long search the royal-rishi (Ambarisha) came upon the Brahmin rishi, Richika, a descendant of Bhrigu, and asked him to sell one of his sons for a victim, at the price of a hundred thousand cows. Richika answered that he would not sell his eldest son and his wife added that she would not sell the youngest ; 'youngest sons' she observed, 'being generally the favourites of their mothers.' The second son, Shunasshepa, then said that in that case he regarded himself as the one who was to be sold, and desired the king to remove him. The hundred thousand cows, with ten millions of gold pieces and heaps of jewels, were paid down and Shunasshepa carried away. As they were passing through Pushkara, Shunasshepa beheld his maternal uncle Vishvamitra who was engaged in austerities there with other rishis, threw himself into his arms, and implored his assistance, urging his orphan, friendless and helpless state, as claims on the sage's benevolence. Vishvamitra soothed him ; and pressed his own sons to offer themselves as victims in the room of Shunasshepa. This proposition met with no favour from Madhushyanda and the other sons of the royal hermit, who answered with haughtiness and derision : 'How is it that thou sacrificest thine own sons and seekest to rescue those of others ? We look upon this as wrong, and like the eating of one's own flesh.' The sage was exceedingly wroth at this disregard of his injunction, and doomed his sons to be born in the most degraded classes, like Vasishtha's sons, and to eat dog's flesh, for a thousand years. He then said to Shunasshepa : 'When thou art bound with hallowed cords, decked with a red garland, and anointed with unguents and fastened to the sacrificial post of Vishnu, then address thyself to Agni, and sing these two divine verses (gathas), at the sacrifice of Ambarisha : then shalt thou attain the fulfilment (of thy desire)'. Being furnished with the two gathas, Shunasshepa proposed at once to king Ambarisha that they should set out for their destination.

[1] Quoted by Muir, Vol. I, pp. 405-407.

When bound at the stake to be immolated, dressed in a red garment, he celebrated the two gods, Indra and his younger brother (Vishnu), with the excellent verses. The thousand-eyed (Indra) was pleased with the secret hymn; and bestowed long life on Shunasshepa."

The last episode recorded in which the two had ranged themselves on opposite sides is connected with king Kalmashapada. The episode is recorded in the Adi Parvan of the Mahabharata[1]:

"Kalmashapada was a king of the race of Ikshvaku. Vishvamitra wished to be employed by him as his officiating priest; but the king preferred Vasishtha. It happened however that the king went out to hunt, and after having killed a large quantity of games, he became very much fatigued, as well as hungry and thirsty. Meeting Shakti, the eldest of Vasishtha's hundred sons, on the road, he ordered him to get out of his way. The priest civilly replied: 'The path is mine, o king; this is the immemorial law; in all observances the king must cede the way to the Brahmin.' Neither party would yield, and the dispute waxing warmer, the king struck the muni with his whip. The muni, resorting to the usual expedient of offended sages, by a curse doomed the king to become a man-eater. It happened that at that time enmity existed between Vishvamitra and Vasishtha on account of their respective claims to be priest to Kalmashapada. Vishvamitra had followed the king; and approached while he was disputing with Shakti. Perceiving, however, the son of his rival Vasishtha, Vishvamitra made himself invisible, and passed them, catching this opportunity. The king began to implore Shakti's clemency; but Vishvamitra wishing to prevent their reconciliation, commanded a Rakshasa (a man-devouring demon) to enter into the king. Owing to the conjoint influence of the Brahman-rishi's curse, and Vishvamitra's command, the demon obeyed the injunction. Perceiving that his object was gained, Vishvamitra left things to take their course, and absented himself from the country. The king having happened to meet a hungry Brahmin, and sent him, by the hand of his cook (who could procure nothing else), some human flesh to eat, was cursed by him also to the same effect as by Shakti. The curse,

[1] Quoted by Muir, Vol. I, pp. 415-417.

being now augmented in force, took effect, and Shakti himself was the first victim, being eaten up by the king. The same fate befell all the other sons of Vasishtha at the instigation of Vishvamitra. Perceiving Shakti to be dead, Vishvamitra again and again incited the Rakshasa against the sons of Vasishtha and accordingly the furious demon devoured those of his sons who were younger than Shakti as a lion eats up the small beasts of the forest. On hearing the destruction of his sons by Vishvamitra, Vasishtha supported his affliction as the great mountain sustains the earth. He meditated his own destruction, but never thought of exterminating the Kaushikas. This divine sage hurled himself from the summit of Meru, but fell upon the rocks as if on a heap of cotton. Escaping alive from his fall, he entered a glowing fire in the forest; but the fire, though fiercely blazing, not only failed to burn him, but seemed perfectly cool. He next threw himself into the sea with a heavy stone attached to his neck; but was cast up by the waves on the dry land. He then went home to his hermitage; but seeing it empty and desolate, he was again overcome by grief and went out; and seeing the river Vipasa which was swollen by the recent rains, and sweeping along many trees torn from its banks, he conceived the design of drowning himself into its waters; he accordingly tied himself firmly with cords, and threw himself in; but the river severing his bonds, deposited him unbound (*Vipasa*) on dry land; whence the name of the stream, as imposed by the sage. He afterwards saw and threw himself into the dreadful Satadru (Sutlej), which was full of alligators, etc., and derived its name rushing away in a hundred directions on seeing the Brahmin brilliant as fire. In consequence of this, he was once more stranded; and seeing that he could not kill himself, he went back to his hermitage."

These are particular instances in which Vasishtha and Vishvamitra had come into conflict with each other. But there was more than these occasional conflicts between the two. There was general enmity between them. This general enmity was of a mortal kind so much so that Vishvamitra wanted even to murder Vasishtha as will be seen from the Shalyaparvan of the Mahabharata. Says the author of the Mahabharata[1] :—

---

[1] Quoted by Muir, Vol. I, pp. 420-422.

"There existed a great enmity, arising from rivalry in their austerities, between Vishvamitra and the Brahmin rishi Vasishtha. Vasishtha had an extensive hermitage in Sthanutirtha, to the east of which was Vishvamitra's. These two great ascetics were every day exhibiting intense emulation in regard to their respective austerities. But Vishvamitra beholding the might of Vasishtha was the most chagrined; and fell into deep thought. The idea of this sage, constant in duty, was the following: 'This river Sarasvati will speedily bring to me on her current the austere Vasishtha, the most eminent of all utterers of prayers. When that most excellent Brahmin has come, I shall most assuredly kill him.' Having thus determined, the divine sage Vishvamitra, his eyes reddened by anger, called to mind the chief of rivers. She being thus the subject of his thoughts became very anxious, as she knew him to be very powerful and very irascible. Then trembling, pallid and with joined hands, the Saraswati stood before the chief of munis like a woman whose husband has been slain; she was greatly distressed, and said to him 'what shall I do?' The incensed muni replied, 'Bring Vasishtha hither speedily, that I may slay him.' The lotus-eyed goddess, joining her hands trembled in great fear, like a creeping plant agitated by the wind. Vishvamitra, however, although he saw her condition, repeated his command. The Sarasvati, who knew how sinful was his design, and that the might of Vasishtha was unequalled, went trembling, and in great dread of being cursed by both the sages, to Vasishtha and told him what his rival had said. Vasishtha seeing her emaciated, pale and anxious, spoke thus, 'Deliver thyself, o chief of rivers; carry me unhesitatingly to Vishvamitra, lest he curse thee.' Hearing these words of the merciful sage, the Sarasvati considered how she could act most wisely. She reflected, 'Vasishtha has always shown me great kindness; I must seek his welfare.' 'Then observing the Kaushika sage praying and sacrificing on her brink, she regarded that as a good opportunity, and swept away the bank by the force of her current. In this way the son of Mitra and Varuna (Vasishtha) was carried down; and while he was being borne along, he thus celebrated the river; 'Thou, o Sarasvati, issuest from the lake of Brahma, and pervadest the whole world with thy excellent streams. Residing in the sky, thou dischargest water into the clouds. Thou alone art all waters. By thee we study.' 'Thou art nourishment, radiance, fame, perfection, intellect, light. Thou art speech; thou art svaha; this world is subject to thee. Thou, in fourfold form, dwellest in all creatures.' Beholding Vasishtha brought near by the Sarasvati, Vishvamitra searched for a weapon with which to make an end of him. Perceiving his anger, and dreading lest Brahmanicide should ensue, the river promptly carried away Vasishtha in an easterly direction thus fulfilling the commands of both sages, but eluding Vishvamitra. Seeing Vasishtha so carried away, Vishvamitra, impatient and enraged by vexation, said to her, 'Since thou, o chief of rivers, hast eluded me, and hast receded, roll in waves of blood acceptable to the chief of demons' (which are fabled to gloat on blood). The Sarasvati being thus cursed, flowed for a year in a stream mingled with blood. Rakshasas came to the place of pilgrimage where Vasishtha had been swept away, and revelled in drinking to satiety the bloody stream in security, dancing and laughing, as if they had conquered heaven. Some rishis who arrived at the spot some time after were horrified to see the blood-stained water, and the Rakshasas quaffing it, and made the most strenuous efforts to rescue the Sarasvati."

The enmity between Vasishtha and Vishvamitra was not an enmity between two priests. It was an enmity between a Brahmin priest and a Kshatriya priest. Vasishtha was a Brahmin. Vishvamitra was a Kshatriya. He was a Kshatriya of royal lineage. In the Rig Veda (iii . 33 . 11) Vishvamitra is spoken of as the son of Kushika. The Vishnu Purana[1] gives further details about Vishvamitra. It says that Vishvamitra was the son of Gadhi who was descended from king Pururavas. This is confirmed by the Harivamsha[2]. From the Rig Veda (iii : 1 : 21) we know that the family of Vishvamitra has been keeping 'fire' kindled in every generation[3]. We also know from the Rig Veda that Vishvamitra was the author of many hymns of that Veda and was admitted to be a Rajarishi He was the author of the hymn which

[1] Quoted in Muir, Vol. I, p. 349.
[2] Quoted in Muir, Vol. I, p. 353.
[3] Quoted in Muir, Vol. I, p. 316.

is held to be the holiest in the whole of the Vedas namely the Gayatri hymn in the Rig Veda (iii . 62 . 10). Another important fact we know about him is that he was a Kshatriya and his family belonged to the clan of the Bharatas[1].

It seems that about this time a dispute was going on between Brahmins and Kshatriyas on the following points:

(1) The right to receive gifts. Gift means payment made without work. The contention of the Brahmins was that nobody could receive gifts. To receive gifts was the right of the Brahmins only[2].

(2) The right to teach the Vedas. The Brahmins' contention was that the Kshatriya had only the right to study the Vedas. He had no right to teach the Vedas. It was the privilege of the Brahmins only.

(3) The right to officiate at a sacrifice. On this point the Brahmins' contention was that the Kshatriya had the right to perform sacrifices, but he had no right to officiate as a purohit (priest) at a sacrifice. That was the privilege of the Brahmins.

What is important to note is that even in disputes on these points and particularly on the third point they did not fail to play their part as the opponents of each other. This is confirmed by the story of Trisanku narrated in the Ramayana[3] and which runs as follows:

"King Trishanku, one of Ikshvaku's descendants, had conceived the design of celebrating a sacrifice by virtue of which he should ascend bodily to heaven. As Vasishtha on being summoned, declared that the thing was impossible (*asakyam*), Trishanku travelled to the south, where the sage's hundred sons were engaged in austerities, and applied to

---

[1] Quoted in Muir, Vol. I, p. 354.

[2] That is why Manu says " if the king wants to make a gift to a Shudra he must make him work."

[3] Muir, Vol. I, pp. 401-404.

them to do what their father had declined. Though he addressed them with the greatest reverence and humility, and added that 'the Ikshvakus regarded their family-priesis as their highest resource in difficulties, and that, after their father, he himself looked to them as his tutelary deities," he received from the haughty priests the following rebuke for his presumption: "Fool, thou hast been refused by thy truth-speaking preceptor. How is it that, disregarding his authority, thou hast resorted to another school (shakha) ? The family-priest is the highest oracle of all the Ikshvakus; and the command of that veracious personage cannot be transgressed. Vasishtha, the divine rishi, has declared that 'the thing cannot be:' and how can we undertake thy sacrifice ? Thou art foolish, king; return to thy capital. The divine (Vasishtha) is competent to act as priest of the three worlds; how can we shew him disrespect ?

Trishanku then gave them to understand, that as his preceptor and "his preceptor's sons had declined compliance with his requests, he should think of some other expedient." In consequence of his venturing to express this presumptuous intention, they condemned him by their imprecation to become a Chandala. As this curse soon took effect, and the unhappy king's form was changed into that of a degraded outcast, he resorted to Vishvamitra (who, as we have seen, was also dwelling at this period in the south), enlarging on his own virtues and piety, and bewailing his fate. Vishvamitra commiscrated his condition and promised to sacrifice on his behalf, and exalt him to heaven in the same Chandala-form to which he had been condemned by his preceptor's curse. 'Heaven is now as good as in thy possession, since thou hast resorted to the son of Kushika.' He then directed that preparations should be made for the sacrifice, and that all the rishis, including the family of Vasishtha, should be invited to the ceremony.

The disciples of Vishvamitra who had conveyed his message, reported the result on their return in these words: "Having heard your message, all the Brahmins are assembling in all the countries, and have arrived, excepting Mahodaya (Vasishtha). Hear what dreadful words those hundred Vasishthas, their voices quivering with rage, have uttered: 'How can the gods and rishis consume the oblation at the sacrifice of that man, especially if he be a Chandala, for whom a Kshatriya is officiating priest ? How can illustrious

Brahmins ascend to heaven, after eating the food of a Chandala, and being entertained by Vishvamitra ?' These ruthless words all the Vasishthas, together with Mahodaya, uttered, their eyes inflamed with anger," Vishvamitra who was greatly incensed on receiving this message, by a curse doomed the sons of Vasishtha to be reduced to ashes, and reborn as degraded outcasts (*mritapah*) for seven hundred births, and Mahodaya to become a Nishada.

"Knowing that this curse had taken effect Vishvamitra then, after eulogizing Trishanku, proposed to the assembled rishis that the sacrifice should be celebrated. To this they assented, being actuated by fear of the terrible sage's wrath. Vishvamitra himself officiated at the sacrifice as Yajaka; and the other rishis as priests (*ritvijah*) (with other functions) performed all the ceremonies."

In this dispute between Vasishtha and Vishvamitra Sudas seems to have played an important part. Vasishtha was the family priest of Sudas. It was Vasishtha who performed his coronation ceremony. It was Vasishtha who helped him to win the battle against the ten kings. Notwithstanding this, Sudas removed Vasishtha from office. In his place he appointed Vishvamitra as his purohita[1] who performed yajna for Sudas. This is the first deed of Sudas which created enmity between Sudas and Vasishtha. There was another deed which Sudas committed which widened and intensified the enmity He threw into fire Shakti the son of Vasishtha and burned him alive. The story is reported in the Satyayana Brahmana[2]. The Satyayana Brahmana does not give the reason for such an atrocious act. Some light is thrown on it by Shadgurusishya[3] in his Commentary on Katyayana's Anukramanika to the Rig Veda. According

[1] There is no direct evidence for this. Tradition accepts this as correct which seems to have been based upon Rig Veda, III. 53. 9. This is confirmed by Yaska in his Nirukta (II. 24) where he says "They then relate a story. The rishi Vishvamitra was the purohita of Sudas, the son of Pijavana."

[2] This is referred to by Sayana in his introduction to Rig Veda, vii. 32 on the authority of the Anukramanika which is quoted by Muir, Vol. I, p. 328.

[3] This is referred to by Sayana in his introduction to verses 15 and 16 of Sukta 53 of the Third Mandal of the Rig Veda, which is quoted by Muir, Vol. I, p. 343.

to Shadgurushishya, a sacrifice was performed by Sudas at which there was a sort of public debate between Vishvamitra and Shakti, the son of Vasishtha and in this debate, to use the words of Shadgurushishya :

> "The power and speech of Vishvamitra were completely vanquished by Shakti, son of Vasishtha ; and the son of Gadhi (Vishvamitra) being so overcome, became dejected."

Here is the reason why Sudas threw Shakti into fire. Obviously, Sudas did it to avenge the dishonour and disgrace caused to Vishvamitra. Nothing could avert a deadly enmity growing up between Sudas and Vasishtha.

This enmity does not seem to have ended with Sudas and Vasishtha. It appears to have spread to their sons. This is supported by the Taittiriya Samhita which says[1] :

> "Vasishtha, when his son had been slain, desired, 'May I obtain offspring ; may I overcome the Saudasas.' He beheld this *ekasmannapanchasa*, he took it and sacrificed with it. In consequence he obtained offspring, and overcame the Saudasas."

This is confirmed by the Kaushitaki Brahmana[2] which says :

> "Vasishtha, when his son had been slain, desired, 'May I be fruitful in offspring and cattle, and overcome the Saudasas.' He beheld this form of offering, the Vasishtha-sacrifice ; and having performed it, he overcame the Saudasas[3]."

II

The conflict between Sudas and Vasishtha is not the only conflict between kings and the Brahmins. The Puranas

---

[1] Muir, Vol. I, p. 328.

[2] *Ibid.*

[3] There seems to be some doubt whether this enmity of Vasishtha had developed against Sudas or against the sons of Sudas. This doubt has arisen because the Satyayana and Kaushitaki Brahmanas speak of Saudasas, thereby suggesting that the quarrel of Vasishtha was with the sons of Sudas and not with Sudas. On the other hand, Manu is definite that it was Sudas who was the offender. Shadgurushishya speaks of Saudasa and not Saudasas while the Brihaddevata in a similar passage gives Sudas. The difficulty could be solved if Saudasas was interpreted to be the family of Sudas, which includes both Sudas and his sons.

record other conflicts also between kings and Brahmins. It is desirable to assemble them here. The first relates to king Vena. The story of his conflict with Brahmins has been told by various authorities. The following account[1] is taken from the Harivamsa :

> " There was formerly a Prajapati (Lord of creatures), a protector of righteousness called Anga, of the race of Atri, and resembling him in power. His son was the Prajapati Vena who was but indifferently skilled in duty, and was born of Sunita, the daughter of Mrityu. This son of the daughter of Kala (Death), owing to the taint derived from his maternal grandfather, threw his duties behind his back, and lived in covetousness under the influence of desire. This king established an irreligious system of conduct ; transgressing the ordinances of the Veda, he was devoted to lawlessness. In his reign men lived without study of the sacred books and without the Vashatkara, and the gods had no Soma-libations to drink at sacrifices. ' No sacrifice or oblation shall be offered '—such was the ruthless determination of that Prajapati, as the time of his destruction approached. 'I,' he declared, ' am the object, and the performer of sacrifice, and the sacrifice itself ; it is to me that sacrifice should be presented, and oblations offered.' This transgressor of the rules of duty, who arrogated to himself what was not his due, was then addressed by all the great rishis headed by Marichi : ' We are about to consecrate ourselves for a ceremony which shall last for many years ; practise not unrighteousness, O Vena ; this is not the eternal rule of duty. Thou art in very deed a Prajapati of Atri's race, and thou hast engaged to protect thy subjects.' The foolish Vena, ignorant of what was right, laughingly answered those great rishis, who had so addressed him ; ' who but myself is the ordainer of duty ? or whom ought I to obey ? Who on earth equals me in sacred knowledge, in prowess, in austere fervour, in truth ? Ye, who are deluded and senseless, know not that I am the source of all beings and duties. Hesitate not to believe that I, if I willed, could burn up the earth, or deluge it with water, or close up heaven and earth.' When owing to his delusion and arrogance Vena could not be governed, then the mighty rishis becoming incensed, seized the vigorous and struggling

[1] Quoted from Muir, Vol. I, p. 302.

king, and rubbed his left thigh. From this thigh, so rubbed, was produced a black man, very short in stature, who, being alarmed, stood with joined hands. Seeing that he was agitated, Atri said to him ' Sit down ' (*nishida*). He became the founder of the race of the Nishadas, and also progenitor of the Dhivaras (fisherman), who sprang from the corruption of Vena."

The next king who came in conflict with the Brahmins was Pururavas. This Pururavas is the son of Ila and grandson of Manu Vaivastava. The details of his conflict with the Brahmins are given in the Adi Parvan of the Mahabharata :[1]

"Subsequently, the wise Pururavas was born of Ila, who, as we have heard, was both his father and his mother. Ruling over the thirteen islands of the ocean, and surrounded by beings who were all superhuman, himself a man of great renown, Pururavas, intoxicated by his prowess, engaged in a conflict with the Brahmins, and robbed them of their jewels, although they loudly remonstrated. Sanatkumara came from Brahma's heaven, and addressed to him an admonition, which, however, he did not regard. Being then straightaway cursed by the incensed rishis, he perished, this covetous monarch, who, through pride of power, had lost his understanding."

The third king in this series in Nahusha. This Nahusha is the grandson of Pururavas, the account of whose conflict with the Brahmins has been recounted above. The story of Nahusha and his conflict with the Brahmins has been told in two places in the Mahabharata, once in the Vanaparvan and again in the Udyogaparvan. The account which follows is taken from the Udyogaparvan.[2] It says :

"After his slaughter of the demon Vritra, Indra became alarmed at the idea of having taken the life of a Brahmin (for Vritra was regarded as such), and hid himself in the waters. In consequence of the disappearance of the king of the gods, all affairs, celestial as well as terrestrial, fell into

[1] Quoted by Muir, Vol. I, p. 307.

[2] Quoted by Muir, Vol. I, pp. 310-313.

confusion. The rishis and gods then applied to Nahusha to be their king. After first excusing himself on the plea of want of power, Nahusha at length, in compliance with their solicitations, accepted the high function. Up to the period of his elevation he had led a virtuous life, but he now became addicted to amusement and sensual pleasure; and even aspired to the possession of Indrani, Indra's wife, whom he had happened to see. The queen resorted to the Angiras Brihaspati, the preceptor of the gods who engaged to protect her. Nahusha was greatly incensed on hearing of this interference; but the gods endeavoured to pacify him, and pointed out the immorality of appropriating another person's wife. Nahusha, however, would listen to no remonstrance, and insisted that in his adulterous designs he was no worse than Indra himself. 'The renowned Ahalya, a rishi's wife, was formerly corrupted by Indra in her husband's lifetime. Why was he not prevented by you? And many barbarous acts, and unrighteous deeds, and frauds were perpetrated of old by Indra; why was he not prevented by you?' The gods, urged by Nahusha, went to bring Indrani; but Brihaspati would not give her up. At his recommendation, however, she solicited Nahusha for some delay, till she should ascertain what had become of her husband. This request was granted. Indrani now went in search of her husband; and by the help of Upashruti (the goddess of night and revealer of secrets) discovered him existing in a very subtle form in the stem of a lotus growing in a lake situated in a continent within an ocean north of the Himalayas. She made known to him the wicked intentions of Nahusha, and entreated him to exert his power, rescue her from danger and resume his dominion. Indra declined any immediate interposition on the plea of Nahusha's superior strength; but suggested to his wife a device by which the usurper might be hurled from his position. She was recommended to say to Nahusha that 'if he would visit her on a celestial vehicle borne by rishis, she would with pleasure submit herself to him.'

The queen of the gods accordingly made this proposal: 'I desire for thee, king of the gods, a vehicle hitherto unknown, such as neither Vishnu nor Rudra, nor the Asuras, nor the Rakshasas employ. Let the eminent rishis, all united, bear thee, lord, in a car; this idea pleases me.' Nahusha receives favourably this appeal to his vanity, and in the course of his reply thus gives utterance to his self-congratulation ; 'He is a personage of no mean prowess who makes the munis his bearers. I am a fervid devotee of great might, Lord of the past, the future, and the present. If I were angry, the world would no longer stand ; on me everything depends. Wherefore, O goddess, I shall, without doubt, carry out what you propose. The seven rishis and all the Brahmin rishis, shall carry me. Behold, beautiful goddess, my majesty and my prosperity."

The narrative goes on :

Accordingly this wicked being, irreligious, violent, intoxicated by the force of conceit, and arbitrary in his conduct, attached to his car the rishis, who submitted to his commands, and compelled them to bear him. Indrani then again resorts to Brihaspati who assures her that vengeance will soon overtake Nahusha for his presumption ; and promises that he will himself perform a sacrifice with a view to the destruction of the oppressor, and the discovery of Indra's lurking place. Agni is then sent to discover and bring Indra to Brihaspati and the latter, on Indra's arrival, informs him of all that had occurred during his absence. While Indra, with Kubera, Yama, Soma and Varuna was devising means for the destruction of Nahusha, the sage Agastya came up, congratulated Indra on the fall of his rival, and proceeded to relate how it had occurred.

Wearied with carrying the sinner, Nahusha, the eminent divine-rishis, and the spotless Brahmin-rishis, asked that divine personage, Nahusha (to solve) a difficulty ; 'Dost thou, O Vasava, most excellent of conquerors, regard as authoritative or not those Brahmana texts which are recited at the immolation of king ?' 'No,' replied Nahusha, whose understanding was enveloped in darkness. The rishis rejoined ; 'Engaged in unrighteousness, thou attainest not unto righteousness ; these texts, which were formerly uttered by great rishis, are regarded by us an authoritative.' Then (proceeds Agastya) disputing with the munis, Nahusha impelled by unrighteousness touched me on the head with his foot. In consequence of this, the king's glory was smitten and his prosperity departed. When he had instantly become agitated and oppressed with fear, I said to him, 'Since thou, a fool, condemnest that sacred text, always held in honour, which has been composed by former sages, and employed by Brahmin-rishis and hast touched my head with thy foot, and employest the Brahma-like and irresistible rishis as bearers to carry thee, therefore, shorn of thy lustre and all thy merit exhausted, sink down, sinner, degraded from heaven to earth. For ten thousand years thou shalt crawl in the form of a huge serpent. When that period is completed, thou shalt again ascend to heaven.' So fell that wicked wretch from the sovereignty of the gods. Happily, O Indra, we shall now prosper, for the enemy of the Brahmins has been smitten. Take possession of the three worlds, and protect their inhabitants, O husband of Shachi (Indrani), subduing the senses, overcoming thine enemies, and celebrated by the great rishis."

The fourth king to come into conflict with the Brahmins was Nimi. The details of the story are related in the Vishnu Purana[1] which says:

"Nimi had requested the Brahmin-rishi, Vasishtha to officiate at a sacrifice, which was to last a thousand years. Vasishtha in reply pleaded a pre-engagement to Indra for five hundred years, but promised to return at the end of that period. The king made no remark, and Vasishtha went away, supposing that he had assented to his arrangement. On his return, however, the priest discovered that Nimi had retained Gautama (who was, equally with Vasishtha, a Brahmin-rishi) and others to perform the sacrifice; and being incensed at the neglect to give him notice of what was intended, he cursed the king, who was then asleep, to lose his corporeal form. When Nimi awoke and learnt that he had been cursed without any previous warning, he retorted by uttering a similar curse on Vasishtha, and then died. Nimi's body was embalmed. At the close of the sacrifice which he had begun, the gods were willing, on the intercession of the priests, to restore him to life; but he declined the offer; and was placed by the deities, according to his desire, in the eyes of all living creatures. It is in consequence of this that they are always opening and shutting (*Nimisha* means 'the twinkling of the eye')."

These foregoing cases of conflict have been referred to by Manu in his Smriti:[2]

"Through a want of modesty many kings have perished,

---

[1] Quoted by Muir, Vol. I, p. 316.

[2] Max Muller's 'Sacred Books of the East,' Vol. XXV, p. 222.

together with their belongings ; through modesty even hermits in the forest have gained kingdoms.

Through a want of humility Vena perished, likewise king Nahusha, Sudas, the son of Pijavana, Sumukha, and Nimi."

Unfortunately, the bearing of these cases on the position of the Shudra has not been realized as fully as it should have been. The reason is that nobody has realized that this conflict was a conflict between Brahmins and Shudras. Sudas definitely was a Shudra. The others although they have not been described as Shudras are described as having been descended from Ikshvaku. Sudas is also described as a descendant of Ikshvaku. There is nothing far-fetched in saying that they were all Shudras. Even Manu had no idea of this. He represents these cases as cases of conflict between Brahmins and Kshatriyas. Dr. Muir has failed to realize that Sudas was a Shudra and has in recounting these stories represented that the parties to these conflicts were Brahmins on the one hand and the Kshatriyas on the other. In a sense, it is true that the conflict was between Brahmins and Kshatriyas because the Shudras were also a branch of the Kshatriyas. It would, however, have been far more illuminating if they had been described in more precise terms as conflicts between Brahmins and Shudras. The misunderstanding having been caused, it has remained and has continued to conceal the real nature of so important a part of the history of the Indo-Aryan society. It is to clear this misunderstanding that the heading given to this Chapter is 'Brahmins *versus* Shudras' and not 'Brahmins *versus* Kshatriyas.' Understood as a history of conflict between Brahmins and Shudras, it helps one to understand how the Shudras came to be degraded from the second to the fourth Varna.

CHAPTER X

THE DEGRADATION OF THE SHUDRAS

WHAT is the technique which the Brahmins employed to bring about the degradation of the Shudras from the rank of the second to the rank of the fourth Varna?

The discussion has so far centred round two questions as to whether or not the Shudras were originally a part of the second or Kshatriya Varna and whether or not the Brahmins had not received sufficient provocation to degrade the Shudras. It is now necessary to deal with the question, which is logically next in order of sequence. What is the technique of degradation employed by the Brahmins?

My answer to the question is that the technique employed by the Brahmins for this purpose was to refuse to perform the Upanayana of the Shudras. I have no doubt that it is by this technique that the Brahmins accomplished their end and thereby wreaked their vengeance upon the Shudras.

It is perhaps necessary to explain what Upanayana means and what importance it had in the Indo-Aryan Society. The best way to give an idea of Upanayana is to give a description of the ceremony.

As a rite *Upanayana* was originally a very simple ceremony. The boy came to the teacher with a *samidh* (a grass blade) in his hand and told the teacher that he desired to become a Brahmachari (i.e. a student) and begged the teacher to allow him to stay with him for purposes of study. At a later date it became a very elaborate ceremony. How elaborate it had become may be realised from the following description of *Upanayana* in the Ashvalayana Grihya sutra[1] :

"Let him initiate the boy who is decked, whose hair (on the head) is shaved (and arranged), who wears a new garment or an antelope skin if a Brahmana, ruru skin if a Kshatriya, a goat's skin if a Vaishya ; if they put on garments they should put on dyed ones, reddish-yellow, red and yellow (for a Brahmana, Kshatriya, Vaishya respectively); they should have girdles and staffs (as described above). While the boy takes hold of (the hand of) his teacher, the latter offers (a homa of clarified butter oblations) in the fire (as described above), and seats himself to the north of the fire with his face turned to the east, while the other one (the boy) stations himself in front (of the teacher) with his face turned to the west. The teacher then fills the folded hands of both himself and of the boy with water and with the verse 'we choose that of Savitri (Rg. V. 82 . I) the teacher drops down the water in his own folded hands on to the water in the folded hands of the boy ; having thus poured the water, he should seize with his own hand the boy's hand together with the thumb (of the boy) with the formula 'by the urge (or order) of the god Savitri, with the arms of the two Ashvins, with the hands of Pushan, I seize thy hand, oh so and so'; with the words 'Savitri has seized thy hand, oh so and so' a second time (the teacher seizes the boy's hand) with the words 'Agni is thy teacher, oh so and so' a third time. The teacher should cause (the boy, to look at the sun, while the teacher repeats 'God Savitri, this is thy brahmachari protect him, may he not die' and (the teacher should further) say 'Whose brahmachari art thou ? thou art the brahmachari of Prana. Who does initiate thee and whom (does he initiate) ? I give thee to Ka (to Prajapati).' With the half verse (Rg. III . 8 . 4) 'the young man well attired and dressed, came hither' he (the teacher) should cause him to turn round to the right and with his two hands placed over (the boy's) shoulders he should touch the place of the boy's heart repeating the latter half (of Rg. III . 8 . 4). Having wiped the ground round the fire, the brahmachari should put (on the fire) a fuel stick silently, since it is known (from sruti) 'what belongs to Prajapati is silently done,' and the brahmachari belongs to Prajapati. Some do this (offering of a fuel stick) with a mantra to Agni :

---

[1] Kane, History of Dharmashastra, Vol. II (i), pp. 281-283.

'I have brought a fuel stick, to the great Jatavedas; by the fuel stick mayst thou increase, Oh Agni and may we (increase) through *brahman* (prayer or spiritual lore), svaha.' Having put the fuel stick (on the fire) and having touched the fire, he (the student) thrice wipes off his face with the words 'I anoint myself with lustre,' it is known (from sruti) for he does anoint himself with lustre. 'May Agni bestow on me, insight, offspring and lustre; on me may Indra bestow insight, offspring and vigour (Indriya); on me may the sun bestow insight, offspring and radiance; what thy lustre is, Oh Agni, may I thereby become lustrous; what thy strength is, Agni, may I thereby become strong; what thy consuming power is, Agni, may I thereby acquire consuming power.' Having waited upon (worshipped) Agni with these formulæ, (the student) should bend his knees, embrace (the teacher's feet) and say to him 'recite, Sir, recite, Sir, the Savitri.' Seizing the student's hands with the upper garment (of the student) and his own hands, the teacher recites the Savitri first pada by pada, then hemistich by hemistich (and lastly) the whole verse. He (the teacher) should make him (the student) recite (the Savitri) as much as he is able. On the place of the student's heart the teacher lays his hand with the fingers upturned with the formula 'I place thy heart unto duty to me, may thy mind follow my mind; may you attend on my words single-minded; may Brihaspati appoint thee unto me.' Having tied the girdle round him (the boy) and having given him the staff, the teacher should instruct him in the observances of a brahmachari with the words 'a brahmachari art thou, sip water, do service, do not sleep by day, depending (completely) on the teacher learn the Veda.' He (the student) should beg (food) in the evening and the morning; he should put a fuel stick (on fire) in the evening and morning. That (which he has received by begging) he should announce to the teacher; he should not sit down (but should be standing) the rest of the day."

The Upanayana ends with the teaching by the Acharya to the boy of the Vedic Mantra known as the Gayatri Mantra. Why the Gayatri Mantra is regarded as so essential as to require the ceremony of Upanayana before it is taught it is difficult to say.

From this description of the Upanayana ceremony two things are clear. First is that the purpose of Upanayana was to initiate a person in the study of the Vedas which commenced with the teaching of the Gayatri Mantra by the Acharya to the Brahmachari. The second thing that is clear is that certain articles were regarded as very essential for the Upanayana ceremony. They are (1) two garments one for the lower part of the body technically called *Vasa* and the other for the upper part of the body called *uttariya,* (2) Danda or wooden staff, (3) Mekhala or a girdle of grass tied across the waist.

Any one who compares this description of Upanayana as it was performed in ancient times with the details of the ceremony as performed in later days is bound to be surprised at the absence of any mention of thread called *Yajnopavita* to be worn by the Brahmachari as a part of his Upanayana. The centre of the modern ceremony of Upanayana is the wearing of this thread and the whole purpose of the Upanayana has come to be the wearing of this *Yajnopavita.*[1] So important a part this *Yajnopavita* has come to play that most elaborate rules have come to be framed about its manufacture and its use.

The *Yajnopavita* should have three threads, each thread to be of nine strands well twisted. One *tantu* (strand) stands for one devata (deity).

The *Yajnopavita* should reach as far as the navel,[2] should not reach beyond the navel, nor should it be above the chest.

A person could wear more than one *Yajnopavita.*

---

[1] Yajnavalkya (I, 16 and 133) calls it Bramha Sutra.

[2] Kane, D.S., II (1), p. 292.

The nine devatas of the nine *tantus* (strands) according to the Devala Smriti are, Omkara, Agni, Naga, Sema, Pitris, Prajapati, Vayu, Surya, Vishvedeva. Some change seems to have come about in this view. For Medhatithi (see Kane) says that in *ishtis,* animal sacrifices and soma sacrifices, the Yajnopavita was to have only one thread of three *tantus,* but it was three-fold in three classes of *ahina, ekaha* and *sattra* sacrifices as they required three fires, and in the seven *som*[illegible]

A man must always wear *Yajnopavita.* If he took his meals without wearing the *Yajnopavita,* or answers the call of nature without having the *Yajnopavita* placed on the right ear, he had to undergo prayascitta, viz., to bathe, to mutter prayers and fast.

Wearing of another's *Yajnopavita* along with several other things (such as shoes, ornament, garland and kamandalu) is forbidden.[1]

Three ways of wearing the *Yajnopavita* are recognized: (1) nivita, (2) pracinavita and (3) upavita. When the cord is carried over the neck, both shoulders and the chest and is held with both the thumbs (of the two hands) lower than the region of the heart and above the navel, it is called *nivita.* Suspending the cord over the left shoulder in such a way that it hangs down on his right side, it becomes *upavita.* Suspending it on his right shoulder in such a way that it hangs down on his left side, it becomes *pracinavita.*

How did this *Yajnopavita* come in? Mr. Tilak offers an explanation[2] which is worth quoting. Mr. Tilak says:—

> "Orion or Mrigashiras is called Prajapati in the Vedic works, otherwise called Yajna. A belt or girdle of cloth round the waist of Orion or Yajna will therefore be naturally named after him as *Yajnopavita,* the *upavita* or the cloth of yajna. The term, however, now denotes the sacred thread of the Brahmins, and it may naturally be asked whether it owes its character, if not the origin, to the belt of Orion. I think it does on the following grounds:
>
> The word yajnopavita is derived by all native scholars from *Yajna* + *upavita;* but there is a difference of opinion

seven-fold, and five-fold when viewed with reference to the three savanas and two samdhyas.

A brahmachari was to wear only one yajnopavita, and samnyasins, when they kept yajnopavita at all, also wore only one. A snataka (i.e., one who has returned from the teacher's house after brahmacharya) and householder were to wear two, while one who desired long life may wear more than two. A snataka should always wear two yajnopavitas. A householder may wear any number up to ten.

[1] Kane, *ibid,* p. 293.

[2] Orion, pp. 144-146.

as to whether we should understand the compound to mean an *upavita* for *yajna* i.e. for sacrificial purposes, or, whether it is the 'upavita of Yajnas.' The former is not incorrect, but authority is in favour of the latter. Thus the Prayoga-writers quote a *smriti* to the effect that 'the High Soul is termed *Yajna* by the hotris; this is his *upavita*; therefore it is *yajna-upavita*.' A mantra, which is recited on the occasion of wearing the sacred thread means, 'I bind you with the *upavita* of *yajna*'; while the first half of the general formula with which a Brahmin always puts on his sacred thread is as follows :—

यज्ञोपवीतं परमंपवित्रं प्रजापतेर्यत्सहजं पुरस्तात्।

"The Mantra is not to be found in any of the existing Samhitas, but is given in the Brahmopanishad and by Baudhayana. This verse is strikingly similar to the verse quoted above from the Haoma Yesht. It says, 'yajnopavita is high and sacred; it was born with Prajapati, of old.' The word *purastat* corresponds with *paurvanim* in the Avesta verse and thus decides the question raised by Dr. Haug, while *sahaja*, born with the limbs of Prajapati, conveys the same meaning as *mainyutastem*. The coincidence between these verses cannot be accidental, and it appears to me that the sacred thread must be derived from the belt of Orion. Upavita, from *ve* to weave, literally means a piece of cloth and not a thread. It appears, therefore, that a cloth worn round the waist was the primitive form of *yajnopavita*, and that the idea of sacredness was introduced by the theory that it was to be a symbolic representation of Prajapati's waist-cloth or belt."

This explanation by Mr. Tilak is no doubt very interesting. But it does not help to explain some of the difficulties. It does not explain the relation of the *Yajnopavita* to the two garments, the *Uttariya*, and the *vasa*, which are necessary for a person to wear while undergoing *Upanayana*. Was the *Yajnopavita* in addition to the two garments ? If so, how is it that there is no mention of it in the early description of the ceremony of the *Upanayana*? It does not explain another difficulty. If the thread is a substitute for the cloth, how is it that the wearing of the cloth is retained in the *Upanayana?*

There seems to be another explanation. I offer it for what it is worth. According to it, the wearing of the thread had to do with the adoption of the *gotra.* Its object was to tie oneself to a particular *gotra.* It had nothing to do with the *Upanayana* as such, the object of which was to initiate a person in the study of the Vedas. It is not sufficiently realized that under the Ancient Aryan Law, a son did not naturally inherit the *gotra* of his father. The father had to perform a special ceremony to give his *gotra* to his son. It is only when this ceremony was performed that the son became of the same *gotra* as the father. In this connection, reference may be made to two rules observed by the Indo-Aryan Society. One is the rule of impurities. The other is the rule of adoption. With regard to the rule of impurity, brought about by death, the days of impurity vary with the kinship with the dead. If the kinship is very close, the days of impurity are greater than those in the case where the kinship is less close. The impurities attached to the death of a boy who has not been invested with the thread are very meagre,[1] not extending for more than a few days. With regard to the rule of adoption,[2] it lays down that a boy who was invested with the thread was not eligible for adoption. What is the idea behind these rules? The idea seems to be quite clear. The impurities are nominal because there being no thread, the boy had not formally entered into the *gotra* of his father. Adoption means entering into the *gotra* of the adoptive father. Once the thread ceremony had taken place, the boy had already and irrevocably entered another *gotra.* There was no room for adoption left. Both these rules show that the

[1] See Manu Smriti, Chapter V, Verses 66-70.

[2] Kalikapurana quoted by Vyavahara Mayukha, edited by Kane, p. 114. This plea has been taken in various cases in Courts by litigants to which Mr. Kane makes ref re o

thread ceremony was connected with *gotra* and not with *Upanayana*.

The view that the thread has connection with *gotra* seems to receive support from Jain literature. Shloka 87 of the fourth Parvan of the Padmapurana by Acharya Ravishena reads as follows :[1]

> "Bhagwan ! you have told us the origin of Kshatriya, Vaishya and Shudra. I am anxious to know the origin of those who wear the thread in their neck."

The words 'those who wear the thread in the neck' are very important. There is no doubt that it is a description of the Brahmins. From this it is clear that there was a time when the Brahmins alone wore the thread and no other class did. Read with the fact that the *gotra* relationship was confined only to the Brahmins, it is clear that the thread ceremony was connected with bringing the boy into—actually tying him up to the *gotra*—of his father, and had nothing to do with *Upanayana* which was connected with the initiation in the teaching of the Vedas.

If this is true, then the thread ceremony and the *Upanayana* ceremony had different purposes to serve. At some later date the two merged into one. The reason for this merger appears to be very natural. The *Upanayana* without the thread ceremony involved the danger of the Acharya taking the boy in his *gotra*. It was to avoid the danger that the father of the boy performed the thread ceremony before handing him over to the Acharya. This is the probable reason why the two ceremonies came to be performed simultaneously.

Be that as it may, *Upanayana* means the teaching of the Veda by the Vedic Brahmin.

III

While I am convinced that my thesis is sound, it would be over confident to think that there will not be found

[1] Quoted by Nathuram Promi in his *Jain Sahitya aur Itihas* (Hindi), p. 55a.

persons who will not raise objections to it. I anticipate the following :

(1) Is absence of *Upanayana* the test of Shudradom ;
(2) Did the Shudra ever have the right to *Upanayana?*
(3) How can the loss of *Upanayana* result in the general degradation of Shudras ?
(4) What power did the Brahmins have to deny *Upanayana* to the Shudras ?

Having stated the possible objections to my thesis, I like to give my reply to them.

IV

To begin with the first. The best way to deal with this objection is to refer to the judicial decisions in order to find out what the Courts in India have regarded as the surest criterion for determining who is a Shudra.

The first case to which reference may be made is to be found in 7, M.I.A. 18.[1] It was decided by the Privy Council in 1837. The question at issue was whether at the relevant time there were in India any Kshatriyas. The contention of one side was that there were. The contention on the other side was that there were none. The latter contention was based upon the theory propagated by the Brahmins that the Brahmin Parashurama had killed all the Kshatriyas and that if any were left they were all exterminated by the Shudra king Mahapadma Nanda, so that thereafter there were no Kshatriyas left and that there were only Brahmins and Shudras. The Privy Council did not accept this theory which they regarded as false and concocted by the Brahmins and held that the Kshatriyas still existed in India. The Privy Council did not however lay down any test by which a Kshatriya could be distinguished from a Shudra. In

[1] Chuohirya Run Murdan Syn *vs.* Sahub Purhulad Syn.

their view, the question must be determined in each case on its own facts.

The second case on the subject is to be found in I.L.R. 10 Cal. 688[1]. The question raised in the case was whether the Kayasthas of Bihar were Kshatriyas or Shudras. The High Court decided that they were Shudras. The partisans of the Kayasthas took the position that the Kayasthas of Bihar were different from the Kayasthas of Bengal, the Upper Provinces and Benares and that while those in the Upper Provinces and Benares were Shudras, the Kayasthas of Bihar were Kshatriyas. The court refused to make this distinction and held that the Kayasthas of Bihar were also Shudras.

The validity of this judgment was not accepted by the Allahabad High Court. In I.L.R. 12 All. 328[2], Justice Mahmood at page 334 observed as follows :—

> " I entertain considerable doubts as to the soundness of the view which seems to have been adopted by both the Courts below, that the literary caste of *Kayasthas* in this part of the country, to which the parties belong, falls under the category of *Shudras*, as understood in the division of mankind in the Institute of Manu or elsewhere in authoritative texts of the Hindu Law. The question is one of considerable difficulty not only ethnologically, but also from a legal point of view, so far as the administration of the Hindu Law to this important section of the population is concerned. I do not take the question to be settled by any adjudication of the Lords of the Privy Council either in *Sri Narayan Mitter* vs. *Sree Mutty Kishen Soondoory Dassee*[3], or in *Mahashova Shosinath Ghose* vs. *Srimati Krishna Soondari Dasi*[4], in both of which the cases referred to adoption by *Kayasthas* of Lower Bengal, who may be distinguishable from the twelve castes of Kayasthas in Upper India, such as the North-western Provinces and Oudh. Nor do I think that the unreported decision of the learned Chief Justice and my brother Tyrell in *Chaudhri Hazari Lal* versus *Bishnu Dial* (First Appeal No. 118 of 1886,

---

[1] Raj Coomar Lall *versus* Bissessur Dyal.

[2] Tulsi Ram *versus* Behari Lal.

[3] L.R.I.A. Sup., Vol. 149.

[4] L.R. 7, I.A., 250.

decided on the 15th of June 1887), which was also an adoption case, settles the question. But I need not pursue the subject any further. . . . "

The third case is reported in (1916) 20 Cal. W.N. 901[1]. Here the question raised was whether *Kayasthas* of Bengal were Kshatriyas or Shudras. The High Court of Calcutta held that they were Shudras. The case was taken to the Privy Council by way of appeal against the decision of the Calcutta High Court. The decision of the Privy Council is reported in (1926) 47 I.A. 140. The question whether the Bengali Kayasthas are Shudras or Kshatriyas was not decided upon by the Privy Council but was left open. In between 1916 and 1926 the Calcutta High Court gave two decisions which held that inter-marriages between Kayasthas of Bengal and *Tantis*[2] and *Domes*[3] two of the low castes, were legal on the ground that both of them were sub-castes of Shudras.

These decisions which caused further deterioration in the position of the Kayasthas were followed by another which is reported in I.L.R. 6 Patna 506[4]. In a most elaborate judgment extending over 47 pages Mr. Justice Jwala Prasad went into every Purana and every Smriti in which there was a reference to the Kayasthas. He differed from the Calcutta High Court and held that the Kayasthas of Bihar were Kshatriyas.

Next come cases in which the question at issue was whether the Mahrattas are Kshatriyas or Shudras. The first case in which this issue was raised is reported in 48 Mad. 1[5]. This was an interpleader suit filed by the Receiver of the estate of Raja of Tanjore in which all the descendants as well as the distant agnates and cognates of the Raja were made defendants in the suit. The

---

1 Asita Mohan Ghosh *versus* Nirod Mohan Ghosh Maulik.

2 (1921) 48 Cal. 626. Bishwanath Ghosh *versus* Srimati Balai Dasai.

3 (1924) 51 Cal. 788. Bholanath Mitter *versus* King Emperor.

4 (1926) Ishwari Prasad *versus* Rai Hari Prasad Lal.

5 (1924) Maharaja of Kolhapur *versus* Sundaram Ayyar.

kingdom of Tanjore was founded by Venkoji, otherwise called Ekoji, who was a Mahratta and the brother of Shivaji the founder of the Mahratta Empire. The judgment in the case covers 229 pages and the question whether Mahrattas were Kshatriyas was dealt with in a most exhaustive manner. The decision of the Madras High Court was that the Mahrattas were Shudras and not Kshatriyas as was contended by the defendants.

The next case which also relates to the Mahrattas is reported in I.L.R. (1928) 52 Bom. 497[1]. The Court decided that:

> "There are three classes among the Mahratthas in the Bombay Presidency: (1) the five families; (2) the ninety-six families; (3) the rest. Of these, the first two classes are legally Kshatriyas."

The last case to which reference may be made is reported in I.L.R. (1927) 52 Mad. 1[2]. The issue was whether the Yadavas of Madura were Kshatriyas. The Yadavas claimed themselves to be Kshatriyas. But the Madras High Court negatived the claim and held that they were Shudras.

Such is the course of judicial pronouncements on the issue as to how to determine who is a Kshatriya and who is a Shudra. It is a most confusing medley of opinion which settles little and unsettles much. The Kayasthas of Bihar, of the Upper Provinces (now U.P.) and Benares are Kshatriyas, while the Kayasthas of Bengal are Shudras!! According to the Madras High Court all Mahrattas are Shudras. But according to the Bombay High Court, Mahrattas belonging to five families and 96 families are Kshatriyas and the rest are Shudras!! The Yadava community to which Krishna belonged is popularly believed to be Kshatriyas. But according to the Madras High Court, the Yadavas are Shudras!!

---

[1] Subbarao Hambirao Patil *versus* Radha Hambirao Patil.

[2] Mokka Kone *versus*. A[illegible]

More important for our purpose are the criteria which the courts have adopted in coming to their decisions than the particular decisions in the cases referred to. Among the criteria which the courts have laid down, the following may be noted :

(1) In I.L.R. 10 Cal. 688, the criteria adopted were (*i*) use of *Das* as surname, (*ii*) wearing the sacred thread, (*iii*) ability to perform the *homa*, (*iv*) the period of impurity, (*v*) competence or incompetence of illegitimate sons to succeed.

(2) In I.L.R. 6 Patna 606, the criterion seems to be general repute. If a community is Kshatriya by general repute it is to be treated as a Kshatriya community.

(3) In 48 Madras 1, a variety of criteria were adopted. One was the consciousness of the community. The second was undergoing the ceremony of *Upanayana* as distinguished from wearing the sacred thread. The third criterion was that all non-Brahmins are Shudras unless they prove that they are Kshatriyas or Vaishyas.

(4) In I.L.R. Bom. 497, the tests adopted were (*i*) the consciousness of the caste, (*ii*) its custom, and (*iii*) the acceptance of that consciousness by other castes.

No one who knows anything about the subject can say that the criteria adopted by the various courts are the right ones. A criterion such as the period of impurity is irrelevant and of no value for determining the question. A criterion such as the capacity for performing *homa* is relevant but not valid. It mistakes effect for a cause. The criterion of consciousness is hardly a fair criterion. A community may have lost its consciousness by long disuse of necessary religious observances due to causes over which it has no control. The criterion of *Upanayana* stands on a different footing. The courts have not put it properly. But there is no doubt that rightly understood and properly put the criterion of *Upanayana* is sound. The courts have not made any distinction between the *de facto* position of the community and its position *de jure* in regard to *Upanayana*, and have proceeded on the assumption that what is true *de facto* must also be true *de jure*. It is this fault in the application of the criterion of *Upanayana* which has produced anomalies and absurdities, such as one community having one status in one area and quite a different status in a different area—or allowing any pretender community to wear the thread and by continuing its pretence for a period to acquire a vested right, or contrariwise punishing a community by declaring that it had no *de jure* right to wear the thread merely because it has not been wearing it *de facto*. The real criterion is not the wearing of the sacred thread but the right to wear the sacred thread. Understood in its proper sense, it may be said without fear of contradiction that the right to *Upanayana* is the real and the only test of judging the status of a person whether he is a Shudra or a Kshatriya.

V

The second objection is quite untenable. To assume, as the objection does, that from the very beginning the Aryan Society treated its different classes differently in the matter of *Upanayana* is to my mind a very unnatural supposition. Primitive society does not begin with differentiation. It begins with uniformity and ends in diversity. The natural thing would be to suppose that in the matter of the *Upanayana* the ancient Aryan society treated all its classes on the same footing. It may however be argued, on the other side, that such an original tendency in favour of uniformity need not be accepted as being universal, that it may well be that in the ancient Aryan society the Shudras and the women were excluded from

Upanayana. Fortunately for me, it is not necessary for me to rely on logic alone though I contend that logic is on my side. For there is ample evidence both circumstantial as well as direct to show that both Shudras as well as women had at one time the right to wear the sacred thread.

That the ancient Aryan society regarded *Upanayana* as essential for all will be evident if the following facts are borne in mind.

Upanayana was allowed for the deaf, the dumb, the idiot and even the impotent. A special procedure was prescribed for the *Upanayana* of the deaf and dumb and idiots. The principal points in which their *Upanayana* differs from that of others are that the offering of *Samidh*, treading on a stone, putting on a garment, the tying of *mekhala*, the giving of deer skin and staff are done silently, that the boy does not mention his name, it is the *acharya* himself who makes offering of cooked food or of clarified butter, all the *mantras* are muttered softly by the *acharya* himself. The same procedure is followed as to other persons who are impotent, blind, lunatic, suffering from such diseases as epilepsy, white leprosy or black leprosy, etc.

The six *anuloma* castes were also eligible for *Upanayana*; this is clear from the rules[1] for the *Upanayana* of Kshatriyas, Vaishyas and of mixed castes like Rathakara, Ambashtha, etc.

Upanayana was permitted to *Patitasavitrikas*. The proper age for the *Upanayana* of a Brahman boy was 8th year from birth, of a Kshatriya 11th year and of a Vaishya 12th year. But a certain latitude was allowed so that the time for *Upanayana* was not deemed to have passed upon the 16th, the 22nd and the 24th year in the case of Brahmins, Kshatriyas and Vaishyas respectively. After these years are passed without *Upanayana* taking place,

[1] Baud. Gr. Sutra (II.8), Kane: History of Dharmashastra, II (1), p. 299.

a person was held to have become incompetent thereafter for learning the Savitri (the sacred Gayatri verse). Such persons were then called *patitasavitrika* or *savitripatita.* According to the strict interpretation of rules, no *Upanayana* is to be thereafter performed for them, they are not to be taught the Veda, nor is anyone to officiate at their sacrifices and there is to be no social intercourse with them (i.e., no marriage takes place with them). But even in their case, there was readiness to relax the rules[1] subject to certain penances.

Upanayana was permitted in the case of Brahmaghnas. A Brahmaghna is a person whose father or grandfather had failed to perform Upanayana. The original rule[2] was that if a person's father and grandfather also had not the Upanayana performed for them then they (i.e., the three generations) are called slayers of *brahma* (holy prayers or lore); people should have no intercourse with them, should not take their food nor should enter into marriage alliance with them. But even in their case the rule was relaxed and they were allowed Upanayana if they desired, provided they performed the prescribed penance.

---

[1] Ap. Dh. S., I. 1. 1. 28-31, prescribes that after the 16th or 24th year, the person should undergo the rules of studenthood two months just as those who meant to study the three vedas and whose Upanayana has been performed, observe (viz., begging for food, etc.), then his Upanayana should be performed, then for one year he should bathe (thrice if possible) every day and then he should be taught the Veda. This is a somewhat easy penance. But others prescribe heavier penalties. Vas. Dh. S. XI, 76-79 and the Vaik. Smarta, 11. 3 prescribes that one who is *patitasavitrika* should either perform the Uddalaka vrata or should take a bath along with the performer of an Ashvamedha sacrifice or should perform the Vratyastoma sacrifice. See Kane, *ibid,* p. 377.

[2] Ap. Dh.S., I.1.1.32-2.4 The penance prescribed was that of observing the rules of studenthood one year for each generation (that had not the Upanayana performed), then there is Upanayana and then they have to bathe (thrice or once) every day for a year with certain mantras, viz., the seven Pavamani verses beginning with 'yad anti yacca durake' (Rg. IX. 67. 21-27) with the Yajus Pavitra (Tai. S., I. 2. 1. 1=Rg. X. 17. 10) with the *samapavitra* and with the mantra called Angirasa (Rg. IV. 40. 5) or one may pour water only with the Vyahritis. After all this is done, one may be taught the Veda. See Kane, *ibid,* p. 378.

A further relaxation was made in the case of a person whose generation beginning with the great grandfather had not the Upanayana performed on them.[1] Even they were allowed to have their Upanayana performed if they desired, provided they performed penance which included studenthood for twelve years and bath with the Pavamani, and other verses. On his Upanayana, instruction in the duties of the householder was imparted to him, and though he himself could not be taught the Veda, his son may have the samskara performed as in the case of one who is himself a *patitasavitrika* so that his son will be 'one like other Arya.'

Upanayana was permitted to the Vratyas. It is difficult to state exactly who the Vratyas were, whether they were Aryans who had for more than three generations failed to perform the Upanayana or whether they were non-Aryans who were never within the Aryan fold and whom the Brahmins wanted to convert to the Aryan faith. It is possible that it included both. Be that as it may, there is no doubt that Upanayana was open to the Vratyas provided they performed Vratyastomas. Vratyas were those who lead the Vratya life, were base and were reduced to a baser state since they did not observe studenthood (brahmacharya) nor did they till the soil nor engage in trade. There were four vratyastomas, the first of which is meant for all Vratyas, the second is meant for those who are *Abhishasta* who are wicked or guilty of heavy sins and are censured and lead a Vratya life, the third for those who are the youngest and lead a Vratya life, and the fourth for those who are very old and yet lead a Vratya life. In each of the four Vratyastomas, Sodasastoma[2] is always performed. It is by the Sodasastoma that they

---

[1] Ap. Dh. S.,I. 1 . 2. 5-10.

[2] Kane (*ibid*, p. 385) refers to the Tandya Brahmana 17.1.1 which tells the story that when the gods went to the heavenly world some dependents of theirs who lived the *vratya* life were left behind on the earth. Then through the favour of the gods the dependents got at the hands of Maruts the Sodasastoma (containing 16 stotras) and the metre (viz., anustubh) and then the dependents secured heaven.

can attain this (superior status). The Sodasastoma was supposed to have the power to remove the guilt of these. By performing the Vratyastoma sacrifice, they should cease to be Vratyas and become eligible for social intercourse with the orthodox Aryas, to have the sacrament (samskara of Upanayana) performed of them and then be eligible to study the Veda.

In the Vratyata-shuddisamgraha[1] provision is made for the purification of Vratyas even after twelve generations subject to appropriate penances.

Upanayana was so highly thought of that Baudhayana (ii . 10) allowed Upanayana for the Asvattha tree.

Given these facts, it is difficult to believe that the women and Shudras were excluded from the Upanayana by the Aryan society from the very beginning. In this connection, attention may be drawn to custom prevalent among the Indo-Iranians who were very closely related to the Indo-Aryans in their culture and religion. Among the Indo-Iranians, not only both men and women but men and women of all classes are invested with the sacred thread. It is for the opponents to prove why the system was different among the Indo-Aryans.

It is, however, not quite necessary to depend upon circumstantial evidence. There is enough direct evidence to show that there was a time when both women and Shudras had the right to Upanayana and did have it performed.

As to the Upanayana of women the statements[2] contained in the Hindu religious books are quite explicit. Anyone who examines them will find that Upanayana was open to women. Women not only learned the Vedas but they used to run schools for teaching the Vedas, are even known to have written commentaries on the Women Purva Mimamsa.

---

[1] Kane, *ibid*, p. 387.

[2] See Purushartha Number for September 1940 where all authorities are collected in one place.

As to the Shudras, the evidence is equally positive. If Sudas was a king, if Sudas was a Shudra, if his coronation ceremony was performed by Vasishtha and if he performed the Rajasuya Yaga, then there can be no doubt that the Shudras did at one time wear the sacred thread. In addition to circumstantial evidence and the evidence of the authors mentioned before, the Sanskara Ganapati cited by Max Muller[1] contains an express provision declaring the Shudra to be eligible for Upanayana.

The only difference between the women and the Shudras is that in the case of women there is some plausible explanation given as to why the Upanayana of women was stopped, while there is no such explanation for stopping the Upanayana of the Shudras. It is argued that the Upanayana of women continued as long as the age of Upanayana and the age of marriage continued to be different. It is said that in ancient times the age of Upanayana was 8 and the age for marriage was considerably later. But at a later stage, the age of marriage was brought down to 8, with the result that the Upanayana as an independent ceremony ceased to exist and became merged in marriage. Whether this explanation is right or wrong is another matter. The point is that in the case of the Shudra, the Upanayana was at one time open to him, that it was closed to him at a later stage and that there is no explanation for this change.

Those who, in spite of the evidence to which I have referred, think that they must insist upon their objection should remember the weakness of their side. Assuming that the Shudras had never had the benefit of Upanayana, the question they have to face is why were the Shudras not allowed the benefit of the Upanayana. The orthodox theory merely states the fact that there is no Upanayana for a Shudra. But it does not say why the Shudra is not to have his Upanayana performed. The explanation

[1] History of Ancient Sanskrit Literature (1860), p. 207.

that there was no Upanayana of the Shudra because he was a non-Aryan is a modern invention which has been shown to be completely baseless. Either there was once an Upanayana and it was stopped or the Upanayana was from the very beginning withheld. Either may be true. But before one or the other is accepted to be true, it must be accompanied by reasons. There being no reason why the benefit of the Upanayana was withheld from the Shudra, the presumption must be in favour of my thesis which states that they had the right to Upanayana, that they were deprived of it and gives reasons why they were deprived of its validity.

VI

The third objection is no objection at all. Only a person who does not know fully all the incidents of Upanayana can persist in upholding its validity.

The Aryan society regarded certain ceremonies as Samskaras. The Gautama Dharma Sutra (VIII. 14-24) gives the number of Samskaras as forty. They are :

> Garbhadhana Pumsavana, Simantonnayana, Jatakarma, namakarana, annaprasana, caula, Upanayana, the four vratas of the Veda, Snana (or Samavartana), vivaha, five daily mahayajnas (for deva, pitri, manushya, bhuta, and Brahma); seven pakayajnas (viz., astaka, parvanasthalipaka, sraddha sravani, agrahayani, caitri, asvayuji) ; seven haviryajnas (in which there is burnt offering but no Soma, viz., Agnyadheya, Agnihotra, Darsapurnamasa, Agrayana, Caturmasyas, Nirudhapasubandha and Sautramani) ; seven soma sacrifices (Agnistoma, Atyagnistoma, Ukthya, Sodasin, Vajapeya, Atiratra, Aptoryama).

At a late stage a distinction appears to have been drawn between Samskaras in the narrower sense and Samskaras in the wider sense. Samskaras in the wider sense were really sacrifices and were therefore not included in the

Samskaras in the proper sense, which were reduced to sixteen.

There is nothing strange about the Samskaras. Every society recognises them. For instance, the Christians regard Baptism, Confirmation, Matrimony, Extreme Unction, Eucharist, the Lord's Supper and the Holy Communion as sacraments. There however seems to be a difference between the notions of the Indo-Aryans and say the Christians about the Samskaras. According to Christian notions, the Samskara or Sacrament is a purely spiritual matter-drawing in of God's grace by particular rites. It had no social significance. Among the Indo-Aryans the Samskaras had originally a purely spiritual significance. This is clear from what Jaimini the author of the *Purva Mimamsa* has to say about the Samskaras. According to Jaimini the general theory is that Samskaras impart fitness. They act in two ways. They remove taints and they generate fresh qualities. Without such Samskaras, a person may not get the reward of his sacrifice on the ground that he is not fit to perform it. Upanayana was one of the Samskaras and like other Samskaras, its significance was just spiritual. The denial of the Upanayana to the Shudras necessarily brought about a change in its significance. In addition to its spiritual significance it acquired a social significance which it did not have before.

When Upanayana was open to everyone, Aryan or non-Aryan, it was not a matter of social significance. It was a common right of all. It was not a privilege of the few. Once it was denied to the Shudras, its possession became a matter of honour and its denial a badge of servility. The denial of Upanayana to the Shudras introduced a new factor in the Indo-Aryan society. It made the Shudras look up to the higher classes as their superiors and enabled the three higher classes to look down upon the Shudras as their inferiors. This is one way in which the loss of Upanayana brought about the degradation of the Shudras.

There are other incidents of Upanayana. Some idea of these can be had if one refers to the rules laid down in the *Purva Mimamsa.*[1] One of these rules is that all property is meant primarily for the purpose of providing a person with the means of performing a sacrifice. The right to property is dependent upon capacity to sacrifice.[2] In other words, anyone who suffers from an incapacity to perform a sacrifice has no right to property. Capacity to sacrifice depends upon Upanayana. This means that only those who are entitled to Upanayana have a right to own property.

The second rule of the *Purva Mimamsa* is that a sacrifice must be accompanied by Veda mantras. This means that the sacrificer must have undergone a course in the study of the Veda. A person who has not studied the Vedas is not competent to perform the sacrifices. The study of the Veda is open only to those persons who have undergone the Upanayana ceremony. In other words, capacity to acquire knowledge and learning—which is what the study of Veda means—is dependent upon Upanayana. If there is no Upanayana the road to knowledge is closed. Upanayana is no empty ceremony. Right to property and right to knowledge are the two most important incidents of Upanayana.

Those who cannot realise how loss of Upanayana can bring about the degradation of the Shudras should have no difficulty in understanding the matter if they will bear in mind the rules of the *Purva Mimamsa* referred to above. Once the relation of Upanayana to education

---

[1] See Ganganath Jha—*Purva Mimamsa*, pp. 368-369 and 171-172.

[2] Not a few are unable to understand why the Manu Smriti and other Smritis deny women and Shudra the right to hold property and to study the Vedas. All difficulty, however, vanishes if one bears in mind that the disabilities are the natural consequences of the rule laid down in the Purva Mimamsa. Women and Shudras cannot hold property, not because they are women and Shudras, but because they are debarred from performing sacrifices.

and property is grasped, all difficulty in accepting the thesis that the degradation of the Shudra was entirely due to loss of Upanayana must vanish.

It will be seen, from what has been said above, how the sacrament of Upanayana was in the ancient Aryan society fundamental and how the social status and personal rights of persons depended upon it. Without Upanayana, a person was doomed to social degradation, to ignorance and to poverty. The stoppage of Upanayana was a most deadly weapon—discovered by the Brahmins to avenge themselves against the Shudras. It had the effect of an atomic bomb. It did make the Shudra, to use the language of the Brahmins, a graveyard.

VII

That the Brahmins possessed the power to deny Upanayana is beyond question. The doubt probably arises from the fact that there is nowhere an express statement showing the conferment of such a power upon the Brahmins. All the same, whatever doubt there may be lurking in the minds of persons who are not aware of the operative parts of the religious system of the Indo-Aryans must vanish if account is taken of two things: (1) the exclusive right of the Brahmin to officiate at the Upanayana and (2) the penalties imposed upon the Brahmin for performing unauthorised Upanayana.

It is probable that in most ancient times it was the father who taught his son the *Gayatri*, with which the study of the Veda begins and for which the ceremony of Upanayana was devised at a later stage. But it is beyond question that from a very early time the function of performing Upanayana had been assigned to a guru or a teacher called the Acharya and the boy went and stayed in the Acharya's house.

The questions as to who should be the Acharya and what should be his qualifications have been the subject of discussions from very ancient times.

The Acharya must be a man learned in the Vedas. A Brahmana text[1] says "he, whom a teacher devoid of learning initiates, enters from darkness into darkness and he also (i.e. an acharya) who is himself unlearned (enters into darkness)."

The Ap. Dh. S. (I . 1 . 1 . 12—18), lays down that an Acharya selected for performing one's Upanayana should be endowed with learning and should be one whose family is hereditarily learned and who is serene in mind, and that one should study Vedic lore under him up to the end (of brahmacharya) as long as the teacher does not fall off from the path of Dharma.[2]

But the first and foremost qualification of an Acharya is that he must be a Brahmana : It was only in times of difficulty (i.e., when a Brahmana is not available) that a person was allowed to have a Kshatriya or a Vaishya teacher.[3] This exception was permitted only during the period when the distinction between the right to learn the Vedas and the right to teach the Vedas had not been made. But when that distinction came to be made—and it was made in very early times—in fact, the conflict between Vasishtha and Vishvamitra was just on this very point—the Brahmin alone came to possess the right to be an Acharya fit to officiate at an Upanayana.

---

[1] Quoted in the Ap. Dh. S.,I. i . i . 11, Kane, II (I), p. 324.

[2] According to Vyasa (quoted in Sam. p.,p. 408) the Acharya should be one who is solely devoted to the Veda, who knows Dharma, is born of a good family, who is pure, is a *shrotriya* that has studied his Vedic sakha and who is not lazy. Shrotriya has been defined as one who has studied one *sakha* of a Veda.

[3] It is curious to note that in such cases the only service a Brahmana student was required to render to his Kshatriya or Vaishya guru was to follow after him ; he had not to render bodily service (such as shampooing or washing the feet, etc.). *Vide* Ap. Dh. S., II, 2 . 4, 25-28 Gaut. 7, 1-3, Baud. Dh. S.,I. 2 . 40-42, Manu, II . 241. It was also premised that a Kshatriya or a Vaishya should teach a Brahmana only when urged by him and not at his sweet will.

One thing therefore must be taken as well-established, namely, that none but a Brahmin could perform the Upanayana ceremony. Upanayana performed by anybody else is not a valid Upanayana.

The other operative part of the Indo-Aryan religious system is the obligation imposed upon the Brahmin not to do any unauthorized act of a religious character. A Brahmin guilty of any such conduct was liable to punishment or penance. Many such penalties are to be found in the ancient Law Books. I refer to Manu and Parashara.

Manu (III . 150ff.), lays down what class of Brahmins are to be deemed unworthy (to partake) of oblations to the gods and manes. In this list he includes:

> III, 156.—" He who teaches for a stipulated fee and he who is taught on that condition, he who instructs Shudra pupils and he whose teacher is a Shudra, he who speaks rudely, the son of an adulteress, and the son of a widow."

Parashara says :[1]

> " That Brahmana, who for the sake of dakshina (gift of money or fee) offers oblation into fire on behalf of a Shudra, would become a Shudra, while the Shudra (for whom he offers) would become a Brahmana;" that, according to Madhava, propounds that the merit of the rite " goes to the Shudra and the Brahmana incurs sin."

Those who may ask what powers the Brahmins had to deprive the Shudra of his right to Upanayana may consider the combined effect of these two facts: (1) the Brahmin's exclusive right to officiate at an Upanayana, and (2) the penalties to which he is made liable for performing an unauthorized Upanayana. If they do, they will have no doubt that the combined effect of these two factors was to vest in the Brahmin the power of performing as well as of denying Upanayana. It is true that such a power has not been expressly vested in the Brahmin. That was because it was unnecessary to do by express

[1] Quoted by Vyavahara Mayukha (edited by Kane, p. 115).

terms what was in fact done by indirect but more effectual means.

That the Brahmins are conscious of the possession of this power to deny Upanayana is also beyond doubt. So far as the records go, there are 16 reported cases in which they have threatened various communities by putting it into operation against them. In nine cases, they challenged the Kayasthas, in four they challenged the Panchalas, in one they challenged the Palshes. What is important is that they challenged even two Maratha Kings. These instances have occurred between 556 to 1904 A.D. It is true that they do not belong to ancient times. It must however be remembered that these instances are mere evidences of the exercise by the Brahmins of their power to deny Upanayana. The power itself must have been acquired in much more ancient times. That they have acquired it earlier is not an empty assertion without support. Satyakama Jabali's instance which is very ancient is cited generally to prove that the Varna of a man was determined by his *guna* (mental and moral qualities) and not by his birth. While this is true, it is equally true that Jabali's case proves that even in ancient times the Brahmins had acquired the right to refuse to perform Upanayana.

The enumeration of these cases has very little value for the purpose in hand unless we know the deductions that could be drawn from the decisions arrived at in them. To be able to do this, we must know the details of each case. Unfortunately, in most of them beyond the decision other details are not sufficiently full for the purpose. There is only one case that of the Brahmins *versus* Shivaji in respect of which the details are full and well-known. The case is sufficiently important and it is therefore well worth detailed examination. The deductions deducible from it are not only interesting and instructive but they throw a flood of light on the point under discussion.

VIII

As is well known, Shivaji after having established a Hindu independent kingdom in the western part of Maharashtra thought of proclaiming himself a king by having his coronation performed. It was felt by Shivaji and his friends that the coronation ceremony if it was at all to be of any value must be performed according to Vedic rites. But in carrying out his wishes Shivaji found himself faced with many difficulties. He found that whether his coronation could be performed with Vedic rites depended entirely upon the Brahmins. Nobody was from religious point of view qualified to perform the ceremony except a Brahmin. Secondly, he found that no such ceremony could be performed unless it was proved that he was a Kshatriya. There was a third difficulty, namely, that even if he was found to be a Kshatriya, he was past the age of Upanayana and without Upanayana there could be no coronation. The third difficulty was a minor one for it could be got over by the performance of the Vratya Stoma ceremony. The first difficulty was the greatest stumbling block. It related to Shivaji's status. The question was, was he a Kshatriya ? If that could be got over, the rest was easy. Shivaji's claim that he was a Kshatriya was opposed by many. His principal opponents were Brahmins who were led by his own Prime Minister Moro Pant Pingle. Unfortunately for Shivaji even his Maratha Sardars had refused to give him social precedence[1]

---

[1] Kinkaid has some interesting observations to make as to how the idea of coronation originated. He says :—

" For although the high-spirited Deccan nobles gladly followed Shivaji in the field, they were unwilling in private life to concede to him any precedence. And at State dinners they resented that a Bhosle should sit on a seat raised above those assigned to Mohites, and Nimbalkars, Savants and Ghorpades. He spoke of the matter to his Secretary, Balaji Avji Chitnis and the latter urged him to take the royal crown from the hands, not of the Moghul Emperor, but of a Benares priest. The king consulted his mother, Jijabhai, the saintly Ramdas and his favourite and had ranged themselves against him. In their view, he was a Shudra. Shivaji's claim was also in direct conflict with the well-established thesis long insisted upon by the Brahmins that there were no Kshatriyas in the Kali age. Shivaji was living in the Kali age. Obviously he could not be a Kshatriya. This objection to his claim for the status of a Kshatriya was further strengthened by the non-performance of the ceremony of Upanayana or the investiture of the sacred thread at the proper time, which was fixed by the Sastras to be the eleventh year in the case of the Kshatriyas. This was taken to be evidence of his being a Shudra. He was however fortunate in securing the services of one Gagabhat, a renowned Brahmin, resident of Benares, learned both in the Vedas and Sastras. Gagabhat solved all difficulties and performed Shivaji's coronation[1] on 6th June 1674 at Raigad first after performing the Vratya Stoma and then the Upanayana.

---

goddess Bhavani and found them all favourable to his Secretary's suggestions."
—*History of Maharashtra*, p. 244.

From this it appears that the idea behind Vedic coronation was to obtain social precedence and not so much to obtain legal and political sovereignty.

---

[1] It seems that some Brahmins were prepared to perform Shivaji's coronation but with non-Vedic, i.e., with Pauranic rites as is done in the case of the Shudras. They predicted all sorts of evils to happen if Shivaji had his coronation performed with Vedic rites. Unfortunately these evils did take place and Shivaji who undoubtedly was superstitious had another coronation performed according to non-Vedic rites. The following account of this second coronation taken from Mr. C. V. Vaidya makes interesting reading :

" Obstructive and dissatisfied Brahmins there were even then as always. They did not deem the ceremony satisfactory, though it was acclaimed by the whole of Maharashtra. A poem named Rajyabhisheka Kalpataru, a copy of which is in the Library of the Bengal Royal Asiatic Society and which has been published from it by Itihasa S. Mandal of Poona (Quarterly, Vol. X-1), embodies some objections raised against the coronation ceremony gone through. This poem is not quite contemporary, as it mentions the later idea that Shivaji was an incarnation of Siva (not of Vishnu as represented by the earlier Shivabharata) though it is of the time of Rajaram. It gives an imaginary conversation between Nis'chalapuri, a learned Brahmin ascetic of Benares who was an opponent of Gagabhat, and Govindbhat Barve as taking place in Konkan. It recounts the ill omens which preceded and followed the coronation, such as the death of Prataprao Gujar, the death of Kashibai, wife of Shivaji, etc., and the wound caused to Gagabhat himself on the nose by the falling of a rafter. The poem expressly says that Gagabhat

Shivaji's case is important for several reasons. It is important because it proves that nobody except a Brahmin has the right to perform the Upanayana and that nobody can compel a Brahmin to perform it if he is not prepared to do so. Shivaji was the ruler of an independent kingdom and had already started styling himself Maharaja and Chhatrapati. There were many Brahmins who were his subjects. Yet, Shivaji could not compel anyone of them to perform his coronation.

It is important because it proves that the ceremony to be valid must be performed by a Brahmin. A ceremony performed by a non-Brahmin would be infructuous. It was open to Shivaji to have his coronation performed by a non-Brahmin. But he did not dare[1] to do it. For he knew it would be without any social or spiritual efficacy.

In the third place, it is important because it proves that the power of determining the status of a Hindu depends entirely upon the will of the Brahmins. The decision in favour of Shivaji is sought to be justified by the geneology which was brought from Mewar by Shivaji's friend, Balaji Avaji, and which connected Shivaji with

engaged for the ceremony those Brahmins only who were his followers and refused to employ those recommended by Nis'chalapuri. Many defects in the ceremony itself, are next mentioned. Thus when Shivaji was getting into the chariot after the ceremony of ascending the throne Gagabhat himself first sat in the chariot and then Shivaji. After seeing the whole ceremony through, Nis'chalapuri left the fort but told Shivaji that bad events would happen on the 13th, 22nd, and 55th days. On the 13th day accordingly, Shivaji's mother died. Next a horse-shed was burnt at Pratapgad with good many horses in it and an elephant died on Sinhgad. These incidents induced Shivaji to call Nis'chalapuri back and through him and his Brahmins Shivaji performed afresh the ceremony of ascending the throne, not with Vedic rites, but Tantrik or magical. This ceremony is also described in detail. There are mentioned some Vedic mantras from Sama Veda as recited; but the ceremony was not Vedic. It was performed on Ashvin Suddha 5 (Lalita Panchami day S. 1596), as is stated at the end of the poem. This ceremony is also mentioned by J and Nis'chalapuri is also spoken of in a Mahomedan record." —*Shivaji the Founder of Maratha Swaraj*, pp. 252-253.

[1] The Kayasthas had at one time resolved to perform their own ceremonies as a protest against the constant challenge by the Brahmins to their status. But they did not put their resolve into action. The reason must be the same.

the Sisodyas of Mewar who were reckoned as Kshatriyas. It has been alleged that the geneology was a fabrication got up for the occasion. Assuming it was not a fabrication,[1] how can it justify the recognition of Shivaji's claim to be a Kshatriya ? Far from establishing that Shivaji was a Kshatriya, the geneology could do no more than raise another question, namely, whether the Sisodiyas were Kshatriyas. The Sisodiyas were Rajputs. There is considerable doubt as to whether the Rajputs are the descendants of the original Kshatriyas who formed the second Varna of the ancient Indo-Aryan community. One view is that they are foreigners, remnants of the Huns who invaded India and established themselves in Rajputana and whom the Brahmins raised to the status of Kshatriyas with the object of using them as means to suppress Buddhism in Central India by a special ceremony before the sacred fire and who were therefore known as the Agnikul Kshatriyas. This view has the support of many erudite scholars who are entitled to speak on the subject. Vincent Smith says :[2]

> " In this place I want to draw attention to the fact, long suspected and now established by good evidence that the foreign immigrants into Rajputana and the upper Gangetic valley were not utterly destroyed in the course of their wars with the native princes. Many of course perished but many survived and were mixed in the general population of which no inconsiderable part is formed by their descendants. These foreigners like their fore-runners the Sakas and the Yue-chi universally yielded to the wonderful assimilative power of Hinduism and rapidly became Hinduised. Clans or families which succeeded in winning chieftainships were admitted readily into the frame of Hindu polity as Kshatriyas

[1] The Sisodiya family of Mewar was important for two reasons : (1) They were a branch of the Sisodiyas of Udaipur who were descendants of the family of Lava the eldest son of Rama, the hero of Ramayana, (2) The Sisodiyas of Mewar were pure because they had refused to give their females in marriage to the Moghul emperors and had refused to intermarry with other Rajput families such as Jaipur and Jodhpur who had done so. Was it because of these reasons that this attempt to establish that Shivaji was the descendant of the Sisodiyas of Mewar was made ?

[2] Quoted by C. V. Vaidya in his History of Mediaeval India, Vol. II, p. 8.

or Rajputs and there is no doubt that the Parjhars and many other famous Rajput clans of the north were developed out of the barbarian hordes which poured into India during the fifth and sixth centuries. The rank and file of the strangers became Gujars and the castes ranking lower than Rajputs in their precedence. Further to the south, various indigenous or aboriginal tribes and clans underwent the same process of Hinduised social promotion in virtue of which Gonds, Bhars, Kharwas and so forth emerged as Chandels, Rathors, Gaharwars and other well-known Rajput clans duly equipped with pedigree reaching back to the sun and the moon."

William Crooke[1] says :

"Recent research has thrown much light on the origin of Rajputs. A wide gulf lies between the Vedic Kshatriyas and the Rajputs of mediæval times which it is now impossible to bridge. It is now certain that the origin of many clans dates from the Saka or Kushan invasions or more certainly from that of the White Huns who destroyed the Gupta empire about 480 A.D. The Gurjar tribe connected with the latter people adopted Hinduism and their leaders formed the main stock from which the higher Rajput families sprang. When these new claimants to princely honour accepted the faith and the institution of Brahmanism the attempt would naturally be made to connect them with the heroes of the Mahabharata and the Ramayana. Hence arose the body of legend recorded in these annals by which a fabulous origin from the sun and the moon was ascribed to these Rajput families. . . . The group denoted by the name Kshatriya or Rajput depended on status rather than on descent and it was therefore possible for foreigners to be introduced into these tribes without any violation of the prejudices of caste, which was then only partially developed. But it was necessary to disguise this admission of foreigners under a convenient fiction. Hence arose the legend how by a solemn act of purification or initiation under the superintendence of the ancient Vedic Rishis, the *fire-born* septs were created to help the Brahmins in repressing Buddhism and other heresies. This privilege was confined to four septs known as Agnikula or fire-born—viz., the Paramar, Parihar, Chalukya and Chanhan."

[1] Quoted by Vaidya, *ibid*, p. 9.

Dr. D. R. Bhandarkar[1] also holds the same view. According to him, the Rajputs are the descendants of Gujars, the Gujars were foreigners and that the Rajputs are therefore the descendants of foreigners.

The Brahmins engaged for the coronation could not have been ignorant of the origin of the Rajputs, and their claim to be descended from the Kshatriyas. But assuming that they did not know this fact they knew that there was already a previous decision of the Brahmins, namely, that there were no Kshatriyas in the Kali age. This was an old, long-standing decision. And if the Brahmins had respect for precedent, they were bound to throw out the claim of Sisodiyas as well as of Shivaji. Nobody would have blamed them if they had done so. But the Brahmins had never accepted the law of precedent as binding upon them. With them there was no such thing as *stare decisis*.

Fourthly, it is important because it shows that the decisions of the Brahmins on matters of status were open to sale like the indulgences of the Catholic clergy. That the decision of Gagabhat was not an honest decision is obvious from the amount of money which Gagabhat and other Brahmins received as officiating priests. The amount of money spent on the coronation by Shivaji and how much of it went to Gagabhat and the Brahmins will be seen from the following details collected by Mr. Vaidya :[2]

> "These ministers were presented each with one lakh of hon, one elephant, one horse, garments and ornaments. Gagabhat was given one lakh of rupees for seeing the whole ceremony through. The Dakshinas granted by Shivaji on the several occasions of the coronation ceremony were very large, as was suited to the occasion. Sabhasad reports that the whole expenditure amounted to one crore and forty-two lakhs of hons or 426 lakhs of rupees.

---

[1] Quoted by Mr. Vaidya, *ibid*, p. 10. Mr. Vaidya combats the view and tries to prove that the Rajputs are not foreigners but are the descendants of original Aryan-Kshatriyas. What Mr. Vaidya says does not appear to be very convincing.

[2] *Shivaji, the Founder of Maratha Swaraj*, pp. 248 and 252.

Sabhasad relates that 50,000 Vaidika Brahmins had collected on the occasion of Shivaji's coronation.[1] Besides these there were Jogis, Sanyasis, etc., by thousands. These were fed or given corn below the fort. It is related in contemporary papers that Shivaji, before coronation, was weighed against gold and almost every other metal as well as auspicious thing. Dutch record describing the ceremony in detail on 3rd October PS. 1684 states that Shivaji weighed 17,000 hons or 160 lbs. and he was also weighed against silver, copper, iron, etc., and against camphor, salt, sugar, butter, various kinds of fruit, betel-nuts, etc., and the value of the whole was distributed amongst Brahmins. On the 7th June, the day after the coronation, Dakshina was given in general and every Brahmin got three to five rupees and everyone else, whether woman or child two rupees and one rupee. In all, the Dakshina amounted to one and a half lakhs of hon[2] in value.

"Oxenden also states in his diary from 13th May to 13th June that Shivaji was weighed against gold and the weight 16,000 hons, together with one lakh of hons in addition were distributed as Dakshinas among Brahmins.

"The above noted Dutch record further states that for the Vratya ceremony 7,000 hons were given to Gagabhat and 17,000 to other Brahmins. On the 5th of June Shivaji bathed in holy Ganges water and every Brahmin present was given 100 hons."

Can the amount paid to Gagabhat be taken as representing nothing more than a fee[3] properly payable to a priest ? There is one circumstance which may be depended upon to show that Gagabhat was not even paid enough. It is that what Gagabhat got was comparatively much less than what the Ministers of Shivaji got. Two facts must however be noted as telling on the other side before any conclusion is drawn from this fact. They completely nullify the argument. The first is that the

[1] Mr. Vaidya says this must be a mistake for 5,000. He gives no reason in support of his 'must.'

[2] A *Hon* was equal to 3 rupees.

[3] It must not be supposed that Gagabhat got only Rs. 1 lakh. He got in addition 7,000 *hons* or 21,000 rupees for Vratya Stoma. Further he must have received some part of the gold and the value of other things against which Shivaji was weighed and which was distributed among the Brahmins.

ministers themselves had made large presents[1] to Shivaji on his coronation. Moropant Pingle the Peshwa or Prime Minister of Shivaji, the Mujamdar had paid 7,000 hons and the other two ministers 5,000 hons each. Deducting these, the presents given to them by Shivaji must be said to be much smaller than they appear to be.

The second fact is that these ministers of Shivaji were the greatest opponents of Shivaji in this project of coronation. They were staunch in their view that he was a Shudra and that he was not entitled to have his coronation performed as it was a right which belonged to the Kshatriya only. It is therefore no surprise if Shivaji gave them large presents with a view to silence them and win them over permanently to his side. The amount of money paid to the ministers by Shivaji is therefore no criterion to determine whether the amount paid to Gagabhat was no more than a fair fee for officiation. Indeed there are so many twists and turns taken by Gagabhat that one is forced to the conclusion that it was more than fair fee and that it included some part as illegal gratification to keep him straight.

In this business of coronation the man who took the most leading part in bringing it about was a Kayastha from Maharashtra by name Balaji Avaji who was the Personal Secretary to Shivaji. The first step Balaji took was to send three Brahmins[2] as messengers from Shivaji to fetch Gagabhat from Benares with full information as to the status and purpose of Shivaji. What did Gagabhat do ? He sent back the three messengers with a letter refusing to accept the invitation on the ground that in his view Shivaji was a Shudra and was therefore not fit for coronation. The next step Balaji took was to collect evidence in support of Shivaji's claim to the status of a Kshatriya. He succeeded in obtaining a genealogy which

---

[1] Vaidya, *ibid*, p. 247.

[2] They were (1) Keshav Bhat, (2) Bhalachandra Bhat, and (3) Somanath Bhat.

showed that Shivaji was a Kshatriya descended from the Sisodyas who were Rajputs and rulers of Mewad. This evidence he sent with another Messenger[1], to Gagabhat. Gagabhat seemed to have been impressed by the evidence for he agreed to come to Raigad to perform the coronation ceremony. What did Gagabhat do on his arrival ? He said that he had re-examined the evidence and had come to the conclusion that Shivaji was a Shudra and was therefore unfit for coronation.

This is not the only somersault which Gagabhat took in this business. He took another and a very queer turn and declared that he was prepared to perform the coronation of Balaji Avaji for he was a Kayastha and therefore a Kshatriya but not of Shivaji who was a Shudra. Gagabhat did not stop there. He again turned round and gave his opinion that Shivaji was a Kshatriya and that he was prepared to perform his coronation and even went so far as to write a treatise known as Gagabhatti in which he sought to prove that the Kayasthas were bastards.

What do these twists and turns show ? Do they not show he was a most unwilling priest and that his willingness has had to be bought by cash ? If this argument is sound then there is no doubt that his decision that Shivaji was a Kshatriya was sold by him for illegal gratification[2].

[1] The name of the messenger was Nilo Yesaji. He was a Kayastha. The three Brahmins who went on the first occasion to fetch Gagabhat were suspected to have committed a foul play by acting contrary to their instructions and betraying the interests of Shivaji to which as Brahmins they were opposed. It is possible that Balaji felt that the letter brought by them was a piece of manoeuvre. That is why Balaji this time sent a Kayastha, a man of his own caste.

[2] For facts about Gagabhat's twists and turns stated above, I have drawn on Mr. K. S. Thakare's Marathi booklet *'Gnamanyacha Itihas*. Mr. Thakare has in his turn drawn upon the Bakhars or Chronicles. How far they are reliable it is difficult to say. It must however be admitted that the twists and turns of Gagabhat appear to be true because without them it would be difficult to explain certain relevant and disturbing facts. For instance, take the following question. Did Gagabhat change after coming to Raigad and if so, why ? The change and the reason for it is to be found in the discovery by Gagabhat that another Brahmin by

Lastly Shivaji's case is important because it shows that the Brahmins in the matter of status did not recognize as being bound by the principle of *res judicata*. They regard themselves as free to reopen a case already decided by them. For how long did the Brahmins respect their decision that Shivaji was a Kshatriya ?

Shivaji started a new era from the day of his coronation, namely, 6th June 1674 which he called the Rajyabhisheka Era. How long did it remain in vogue ? Only so long as Shivaji and his descendants remained as active rulers on the throne. The moment effective sovereignty passed into the hands of the Brahmin Peshwas, they issued an order[1] to discontinue it. Not only did they stop the use of the Era, they began using the style of the Muslim Emperors, namely, the Fasli year. The Brahmins did not stop there. They went further and began to question the very status of Shivaji's descendants as Kshatriyas[2]. They could do nothing to the two sons of Shivaji, Sambhaji and Rajaram. Shivaji had their Upanayana performed in his life-time by Brahmins with Vedic rites. They could do nothing to his grandson, Shahu because the Brahmins had no ruling power in their hands. The moment Shahu transferred his sovereign powers to his Brahmin Peshwa their road to repudiation became clear. There is no evidence whether Ramjee Raje the successor and adopted son of Shahu, who was a minor and whose guardians were the Peshwas, had his Upanayana performed and if so, whether it was performed with Vedic rites. But there is definite evidence that the Upanayana

name Moropant Pingle who was no less than the Prime Minister of Shivaji was deadly opposed to Shivaji's claim to be a Kshatriya. It is likely that the two Brahmins on meeting together saw eye to eye which made Gagabhat change. Why did Moropant who was a strong opponent became later on a strong supporter of Shivaji's coronation ? If it is a fact that Gagabhat did propose that Balaji should be proclaimed king it gives a complete explanation of Moropant's change of front. Balaji being Kayastha and the Kayasthas being the deadliest enemies of the Brahmins, Moropant consented to Shivaji's coronation as a lesser of the two evils.

[1] Sardesai—Marathi Riyasat, II, p. 363, and Vaidya's Shivaji, p. 251.

[2] What follows is taken from *Siddhanta Vijaya*, edited by Rao Bahadur Dongre.

ceremony of his successors, Shahu II, who was adopted in 1777 had been performed with *Pauranic* rites and by the direction of the Peshwa[1]. The performance of Upanayana of Shahu II with *Pauranic* rites was tantamount to his being regarded by the Peshwas as a Shudra. For it is only in the case of a Shudra that the ceremonies are performed with Pauranic rites. What happened to Maharaja Pratapsingh who succeeded Shahu II in 1808 whether or not his Upanayana was performed and if performed whether it was performed with Vedic rites or *Pauranic* rites it is not possible to be definite. One thing, however, is definitely known that in about 1827 the Shankaracharya of Karvir in his judgment about the status of the Kayasthas of Sangli stated[2] "*that there were no Kshatriyas in the Kali age and that documents showing that neither Shivaji, nor Sambhaji, nor Shahu were Kshatriyas exist in his Daftar.*" It is alleged that this statement is not to be found in the original judgment but was interpolated by the Brahmin Raja of Sangli. Be that as it may be, it was a direct challenge to the status of Pratapsinha as a descent of Shivaji. Pratapsinha had to put the issue to a conference of Brahmins which was held in Satara in 1830. The majority gave a decision in favour and saved Pratapsinha from being degraded to the status of a Shudra.

Foiled in their attempt to level down one line of Shivaji to the status of a Shudra, the Brahmins began their attack on the status of the second line of Shivaji which had established itself at Kolhapur. In the reign of one of the rulers of Kolhapur by name Babasaheb Maharaj, the Palace Priest by name Raghunath Sastri Parvate took into his head to perform all ceremonies in the Palace with *Pauranic* rites. It is said that he was stopped from continuing the practice. Babasaheb died in 1886. From 1886 to 1894, all rulers were minors and the administration

[1] Dongre, Introduction, p. 6.

[2] Dongre, Introduction, p. 9.

was in the hands of the British. There is no direct evidence as to the exact manner and mode of ceremonial performances adopted by the Palace priest. In 1902, the late Shahu Maharaj issued orders to the Palace Priest to perform all ceremonies in the *Vedic* manner. The priest refused and insisted on performing it in the *Pauranic* manner suggesting thereby that the rulers of Kolhapur were Shudras and not Kshatriyas. The part played by Sankaracharya of Karvir Math in this affair is very noteworthy. At the time of the controversy the head of the Math called Guru, had adopted a disciple (Sishya) by name Brahmanalkar and had given him all the rights of the head of the Math. At first both the Guru and the Sishya were on the side of the Palace Priest and against the Maharaja. Later on, the disciple took the side of the Maharaja and accepted his status as a Kshatriya. The Guru who remained on the side of the Priest excommunicated the Sishya. The Maharaja later on tried to create his own Sankaracharya[1] but he too proved false to the Maharaja.

Shivaji was recognised as a Kshatriya. Obviously, that status was not a personal honour conferred on him. It was a status in tail and belonged to his family as well as to his descendants. Nobody could question it. It could be lost by a particular descendant by doing some act which was inconsistent with it. If could not be lost generally. No act inconsistent with the Kshatriya status was attributed to any of the descendants of Shivaji. Yet the Brahmins came forward to repudiate the decision on their status.

This could happen only because the Brahmins claimed the power to do and undo the status of any Hindu at any time. They can raise a Shudra to the status of a Kshatriya. They can degrade the Kshatriya to the status of a Shudra. Shivaji's case proves that their sovereignty in this matter is without limit and without challenge.

---

[1] He is known [illegible] Dr. [illegible]

These instances[1] are no doubt drawn from the Bombay Presidency only. But the principles from them are clear and general in their application. They are :

(1) That the Brahmins have the exclusive right to perform the Upanayana. Neither Shivaji, nor Pratap Sinha nor the Kayasthas, Panchalas or Palashes wanted the Upanayana to be performed by a non-Brahmin. It is only once that the Kayasthas resolved to have their ceremonies performed by Kayasthas. But it was only a paper resolution.

(2) The Brahmin has the right to say whose Upanayana he will perform and whose he will not perform. In other words, the Brahmin is the sole judge of deciding whether a given community is entitled to Upanayana.

(3) The support of the Brahmins for the performance of Upanayana need not be based on honest grounds. It could be purchased by money. Shivaji got the support of the Brahmin Gagabhat on payment of money.

(4) The denial of Upanayana by the Brahmins need not be on legal or religious ground. It is possible for the denial to be based on purely political grounds. The refusal by the Brahmins of Upanayana to Kayasthas was entirely due to political rivalry between the two.

(5) The right of appeal against the denial of an Upanayana by a Brahmin is only to a Vidvat-Parishad and the Vidvat-Parishad is an assembly for which a Brahmin alone is eligible to be a member.

From the foregoing discussion, it must be clear to all that the Brahmins did possess the power to deny Upanayana. Given the power and the motive, there is nothing strange if they used it against the Shudras.

---

[1] For details of each see a Marathi publication—Gramanyacha Itihas, by K. S. Thakare, published in 1919.

Chapter XI

THE STORY OF RECONCILIATION

So far I have attempted to establish the following propositions:

(1) That it is the Brahmins who brought about the fall of the Shudras from the second to the fourth Varna in the Indo-Aryan Society;

(2) That the technique adopted by the Brahmins to degrade the Shudras was to deny them the benefit of the Upanayana;

(3) That this act of degradation was born out of the spirit of revenge on the part of the Brahmins who were groaning under the tyrannies and oppressions and indignities to which they were subjected by the Shudra kings.

While all this is crystal clear, there may be some who may yet have some such questions to ask, namely:

(i) Why should a quarrel with a few kings make the Brahmins the enemies of the whole Shudra community?

(ii) Was the provocation so great as to create a feeling of hatred and desire to seek vengeance?

(iii) Were not the parties reconciled? If they were, then there was no occasion for the Brahmins to degrade the Shudras.

(iv) How did the Shudras suffer this degradation ?

These questions I admit have in them enough force and substance to call for serious consideration. It is only proper that they should be answered.

I

The question why the Brahmins, because of their quarrels with a few kings, should proceed to degrade the whole community of Shudras is not only relevant but is also very pertinent. There would, however, be no difficulty to answer this question if two things are borne in mind.

In the first place, the conflicts described in Chapter IX between the Brahmins and the Shudra kings were not individual conflicts though they appear to be so. On the side of the Brahmins there is no doubt that the whole class was involved. Barring the episode relating to Vasishtha, all other episodes relate to Brahmins in general. On the side of the kings, it is true that the episodes mention individual kings as being involved in this conflict with the Brahmins. But it must not be forgotten that they all belonged to the same line to which Sudas belonged.

In so far as Sudas is concerned, the conflict was between the Brahmins and the Shudra clan of Kshatriyas. Of this, there can be no doubt. We have no direct evidence to say that the other offending kings also belonged to the Shudra clan of Kshatriyas. But we have other evidence which leads to the conclusion that they belonged to the same line of descent as Sudas.

Attention is invited to the following genealogical tree which is taken from the Adi Parvan of the Mahabharata[1] :

---

[1] Muir, Vol. I, p. 126.

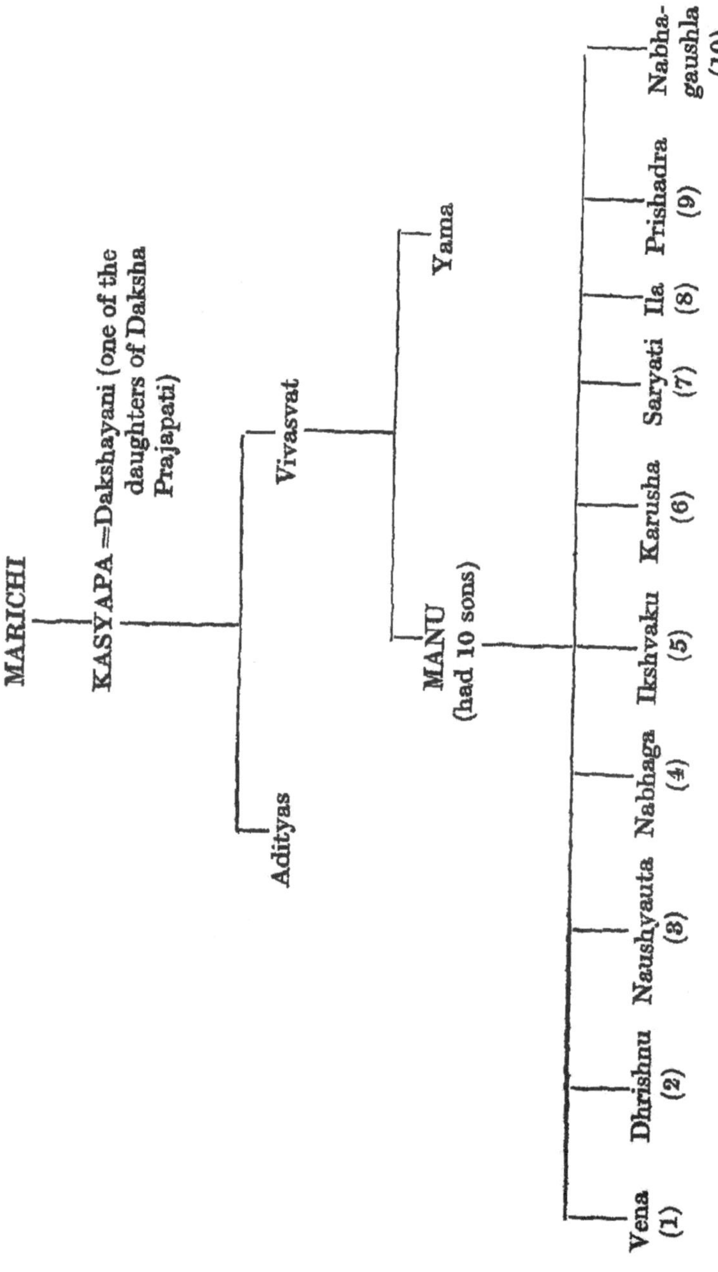
MARICHI
KASYAPA =Dakshayani (one of the daughters of Daksha Prajapati)
Adityas
Vivasvat
Yama
MANU (had 10 sons)
Vena (1)
Dhrishnu (2)
Naushyauta (3)
Nabhaga (4)
Ikshvaku (5)
Karusha (6)
Saryati (7)
Ila (8)
Prishadra (9)
Nabhagaushla (10)

The inter-relationship of the Kshatriya kings who came in conflict with the Brahmins throws some interesting light on the subject. *Pururavas*[1] is the son of Ila and the grandson of Manu Vaivasvata. *Nahusha*[2] is the grandson of Pururavas. *Nimi*[3] is the one of the sons of Ikshvaku, who is the son of Manu Vivasvat. *Trishanku*[4] is 28th in descent from Ikshvaku. *Sudas*[5] is descended from Ikshvaku and is 50th in descent from him. *Vena*[6] is the son of Manu Vaivasvata. All of them claimed descent from Manu, some from him and some from Ikshvaku. Being descendants of Manu and Ikshvaku, it is possible to argue that they were all kindred of Sudas. Given the fact that Sudas is a Shudra, it follows logically that all these kings belonged to the Shudra group.

We have no direct evidence, but there would be nothing unnatural in supposing that in these conflicts with the Brahmins, the whole Shudra community, not merely a few Shudra kings, was involved. This conflict, it must be remembered, has taken place in the ancient past when life was tribal in thought and in action, and when the rule was that what was done by one individual belonging to the tribe was deemed to be done by the whole tribe. In all ancient societies the unit was the tribe or the community and not the individual, with the result that the guilt of the individual was the guilt of the community and the guilt of the community was the guilt of every individual belonging to it. If this fact is borne in mind, then it would be quite natural to say that the Brahmins did not confine their hatred to the offending kings, but extended it to the whole of the Shudra community and applied the ban against Upanayana to all the Shudras.

---

[1] Muir, Vol. I, p. 126.

[2] Muir, Vol. I, p. 307.

[3] Muir, Vol. I, p. 316.

[4] Muir, Vol. I, p. 362.

[5] Muir, Vol. I, p. 362.

[6] Divodasa, the father of Sudas, is spoken of in the Rig Veda as king of Purus and Purus are described as Ikshvakus.

II

As to whether there was enough provocation, the matter is hardly open to question. Tempers must have risen high on both sides. There was enough combustible material on both sides for an explosion to take place.

On the side of the Brahmins, it is evident that their pretensions to social superiority and their claim for special privileges had become outrageous in character and unbearable in extent.

The following is a catalogue[1] of the pretensions put forth by the Brahmins :

(i) The Brahmin must be acknowledged to be the guru to all Varnas by the mere fact of his birth ;

(ii) The Brahmana has the sole right of deciding upon the duties of all other classes, what conduct was proper to them and what should be their means of livelihood; and the other classes were to abide by his directions and the king was to rule in accordance with such directions ;

(iii) The Brahmana is not subject to the authority of the king. The king was the ruler of all except the Brahmana ;

(iv) The Brahmana is exempt from (1) whipping ; (2) fetters being put on him ; (3) the imposition of fines ; (4) exile ; (5) censure and (6) abandonment.

(v) A Shrotriya (a Brahmana learned in Vedas) is free from taxes.

(vi) A Brahmana is entitled to claim the whole of the treasure trove if he found it. If the king found it he must give half to the Brahmana.

(vii) The property of a Brahmana dying without an heir shall not go to the king, but shall be distributed among Shrotriyas or Brahmanas.

(viii) The king meeting a Shrotriya or a Brahmana on the road must give way to the Brahmana.

(ix) The Brahmana must be saluted first.

(x) The person of a Brahmana is sacred. No death sentence could be passed against a Brahmana even if he is guilty of murder.

---

[1] This summary is based on the catalogue given in Kane's Dharma Shastra Vol. II (I), pp. 138-153.

(xi) Threatening a Brahmana with assault, or striking him or drawing blood from his body is an offence.

(xii) For certain offences the Brahmana must receive a lesser punishment than members of other classes.

(xiii) The king should not summon a Brahmana as a witness where the litigant is not a Brahmana.

(xiv) Even when a woman has had ten former husbands who are not Brahmanas, if a Brahmana marries such a woman, it is he alone who is her husband and not a Rajanya or a Vaishya [1] to whom she may have been married.

After discussing these pretensions and privileges claimed by the Brahmanas, Mr. Kane says[2]:

> "Further privileges assigned to Brahmanas are: free access to the houses of other people for the purpose of begging alms; the right to collect fuel, flowers, water and the like without its being regarded as a theft, and to converse with other men's wives without being restrained (in such conversation) by others; and the right to cross rivers without paying any fare for the ferry-boat and to be conveyed (to the other bank) before other people. When engaged in trading and using a ferry boat, they shall have to pay no toll. A Brahmana who is engaged in travelling, who is tired and has nothing to eat, commits no wrong by taking two canes of sugar or two esculent roots."

These privileges have no doubt grown in course of time and it is difficult to say which of them had become vested rights when these conflicts were raging. But there is no doubt that some of the most annoying ones such as (i), (ii), (iii), (viii) and (xiv) had then come into existence. These were enough to infuriate any decent and self-respecting body of men.

On the side of the Kshatriya kings they could not be supposed to be willing to take things lying low. How could they ? It must not be forgotten that most of the Kshatriya kings who came into conflict with the Brahmins,

---

[1] No. (xiv) is not mentioned by Kane, but is mentioned in the Atharva Veda V. 17. 8-9; see Muir, Vol. I, p. 280.

[2] *Ibid*, pp. 153-4.

belonged to the solar line.[1] They differed from the Kshatriyas of the lunar line in learning, in pride and in martial spirit. The Kshatriyas who belonged to the solar line were a virile people, while those who belonged to the lunar line were an imbecile lot without any self-respect. The former challenged the Brahmins. The latter succumbed to them and became their slaves. This was as it should be. For while the Kshatriyas of the lunar line were devoid of any learning, those belonging to the solar line were not merely the equals of Brahmins in the matter of learning, they were their superiors. Several of them were the authors of the Vedic hymns and were known as Rajarishis. This was particularly true of those who came into conflict with the Brahmins.

According to the Anukramanika to the Rig Veda as well as according to tradition the following hymns are said to have been composed by the undermentioned kings[2]:

> "vi. 15 : Vitahavya (or Bharadvaja); x. 9 : Sindhuvipa, son of Ambarisha (or Trisiras, son of Tvashtri); x. 75 : Sindhukshit son of Priyamedha; x. 133, *Sudas* son of Pijavana; x. 134, Mandhatri, son of Yuvanasva; x : 179, Sibi, son of Usinara, Pratardana, son of Divodasa and king of Kasi, and Vasumanas, son of Rohidasva; and x. 148 is declared to have had *Prithi Vainya.*"

---

[1] Only Pururavas and Nahusha belong to the Lunar line of Kshatriyas as may be seen from the following genealogical tree :—

Soma=Tara
|
Budha=Ila
|
Pururavas=Urvashi
|
Ayus
|
Nahusha

If it is borne in mind that Ila the mother of Pururavas was the daughter of Manu Vaivasvata it will be seen that they too were the kith and kin of the solar Kshatriyas who came into conflict with the Brahmins.

[2] Muir, Vol. I, p. 268.

The Matsya Purana also gives the lists[1] of those who composed the hymns of the Rig Veda in a passage which says :

> " Bhrigu, Kashya, Prachetas, Dadhicha, Atmavat, Aurva, Jamadagni, Kripa, Sharadvata, Arshtishena, Yudhajit, Vitahavya, Suvarchas, *Vaina*, *Prithu*, *Divodasa*, Brahmasva, Gritsa, Saunaka—these are the nineteen Bhrigus, composers of hymns. Angiras, Vedhasa, Bharadvaja, Bhalandana, Ritabadha, Garga, Siti, Sankriti, Gurudhira, Mandhatri, Ambarisha, Yuvanasva, Purukutsa, Pradyumna, Shravanasya, Ajamidha, Haryashva, Takshapa, Kavi, Prishadashva, Virupa, Kanva, Mudgala, Utathya, Sharadvat, Vajasravas, Apasya, Suvitta, Vamadeva, Ajita, Brihaduktha, Dirghatamas, Kakshivat, are recorded as thirty-three eminent Angirases. These were all composers of hymns. Now learn the Kasyapas . . . *Vishvamitra*, son of Gadhi, Devaraja, Bala, the wise Madhuchhandas, Rishabha, Aghamarshana, Ashtaka, Lohita, Bhritakila, Vedasravas, Devarata, Puranashva, Dhananjaya, the glorious Mithila, Salankayana,—these are to be known as the thirteen devout and eminent Kusikas. Manu Vaivasvata, Ida, king *Pururavas*, these are to be known as the eminent utterers of hymns among the Kshatriyas. Bhalanda, Vandya, and Sanskirti these are always to be known as the three eminent persons among the Vaishyas who were composers of hymns. Thus ninety-one persons have been declared by whom hymns have been given birth to, Brahmanas, Kshatriyas and Vaishyas."

In this list of the authors of the Vedic hymns there are not only names of many Kshatriyas, there are names of many of the Kshatriyas who had come into conflict with the Brahmins. The Kshatriyas were the leaders among the Vedic hymn makers. The most famous Vedic hymn namely the Gayatri mantra is the production of Vishvamitra who was a Kshatriya. It was impossible for the Kshatriyas of this calibre not to take up this challenge of the Brahmins.

Their pride which was born out of their prowess and their learning must have been so greatly wounded by the

[1] See Muir, Vol. I, p. 279.

pretensions of the Brahmins that when they did take up the challenge of the Brahmins they did it in a ruthless spirit. They hit the Brahmins hip and thigh. Vena forced them to worship him and no other god ; Pururavas looted their wealth. Nahusha yoked them to his chariot and made them drag it through the city. Nimi flouted the exclusive and hereditary right of a family priest to perform all the ceremonies in the family and Sudas went to the length of burning alive the son of Vasishtha who was once his family priest. Surely, there cannot be greater cause to provoke the Brahmins to seek their vengeance upon the Shudras.

III

On the point of possible reconciliation between the Brahmins and the Shudras, there is no doubt some evidence on which some people might rely. Before stating my views upon the worth of this evidence, it is desirable to draw attention to it. The evidence consists of stories of reconciliation which are scattered throughout the Mahabharata and the Puranas.

The first story of reconciliation concerns the two tribes, the Bharatas to whom Vishvamitra belonged and the Tritsus to whom Vasishtha belonged. That the Bharatas were enemies of Vasishtha or Tritsus is clear from the Rig Veda itself which says[1] :

> III. 53.24.—" These sons of Bharata, O Indra, desire to avoid (the Vasishthas), not to approach them."

The story of their reconciliation is told in the Adi Parvan of the Mahabharata[2] and runs as follows :—

> " And the hosts of their enemies also smote the Bharatas. Shaking the earth with an army of four kinds of forces, the Panchalya chief assailed him, having rapidly conquered the

[1] Muir, Vol. I, p. 354.

[2] Muir, Vol. I, p. 361.

earth and vanquished him with ten complete hosts. Then the king Samvarana with his wives, ministers, sons and friends fled from that great cause of alarm and dwelt in the thickets of the great river Sindhu (Indus) in the country bordering on the stream, and near a mountain. There the Bharatas abode for a long time, taking refuge in a fortress. As they were dwelling there, for a thousand years, the venerable rishi Vasishtha came to them. Going out to meet him on his arrival, and making obeisance, the Bharatas all presented him with the *arghya*, offering, showing every honour to the glorious rishi. When he was seated, the king himself solicited him: 'Be thou our priest; let us strive to regain my kingdom.' Vasishtha consented to attach himself to the Bharatas, and as we have heard, invested the descendant of Puru with the sovereignty of the entire Kshatriya race, to be a horn (to have a mastery) over the whole earth. He occupied the splendid city formerly inhabited by Bharata, and made all kings again tributary to himself."

The second story relates to the conflict between the Bhrigus and the Kshatriya king Kritavirya and their subsequent reconciliation. It occurs in the Adi Parvan of the Mahabharata[1]:

"There was a king named Kritavirya, by whose liberality the Bhrigus, learned in the Vedas, who officiated as his priests, had been greatly enriched with cows and money. After he had gone to heaven, his descendants were in want of money, and came to beg for a supply from the Bhrigus, of whose wealth they were aware. Some of the latter hid their money underground, others bestowed it on Brahmins, being afraid of the Kshatriyas, while others again gave these last what they wanted. It happened, however, that a Kshatriya while digging the ground, discovered some money buried in the house of a Bhrigu. The Kshatriyas then assembled and saw this treasure, and, being incensed, slew in consequence all the Bhrigus, whom they regarded with contempt, down to the children in the womb. The widows, however, fled to the Himalaya mountains. One of them concealed her unborn child in her thigh. The Kshatriyas, hearing of its existence from a Brahmani informant, sought to kill it, but it issued forth from his mother's thigh with lustre, and blinded the

[1] Muir, Vol I, pp. 448-449.

persecutors. After wandering about bewildered among the mountains for a time, they humbly supplicated the mother of the child for the restoration of their sight; but she referred them to her wonderful infant Aurva, into whom the whole Veda, with its six Vedangas, had entered, as the person who (in retaliation of the slaughter of his relatives) had robbed them of their eye-sight, and who alone could restore it. They accordingly had recourse to him, and their eye-sight was restored. Aurva, however, meditated the destruction of all living creatures, in revenge for the slaughter of the Bhrigus, and entered on a course of austerities which alarmed both gods, asuras and men; but his progenitors (Pitris) themselves appeared, and sought to turn him from his purpose by saying that they had no desire to be revenged on the Kshatriyas. It was not from weakness that the devout Bhrigus overlooked the massacre perpetrated by the murderous Kshatriyas. 'When we became distressed by old age, we ourselves desired to be slaughtered by them. The money which was buried by some one in a Bhrigu's house was placed there for the purpose of exciting hatred, by those who wished to provoke the Kshatriyas. For what had we who were desiring heaven, to do with money?' They added that they hit upon this device because they did not wish to be guilty of suicide, and concluded by calling upon Aurva to restrain his wrath, and abstain from the sin he was meditating: 'Destroy not the Kshatriyas, o son, nor the seven worlds. Suppress thy kindled anger which nullifies the power of austere fervour.' Aurva, however, replies that he cannot allow his threat to remain unexecuted. His anger, unless wreaked upon some other object, will, he says, consume himself, and he argues, on grounds of justice, expediency and duty, against the clemency which his progenitors recommend. He is, however, persuaded by the Pitris to throw the fire of his anger into the sea, where they say it will find exercise in assailing the watery element, and in this way his threat will be fulfilled. It accordingly became the great Hayasiras, known to those who are acquainted with the Veda, which vomits forth that fire and drinks up the waters."

The third story concerns the conflict between Arjuna son of Kritavirya, the king of the Haihayas and Parashurama and the subsequent reconciliation between them. It occurs in the Vanaparvan of the Mahabharata and runs as follows[1]:

"Arjuna, son of Kritavirya and king of the Haihayas, had, we are told, a thousand arms. He obtained from Dattatreya an aerial car of gold, the march of which was irresistible. He thus trod down gods, Yakshas, rishis, and oppressed all creatures. The gods and rishis applied to Vishnu and he along with Indra, who had been insulted by Arjuna, devised the means of destroying the latter. At this time, the story goes on, there lived a king of Kanyakubja, called Gadhi, who had a daughter named Satyavati. The marriage of this princess to the rishi Richika and the birth of Jamadagni, are then told in nearly the same way as above narrated. Jamadagni and Satyavati had five sons, the youngest of whom was the redoubtable Parashurama. By his father's command he kills his mother (who, by the indulgence of impure desire, had fallen from her previous sanctity), after the four elder sons had refused this matricidal office, and had in consequence been deprived of reason by their father's curse. At Parashurama's desire, however, his mother is restored by his father to life, and his brothers to reason; and he himself is absolved from all the guilt of murder; and obtains the boon of invincibility and long life from his father. His history now begins to be connected with that of king Arjuna (or Kartavirya). The latter had come to Jamadagni's hermitage, and had been respectfully received by his wife; but he had requited this honour by carrying away by force the calf of the sage's sacrificial cow, and breaking down his lofty trees. On being informed of this violence, Parashurama was filled with indignation, attacked Arjuna, cut off his thousand arms, and slew him. Arjuna's son, in return slew the peaceful sage Jamadagni, in the absence of Parashurama. Parashurama incensed at the slaughter of his father, having vowed in consequence to sweep away all Kshatriyas from the earth, seized his weapons and slaying all the sons and grandsons of Arjuna, with thousands of the Haihayas, he turned the earth into a mass of ensanguined mud. Having thus cleared the earth of Kshatriyas he became penetrated by deep compassion and retired to the forest. After some thousand of years had elapsed, the hero, naturally irascible,

[1] Muir, Vol. I, pp. 449-454.

was taunted by Paravasu, the son of Raibhya and grandson of Vishvamitra, in a public assembly in these words: 'Are not these virtuous men, Pratardana and the others, who are assembled at the sacrifice in the city of Yayati—are they not Kshatriyas ? Thou hast failed to execute thy threat, and vainly boastest in the assembly. Thou hast withdrawn to the mountain from the fear of those valiant Kshatriyas, while the earth has again become overrun by hundreds of their race.' Hearing these words, Rama seized the weapons. The hundreds of Kshatriyas who had before been spared had now grown powerful kings. Those, however, Parashurama, now slew with their children, and all the numerous infants then unborn as they came into the world. Some, however, were preserved by their mothers. Having twenty-one times cleared the earth of the Kshatriyas, Rama gave her as a sacrificial fee to Kasyapa at the conclusion of an Ashvamedha."

After telling the story of the conflict the author of the Mahabharata proceeds to narrate the story of reconciliation in the following terms[1]:

"Having one and twenty times swept away all the Kshatriyas from the earth, the son of Jamadagni engaged in austerities on Mahendra, the most excellent of mountains. After he had cleared the world of Kshatriyas, their widows came to the Brahmins, praying for offspring. The religious Brahmins, free from any impulse of lust, cohabited at the proper seasons with these women, who in consequence became pregnant, and brought forth valiant Kshatriya boys and girls, to continue the Kshatriya stock. Thus was the Kshatriya race virtuously begotten by Brahmins on Kshatriya women and became multiplied and long-lived. Thence there arose four castes inferior to the Brahmins."

The above instances of conflicts and conciliations between Brahmins and Kshatriyas do not relate to those Kshatriya kings who have figured in history as having declared war on the Brahmins. To turn to instances of their[2] stories of reconciliation with the Brahmins the first is that of

[1] Muir, Vol. I, pp. 451-452.

[2] I am not sure that the kings mentioned in the episodes which follow are the same as those mentioned in Chapter IX. I refer to them because they belong to the Ikshvaku family.

Kalmashapada. He is said to be the son of Sudas[1]. The story is given in the Adi-parvan of the Mahabharata[2]. That part of the story which narrates the enmity between Kalmashpada and Vashistha has already been recounted[3]. The part of the story which deals with reconciliation runs as follows :

"After roaming about over many mountains and countries, he (Vashishtha) was followed home by his daughter-in-law Adrisyanti, Shaktri's[4] widow, from whose womb he heard a sound of the recitation of the Vedas, as she was pregnant with a child, which, when born, received the name of Parasara. Learning from her that there was thus a hope of his line being continued, he abstained from further attempts on his own life. King Kalmashapada, however, whom they encountered in the forest, was about to devour them both, when Vasishtha stopped him by a blast from his mouth, and sprinkling him with water consecrated by a holy text, he delivered him from the curse by which he had been affected for twelve years. The king then addressed Vasishtha thus : 'Most excellent sage, I am Saudasa, whose priest thou art, what can I do that would be pleasing to thee ?' Vasishtha answered: 'This which has happened has been owing to the force of destiny ; go, and rule thy kingdom ; but, o monarch, never condemn the Brahmins.' The king replied, 'Never shall I despise the most excellent Brahmins ; but submitting to thy commands I shall pay thee all honour. And I must obtain from thee the means of discharging my debt to the Ikshvakus. Thou must give me the offspring which I desire.' Vasishtha promised to comply with his request. They then returned to Ayodhya. And Vasishtha having been solicited by the king to beget an heir to the throne, the queen[5] became pregnant by him, and brought forth a son at the end of twelve years."

---

[1] I am not sure which Sudas he is. From the details he seems to be Paijavana Sudas.

[2] Muir, Vol. I, pp. 415-418.

[3] See Chapter IX.

[4] This is probably a mistake for Shakti.

[5] Her name was Madayanti. She is referred to in the Anushashana Parvanas the wife of Mitrasaha, which is another name for Kalmashapada—See Muir, Vol. I, pp. 418, 423 and 514.

The second instance occurs in the Anushasanaparvan of the Mahabharata[1] :

"At the time the eloquent king Saudasa sprung from the race of Ikshvaku proceeded, after salutation, to make an enquiry of his family priest Vasishtha, the eternal saint, the most excellent of rishis, who was able to traverse all the world, and was a treasure of sacred knowledge: 'What, o, venerable and sinless man, is declared to be the purest thing in the three worlds, by constantly celebrating which one may acquire the highest merit ?' Vasishtha in reply expatiates at great length on the merit resulting from bestowing cows, and ascribes to these animals some wonderful properties so that they are the 'support of all beings,' the present and the future, and describes the cow as 'pervading the universe, mother of the past and the future.' The great self-subduing king, considering that these words of the rishi were most excellent, lavished on the Brahmins very great wealth in the shape of cows and obtained the worlds. So here we find the son of Saudasa extolled as a saint."

The third instance relates to the reconciliation in which there is reference to Sudas's descendants. It occurs in the Shanti Parvan of the Mahabharata[2] :

"Having received the dominion over the earth, Kasyapa made it an abode of Brahmins, and himself withdrew to the forest. Shudras and Vaishyas then began to act lawlessly towards the wives of the Brahmins, and in consequence of there being no government, the weak were oppressed by the strong, and no one was master of any property. The earth being distressed by the wicked, in consequence of that disorder, and unprotected according to rule by the Kshatriyas, the guardians of justice, descended to the lower regions. Perceiving her moving from place to place in terror, Kasyapa upheld her with his thigh (*uru*). From this circumstance she derives her name of *urvi*. The goddess Earth then propitiated Kasyapa and supplicated him for protection, and for a king. 'I have,' she said, 'preserved among females many Kshatriyas who have been born in the race of Haihayas ; let them be my protectors. There is the heir of Pauravas, the son of Viduratha, who has been brought up

---

1 Muir, Vol. I, p. 374.

2 Muir, Vol. I, pp. 455-456.

by bears on the mountain Rikshavat; let him protect me. So, too, the heir of Saudasa, has been preserved by the tender-hearted and glorious priest, Parasara who had performed, though a Brahmin, all menial offices for him like a Shudra whence the prince's name Sarvakarman.' After enumerating other kings who had been rescued, the Earth proceeds: 'All these Kshatriya descendants have been preserved in different places, abiding continually among the classes of dyokaras and goldsmiths. If they protect me, I shall continue unshaken. Their fathers and grandfathers were slain on my account by Rama, energetic in action. It is incumbent on me to avenge their cause. For I do not desire to be always protected by an extraordinary person (such as Kasyapa); but I will be content with an ordinary ruler. Let this be speedily fulfilled.' Kasyapa then sent for these Kshatriyas who had been pointed out by the Earth, and installed them in the kingly office."

Such is the evidence. Can anybody accept it as reliable? In my opinion, far from accepting it, one should beware of such evidence.

In the first place, all these stories of reconciliation end, for the Kshatriyas, in peace without honour. In every case, the Kshatriyas are shown to have undergone an abject surrender. The Bharatas are the enemies of Vasishtha. Suddenly there is a famine in their country. They leave the country and lose their kingdom. They implore Vasishtha their age-old enemy and pray that he become their priest and save them from the calamity. In the story of the Bhrigus and the Kshatriyas, the credit is given to the Brahmins as being too proud to fight. In the story of the Haihaya Kshatriyas and the Saudasa such as Kalmashpada, the surrender of the Kshatriyas was so to say purchased by them by offering their women to the victorious Brahmins. The stories are all doctored with a view to glorify the Brahmins and humiliate the Kshatriyas. Who can take such dirty, filthy, abominable and vainglorious stories of reconciliation as true historical facts? Only a supporter of Brahminism can do so.

Such is the general character of the evidence on the

question of reconciliation. Coming to the particular case of reconciliation between the Brahmins and the Shudras, the descendants of Sudas, there is ample evidence to show that no such reconciliation had taken place. In the first place, it cannot be gainsaid that Parasara the son of Shakti or Shaktri, the son of Vasishtha, when he heard of the way in which his father had met his death—namely, that he was burnt alive by Sudas the Shudra king,—determined to execute a general slaughter of all creatures. The general slaughter is, of course, a figurative term. What is meant is that Vasishtha took a vow of general vengeance against the descendants of Sudas, namely, the Shudras. It is no doubt said in the Mahabharata that Vasishtha restrained Parasara and persuaded him not to carry out his threat of vengeance by telling him how the Bhrigus and the Kshatriyas had come into conflict and how the former won against the latter by adopting non-violence. But this story cannot be true; for, like other stories it is doctored with a view to bring glory to the Brahmins.

In the second place, the strongest proof in support of the contention that there was no reconciliation between the Brahmins and the Shudras comes from the legislation enacted by the Brahmins against the Shudras. The laws against the Shudras have already been referred to. Their growth and their extraordinary character have been pointed out. All that remains to do is to say that against this background of black laws any suggestion regarding reconciliation must appear to be wholly untenable. The Brahmins not only did not forgive the Shudras, they pursued even the progeny of the Shudras with the same spirit of relentless revenge. As many people do not seem to have any idea of this, it may be desirable to state a few facts regarding the Chandala and the Nishada.

The Chandala and Nishada are the issues of mixed marriages. Nishada is an anuloma while the Chandala is a Pratiloma. The anulomas[1] are held to be eligible for Upanayana. But curiously enough an exception is made to this rule. Nishada who is the son of a Brahman from a Shudra woman, though an anuloma, is held not to be eligible for Upanayana. It is interesting to know why this exception was made. The only answer seems to be that this arbitrary act is an act of revenge against the children of one's enemy.

Turning to the Pratilomas[2], Manu no doubt calls, all of them as the basest of men. At the same time, the stigma on the Pratilomas is not evenly distributed among all of them. In the matter of rights and privileges, the Ayogava and the Kshattar are treated with incredible consideration, while the Chandala is subjected to unspeakable condemnation. As an illustration of this discrimination one can cite the following provisions in the Manu Smriti :

As to the Ayogava, the *Manu Smriti* merely says:

> "Carpenting (shall be the occupation) of an Ayogava." —x. 46.

As to the Kshattar the *Manu Smriti* says :

> ". . . catching and killing animals that live in holes (is the occupation) of Kshattar."—x. 49.

They are only assigned low occupations.

---

[1] There are six anulomas as shown in the following table :—

Father	*Mother*	*Name of the progeny*
Brahmin	Kshatriya	Murdhavasikta
Brahmin	Vaishya	Ambashtha
Brahmin	Shudra	Nishada
Kshatriya	Vaishya	Mahishya
Kshatriya	Shudra	Urga
Vaishya	Shudra	Karana

[2] Gaut. Dh. S., IV. 21, quoted by Kane, II, Part I, p. 229.

Father	*Mother*	*Name of the case*
Shudra	Brahmin	Chandala
Shudra	Kshatriya	Kshattar
Shudra	Vaishya	Ayogava
Vaishya	Brahmin	Suta
Vaishya	Kshatriya	Vaidehaka
Kshatriya	Brahmin	Magadha

Compare with this what the *Manu Smriti* has to say about the Chandala :

" A Chandala and a boar, a cock and also a dog, and a woman in her courses and an eunuch, may not see the Brahmins eating."—iii . 239.

" One may not abide with outcasts, nor Chandalas, nor Pukkasas, nor idiots, nor proud (people), nor with the low-born (people) nor with Antyavasayins."— iv . 79.

" One becomes pure by bathing if one has touched a Chandala, or a woman in her courses, an outcaste, also a woman lying-in, a corpse or one who has touched it."—v . 85.

" Manu declared the flesh of (a beast) killed by dogs (to be pure) ; also the flesh of an animal killed by other carnivorous (animals) (or) by Chandala (and) other Dasyus." —v . 131.

" Two-fold should be the fine of a criminal sentenced within a year, and just as much if one cohabit with a Vratya woman or a Chandala woman."—viii . 373.

" The man, however, who foolishly allows this to be done by any other (wife) than the one of his own caste when the latter is at hand, has been, of old, looked upon as (no whit better than) a Chandala."—ix . 87.

" The dwelling of Chandalas and Svapacas (should be) outside the village ; they should be deprived of dishes (apapatra) ; their property (consists of) dogs and asses."—x . 51.

" Moreover, Vishvamitra, well knowing right and wrong, being oppressed by hunger proceeded to eat the rump of a dog, having it from the hand of a Chandala."—x . 108.

" At no time should a Brahmin beg property from a Shudra for the sake of sacrifice, for on offering sacrifice after begging (from a Shudra) he is born after death as a Chandala." —xi . 24.

" On having (carnal) intercourse with Chandala women (or low born woman), on eating their food or receiving (presents) from them, a Brahmin (if he has done so) unwittingly, falls ; but (if he has done so) wittingly, he comes to an equality (with them)."—xi . 175.

" The slayer of a Brahmin enters the womb of dogs, boars, asses, camels, cows, goats, sheep, (forest) animals, birds, Chandalas and Pukkasas."—xi . 55.

How different is the treatment accorded to the Chandala as compared to the treatment accorded to the Ayogava and the Kshattar when all of them are Pratilomas? Why should the Chandala be singled out as the most infamous of the Pratilomas? Only because he is the progeny of the hated Shudra. It is just an act of revenge against the children of one's enemy.

All this leaves no doubt that there was no reconciliation between the Brahmins and the Shudras.

IV

Coming to the last objection, it appears that behind it there is a feeling that the Shudras must have been a very large part of the Indo-Aryan society. With such a feeling it does appear rather strange that the Shudras should have suffered silently the perpetration of such an act as the denial of the Upanayana. Because the Shudras in the Hindu Society form such a vast proportion of the population, so the Shudras of the Indo-Aryan Society must also have formed a very large proportion of the population, can be the only basis for such a feeling. Such an inference is without any foundation, for the Shudras of the Indo-Aryan Society are absolutely different in race from the Shudras of the Hindu Society. The Shudras of the Hindu Society are not the racial descendants of the Shudras of the Indo-Aryan Society.

This confusion has arisen because of the failure to realize that the meaning of the word 'Shudra' in the Indo-Aryan society is quite different from the meaning it has in the Hindu society. In the Indo-Aryans the word Shudra was a proper name of one single people. It was the name of a people who belonged to a particular race. The word Shudra, as used in the Hindu society, is not a proper name at all. It is an epithet for a low uncultured class of people. It is a general cognomen of a miscellaneous and heterogeneous collection of tribes and groups, who have nothing in common except that they happen to be on a lower plane of culture. It is wrong to call them by the name Shudras. They have very little to do with their namesakes of the Aryan society, who had offended the Brahmins. It is a pity that these innocent and backward people of later days have been rolled up with the original Shudras and subjected to the same penalties for which they had given no cause.

That the Shudras of the Indo-Aryan and the Shudras of the Hindu Society are different and distinct is a fact which was present at one time to the minds of the Dharma Sutrakaras is quite clear. This is evident from the distinction they made between *Sacchudra* and *asac-chudra* and between *Aniravasita* Shudras and *Niravasita* Shudras. *Sacchudra* means a cultured Shudra and *asac-chudra* means an uncultured Shudra. Niravasita Shudra means a Shudra living in the village community. Anirvasita Shudra means a Shudra living outside the village community. It is quite wrong to say as some[1] do that this division indicates that the condition of Shudras in the eyes of the law-givers was improving, in that some were admitted to social intercourse when formerly none was. The correct interpretation is the Sacchudra and Niravasita Shudra refer to the Shudras of the Aryan society and the *asac-chudra* and the Anirvasita Shudra refer to the Shudras by epithet who had begun to form part of the Hindu society. We are concerned with the Shudra of the Aryan society. They have no connection with the later-day Shudras of the Hindu society. That being so, the fact that the Shudras of the Hindu society form such a large number cannot be made the basis for an argument that the Shudras of the Indo-Aryans must have also been a very large body of people. We do not know exactly whether the Shudras were a tribe, a clan or a moiety or

[1] See Kane, II (I), p. 123. His view that this distinction implies that Shudras were being gradually raised from their low status is quite incorrect.

a group of families. But even if they were as big as a tribe, they could not have been larger than a few thousand. The Bharatas are being expressly spoken of in the Rig Veda, vii . 33 . 6, as being small in number. The Satapatha Brahmana referring to a horse sacrifice performed by the Panchala king Sona Satrasaha[1] says :

> "When Satrasaha makes the Ashvamedha offering, the Taurvasas arise, six thousand and six and thirty, clad in mail."

If it is any indication that the tribe of Taurvasas numbered six thousand, the Shudras could not be very many.

Apart from the question of numbers, what could the Shudras have done to prevent the calamity ? If some Brahmins whom they had offended refused to perform their Upanayana, could they have got the services of other Brahmins whom they had not offended ? Such a possibility would of course depend upon various circumstances. In the first place, we do not know whether all the Brahmins had formed a common front and whether it was possible to break up that front. We do not know that at the time when the issue was a burning issue the Brahmins had become a caste. But it is clear[2] that even in the times of the Rig Veda Brahmins were a class by themselves, had developed class consciousness and were keen on maintaining class interests. In that event it would have been difficult for the Shudras to break up the conspiracy of the Brahmins. Secondly, it might also be that the performance of Upanayana had become the exclusive right of the family priest. The story of king Nimi[3] shows that the performance of sacrifices had become the exclusive right of the family priest. If there is substance in these suggestions, then obviously the Shudras could not have done much to prevent the common front of the Brahmins operating against them.

---

[1] Quoted by Oldenberg—Life of Buddha, p. 404.

[2] Kane, Vol. II (1), p. 29.

[3] *Supra*, p. 175.

Another possibility was the forging of a common front among all the Kshatriyas which might have had the effect of weighing down the opposition of the Brahmins. Whether such a thing was possible can only be a matter of speculation. In the first place, did the Shudras realize what the effect of the loss of Upanayana was going to be on their future status ? I am sure they did not. Secondly, were the Kshatriyas a united body of people ? I doubt if they were. Thirdly, had the other Kshatriya kings any sympathy for the Shudras ? If the story of the Dasharajna Yuddha told in the Rig Veda is true, it is quite obvious that there was not much love lost between the Shudras and the other non-Shudra Kshatriyas.

Taking all these circumstances into consideration, there is nothing strange if the Shudras suffered the denial of the Upanayana by the Brahmins to be a fact.

CHAPTER XII

THE THEORY IN THE CRUCIBLE

I

THE object of this essay was to trace the origin of the Shudras and discover the causes of their degradation. After an examination of historical material and of theories suggested by various writers—orthodox as well as modern—I have put forth a new thesis. In the preceding chapters, it has been presented in parts for the facility of laying the foundation of each part separately. It is time these parts were assembled together for a full and complete understanding of what the thesis is. It may be summarized as follows :

(1) The Shudras were one of the Aryan communities of the Solar race.

(2) The Shudras ranked as the Kshatriya Varna in the Indo-Aryan Society.

(3) There was a time when the Aryan Society recognized only three Varnas, namely, Brahmins, Kshatriyas and Vaishyas. The Shudras were not a separate Varna but a part of the Kshatriya Varna.

(4) There was a continuous feud between the Shudra kings and the Brahmins, in which the Brahmins were subjected to many tyrannies and indignities.

(5) As a result of the hatred towards the Shudras due to their tyrannies and oppressions, the Brahmins refused to invest the Shudras with the sacred thread.

(6) Owing to the loss of the sacred thread the Shudras became socially degraded, fell below the rank of the Vaishyas and came to form the fourth Varna.

It now remains to assess the validity of this thesis. It is usual for the author to leave this to others to do it. I propose to make a departure and myself enter upon the task of putting my thesis to test. I do so because it gives me an opportunity of vindicating my thesis.

II

I can well imagine my critics to allege that my thesis rests upon a single statement from the Mahabharata in which Paijavana is described as a Shudra; that identification of Paijavana with Sudas is not proved beyond the shadow of doubt; that the description of Paijavana as a Shudra does not occur in any other place except in a single place in the Mahabharata. How can a theory built on such weak foundations be acceptable? They are bound to invoke the usual agreement that a chain is not stronger than its weakest link. I am sure that my thesis cannot be discredited and demolished in such an easy manner.

In the first place, I do not admit that a thesis cannot be built up on a single piece of evidence. It is a well-known principle of the law of evidence that witnesses must be weighed and not numbered. The number of witnesses is a less important consideration than the weight to be attached to the individual testimony of each or to the sum of the testimonies of all taken together. There is no reason to doubt the truth of the statement that Paijavana was a Shudra. The author of the Mahabharata has no reason to give a false description. Writing after such a long time, no motive, no partiality could be attributed to him. The only conclusion one can draw is that the author was recording a true tradition.

The fact that Paijavana is not described as a Shudra in the Rig Veda does not militate against the truth of the statement which occurs in the Mahabharata. Many explanations can be given for the absence of the word Shudra from the description of Paijavana in the Rig Veda. The first explanation is that it is wrong to expect such a description in the Rig Veda. The Rig Veda is a book of religion. A description such as Shudra could not be expected in a book of religion. It would be irrelevant. But such a description may well be expected to occur in a book of history such as the Mahabharata wherein as a matter of fact it does.

The other explanation for the infrequent mention of the word Shudra in connection with Sudas which I can think of is that it was unnecessary. Descriptions in terms of kula, gotra, tribe, etc. are really speaking marks of identification. Marks of identification are necessary in the case of lesser people. They are unnecessary in the case of famous men. There is no doubt that Sudas was the most famous man of his time. It was unnecessary to describe him as Shudra for the purpose of identifying him to the people. This is not altogether a mere matter of speculation. One can cite historical instances. Take the case of Bimbisara and Pasenadi, two kings who lived in the time of Buddha. All other kings who were their contemporaries are described in the literature of the time by their *gotra* name. But these two are just spoken of by their personal names. Prof. Oldenberg[1] who noticed this fact explains this on the ground that they were well-known and did not stand in need for being described by their *gotra* names.

III

But it is really wrong to suppose that my theory is based on the solitary passage in the Mahabharata or on the identification of Paijavana with Sudas. Nothing of the

[1] Life of Buddha, p. 414.

kind. The thesis is not supported by a single chain and therefore the argument that a chain is not stronger than its weakest link does not apply to it. The case is supported by several parallel chains. The weakness of a link in one of them cannot be said to weaken the support. The weakness of one link in one chain throws the whole weight on other chains. Consequently, before concluding that the theory has broken down, it is necessary to prove that the other chains are not able to sustain the weight.

The description of Paijavana as Shudra and the identification of Paijavana with Sudas of the Rig Veda is not the only chain which supports the thesis. There are other chains. One of these is the admission in the Satapatha and Taittiriya Brahmanas that there were only three Varnas and the Shudras did not form a separate Varna. The second consists of evidence that Shudras were kings and ministers of State. The third consists of evidence that the Shudras were at one time entitled to Upanayana. All these are strong chains quite capable of taking all extra weight arising out of a possible breakdown of the first chain.

As far as evidence is concerned, absolute certainty amounting to demonstration is seldom to be had and I do not claim absolute certainty for my thesis. But I do claim that the evidence in support of the theory is both direct as well as circumstantial, and where it is conflicting it is supported by strong probabilities in favour of it.

IV

I have shown what strength there is in the thesis I have presented. I will now proceed to show that the thesis is a valid one. There is one test which I think is generally accepted as the right one by which to appraise the validity of a thesis. It is that a thesis which demands acceptance must not only suggest a solution, but must also show that the solution it proposes answers the riddles which surround the problem which it claims to have solved. It is this test that I propose to apply to my thesis.

Let me begin by listing in one place the riddles of the Shudra. The following include the most important of them :

(1) The Shudras are alleged to be non-Aryans, hostile to the Aryans, whom the Aryans are said to have conquered and made slaves. How is it then that the rishis of the Yajur Veda and the Atharva Veda should wish glory to the Shudras and express a desire to be in favour of the Shudras ?

(2) The Shudras are said not to have the right to study the Vedas. How is it then that Sudas, a Shudra, was the composer of the hymns of the Rig Veda ?

(3) The Shudras are said to have no right to perform sacrifices. How is it that Sudas performed the Ashva-Medha sacrifice ? Why does the Satapatha Brahmana treat the Shudra as a sacrificer and give the formula of addressing him ?

(4) The Shudras are said not to have the right to Upanayana. If this was so from the very beginning, why should there be a controversy about it ? Why should Badari and the Samskara Ganapati say that he has a right to Upanayana ?

(5) The Shudra is not permitted to accumulate property. How is it that the Maitrayani and Kathaka Samhitas speak of the Shudras being rich and wealthy ?

(6) The Shudra is said to be unfit to become an officer of the State. How is it then that the Mahabharata speaks of Shudras being ministers to kings ?

(7) It is said that the duty of the Shudra is to serve, in the capacity of a menial, the three Varnas. How is it then that there were kings among the Shudras as testified by the case of Sudas and other cases mentioned by Sayana ?

(8) If the Shudra had no right to study the Vedas, if he had no right to Upanayana, if he had no right to sacrifice, why was he not given the right to have his Upanayana, to read the Vedas and to perform sacrifices ?

(9) The performance of Upanayana of the Shudra, his learning to read the Vedas, his performing the sacrifices, whether they were of any value to the Shudra or not, were certainly occasions of benefit to the Brahmins in as much as it is the Brahmins who had the monopoly of officiating at ceremonies and of teaching the Vedas. It is the Brahmins who stood to earn large fees by allowing the Shudra the right to Upanayana, the performance of sacrifices and the reading of the Vedas. Why were the Brahmins so determined to deny these concessions to the Shudras, when granting them would have done no harm and would have increased their own earnings ?

(10) Even if the Shudra had no right to Upanayana, sacrifices and Vedas, it was open to the Brahmins to concede him these rights. Why were these questions not left to the free will of the individual Brahmins ? Why were penalties imposed upon a Brahmin if he did any of these prohibited acts ?

How can these riddles be explained ? Neither the orthodox Hindu nor the modern scholar has attempted to explain them. Indeed they do not seem to be aware of the fact that such riddles exist. The orthodox Hindu does not bother about them. He is content with the divine explanation contained in the *Purusha Sukta* that the Shudra was born from the feet of the Purusha. The modern scholar is content with the assumption that the Shudra in his origin is a non-Aryan aboriginal, for whom the Aryan quite naturally prescribed a different code of laws. It is a pity that none of these classes of people have cared to acquaint themselves with the riddles which surround the problem of the Shudra, much less have they thought of suggesting a theory of the origin of the position of the Shudra capable of solving them.

With regard to my thesis it will be seen that it can explain everyone of these riddles. Postulates (1) to (4) explain how the Shudras could be kings and ministers and why the rishis should praise them and desire to be in their good books. Postulates (5) and (6) explain why there was a controversy over the Upanayana of the Shudra, also why the law not only denied the right to the Shudra but imposed penalties upon a Brahmin, helping to make it effective. Indeed there is no riddle which the thesis does not solve. The thesis if I may so is a close and a perfect fit. Few theses can therefore have a better title deed than this.

APPENDIX I

References to the word " Arya " (अर्य) in the Rig Veda.

I		II		III		IV		V		VI		VII		VIII		IX		X	
H	M	H	M	H	M	H	M	H	M	H	M	H	M	H	M	H	M	H	M
33	3	23	13	43	2	1	7	2	12	14	3	8	1	1	4	23	3	20	4
70	1	23	15			2	12	33	2	15	3	21	5	19	36	61	11	27	8
71	3	35	2			2	18	33	6	16	27	21	9	21	16	79	1	27	19
73	5					4	6	33	9	20	1	31	5	24	221			34	13
81	6					16	19	34	9	24	5	34	18	34	10			42	1
81	9					20	3	54	12	25	7	48	3	39	2			59	3
116	6					24	8			36	5	56	12	48	8			76	2
118	9					29	1			45	33	60	11	49	12			86	1
121	15					38	2			47	9	64	3	52	7			86	3
122	14					48	1			48	16	68	2	54	9			89	3
169	6					50	11			51	2	83	5	55	12			133	3
184	1									59	8	86	7					148	3
185	9											92	4					191	1
												100	5						

APPENDIX II

References to the word " Arya " (आर्य)

(I) *In the Rig Veda.*

I		II		III		IV		V		VI		VII		VIII		IX		X	
H	M	H	M	H	M	H	M	H	M	H	M	H	M	H	M	H	M	H	M
51	8	11	18	34	9	26	2	34	6	18	3	5	6	24	27	63	6	38	3
59	2	11	19			30	18			22	10	18	7	103	1	63	14	43	4
117	21									25	2	83	1					49	3
130	8									33	3							65	11
156	5									60	6							69	6
																		83	1
																		86	19
																		102	3
																		103	3
																		138	3
																		191	1

(II) *In the Yajur Veda.*

IV		V		VI		XVIII		XIX		XX	
H	M	H	M	H	M	H	M	H	M	H	M
20	4	11	5	63	4	1	21	32	8	18	5
20	8							62	1	85	4

(III) *Atharva Veda.*

IV		XX		XXII	
H	M	H	M	H	M
32	1	11	9	63	4
		17	4		
		18	5		
		36	10		
		85	4		
		89	1		
		95	4		

APPENDIX III

Different meanings of the word " Arya " (अर्य) found in the Rig Veda.

Meaning	I		II		III		IV		V		VI		VII		VIII		IX		X	
	H	M	H	M	H	M	H	M	H	M	H	M	H	M	H	M	H	M	H	M
Enemy	70	1					16	19	33	2	14	3	21	9	48	8	79	1	42	1
	73	5									15	3	34	18	49	12			59	3
	118	9									20	1	48	3					76	2
	121	15									36	5	56	22					89	3
	169	6											68	2						
													92	4						
Respectable Noble	33	3	23	15	43	2	1	7	33	6	24	5	8	1	19	36			20	4
	81	6	35	2			2	12	33	9	25	7	21	5	21	16			27	8
	81	9	43	2			4	6	34	9	47	9	31	5	24	22			27	19
	121	14					20	3					86	7	34	10			34	13
	184	1					24	8					100	5	55	12			86	1
							29	1											86	3
							38	2											116	6
							48	1											148	3
																			191	1
Citizen							2	18												
							20	3												

APPENDIX IV

References to "DASA" in the Rig Veda.

I		II		III		IV		V		VI		VII		VIII		IX		X	
H	M	H	M	H	M	H	M	H	M	H	M	H	M	H	M	H	M	H	M
92	8	11	2	34	1	18	9	30	7	20	6	19	2	5	31			22	8
103	3	11	4			28	4	30	8	20	10	83	1	24	27			23	2
104	2	12	4			30	14	30	9	22	10	86	7	32	2			38	3
158	5	20	6			30	15	33	4	25	2	99	4	40	6			49	6
174	7	20	7			30	21	34	6	26	5			51	9			49	7
						32	10			33	3			56	3			54	1
										47	21			70	10			62	10
										60	6							73	7
																		83	1
																		86	19
																		99	6
																		102	3
																		120	2
																		138	3

APPENDIX V

References to "Dasyu" in the Rig Veda.

I		II		III		IV		V		VI		VII		VIII		IX		X	
H	M	H	M	H	M	H	M	H	M	H	M	H	M	H	M	H	M	H	M
33	4	11	18	29	9	16	9	4	6	14	3	5	6	6	14	41	2	22	8
33	7	11	19	34	6	16	10	7	10	16	15	6	2	14	14	47	2	47	4
33	9	12	10	34	9	16	12	14	14	18	3	19	4	39	8	88	4	48	2
36	18	13	9	49	2	28	3	29	10	23	2			50	8	92	5	49	3
51	5	15	9			28	4	30	9	24	8			51	2			55	8
51	6	20	9			38	4	31	5	29	6			56	2			73	5
51	8							31	7	31	4			70	11			83	3
53	4							70	3	45	24			98	6			83	6
59	6																	95	7
78	4																	99	7
100	18																	105	11
101	5																	170	2
103	3																		
103	4																		
108	12																		
117	3																		
117	21																		

APPENDIX VI

References to the word "Varna" in the Rig Veda.

I		II		III		IV		V		VI		VII		VIII		IX		X	
H	M	H	M	H	M	H	M	H	M	H	M	H	M	H	M	H	M	H	M
73	7	1	12	34	5	5	13									65	8	3	3
92	10	3	5													71	2	124	7
96	5	4	5													71	8		
104	2	5	5													97	15		
113	2	12	4													104	4		
179	6	34	13													105	40		

INDEX